UNWANTED
MEXICAN AMERICANS
in the GREAT DEPRESSION

UNWANTED
MEXICAN AMERICANS
in the
GREAT DEPRESSION

Repatriation Pressures
1929-1939

ABRAHAM HOFFMAN

THE UNIVERSITY OF ARIZONA PRESS
Tucson, Arizona

About the Author . . .

ABRAHAM HOFFMAN's initial interest in the Mexican-American heritage grew out of his early childhood in East Los Angeles and later teaching in the same public schools he had attended as a boy. While pursuing a Ph.D. at UCLA he uncovered much primary source material in government and university archives dealing with the plight of the Mexican American during the depression. From these obscure sources he has woven together a relatively neglected portion of Mexican-American history. Author of numerous articles on ethnic history, Hoffman has contributed to *Pacific Historical Review, Western Historical Quarterly, Journal of Mexican American History,* and *History Teacher.* In 1970, he joined the University of Oklahoma as assistant professor of history and curator of the Western History Collections.

THE UNIVERSITY OF ARIZONA PRESS

I.S.B.N.–0–8165–0366–4
L.C. No. 73–86448

To My Father
and
To the Memory of My Mother

Contents

ILLUSTRATIONS

MAPS

Foreword

REPATRIATION OF OVER 400,000 Mexican aliens (and their American-born children) during the early 1930s stands out as one of the numerous harsh acts committed against Mexicans by Americans over the years that the two have shared a border. Memory can be merciful, and the originators and administrators of this program doubtless have tended for a number of reasons to forget their roles.

But, Mexicans and Mexican Americans who underwent the process find it hard to forget the shame of repatriation. That a mighty nation with high principles could eagerly seek workers from across the border and, after benefiting from their labor, reject them coldly made Mexicans feel like unwanted *things,* rather than people.

Thousands of adults still remember repatriation: the provocations, the provision of funds, and the pressures upon Mexicans to leave their homes because they were not wanted. Remarkably little about repatriation has been written by Mexicans and little more by Americans. In a situation somewhat akin to the treatment of the Indian or the relocation of the Japanese, all concerned seemed to want to forget the discreditable experience.

Much of the feeling of alienation from Anglo-American society among Mexican-American adults today stems from the belief that they are still not wanted except as they serve U.S. economic desires. The importance of this should not be overlooked. Despite the bitterness over repatriation, the depression generation of Mexican Americans produced the GI generation — youth who served with such distinction in World War II as to become the most decorated ethnic group in that conflict. However, in increasing numbers the children of Mexican-American GIs call themselves *Chicanos,* rejecting the cultural implications of "Mexican American," with or without the hyphen. One need only read the stirring lines in Corky González's *I Am Joaquín* to realize that cultural separatism lives on with a vengeance among the children of those who tried so hard to be called Mexican American as a badge of assimilation. Rediscovery of their past and revisionism in Mexican-American history will only tend to heat the dialogue over what really happened to this group. We can thus expect to hear from one direction that such unsavory episodes should be forgiven and forgotten, and from others that we must know the truth whatever the costs.

Unwanted Mexican Americans in the Great Depression: Repatriation Pressures will stand as a primary work on this subject. Although the author concentrates on California, the greatly varied source material — most not used before — sheds light on conditions throughout the Southwest and sections of the Midwest and East, as well as on U.S. and Mexican governmental actions during that time. This work joins the handful of others with which we can renew efforts to reveal what really happened. In too many Anglo-oriented accounts where the Mexican appears at all, he usually has been portrayed as a problem or as the brunt of humor. Hoffman's work will suggest a variety of other approaches to the study of the Mexican American.

I have had personal experience with one area of interest upon which Hoffman touches — namely Mexican immigrants' reactions to their experience in the United States. Many other immigrant groups share experiences with the Mexican. There are, however, some special elements in the Mexican experience. I refer to Mexico's prior sovereignty over the Southwest, a humiliating war of aggression against Mexico, repeated instances of U.S. interference in Mexican affairs, and callous actions such as the uncurbed ejection of pollutants into the Colorado River flowing into Mexico, rendering vast farming areas below the border unusable. In addition to these examples of older, selfish treatment by Americans, we continue to feel the effect of U.S. labor needs on the Mexican supply. The continuation of the World War II Bracero Program into the 1960s, the application of laws — in a capricious fashion — to deal with wetbacks according to U.S. farm labor needs, and the Green Card practice all demonstrate how major U.S. economic interests have shaped the way the United States deals with Mexicans. Because of the difficulty in sorting out Mexican nationals, Mexican Americans in effect often get the same treatment.

In light of all this, it has not been easy for Mexican Americans to love their native land. But the fact is — they do. As one whose family went through part of the repatriation process, my own reactions mirror those of many Mexican Americans who have become active in politics. We want something better for all children than those experiences we find hard to forget completely.

Chicano perceptions of their history are more important every day as their numbers grow in relation to other Americans, and as they expand a phenomenal renaissance evident in their cultural and political life. In California alone, upon which this book focuses extensively, Spanish surnames increased from about 1.4 million in 1960 to about 3.1 million in 1970. I say "about" because students of this group feel certain the census undercounts Mexican Americans. In the light of more traditional attitudes favoring larger families, as well as other factors such as poverty and immigration from Mexico, can we expect some 9 million Mexican Americans in California by 1980? What about 1990? As other Americans approach population growth rate zero, we must take note of the fact that Mexican Americans will increase in numbers and importance as they enter various parts of our social, cultural, and political life with greater vigor and pride in their origins.

JULIAN NAVA
California State University
Northridge, California

Author's Note

> The term "Mexican American" refers to persons living in the United States who are themselves of Mexican origin or whose parents or more remote ancestors came to the United States from Mexico or whose antecedents resided in those parts of the Southwestern United States which were once part of the Mexican Natión. . . .
>
> — United States Commission on Civil Rights, *Mexican Americans and the Administration of Justice in the Southwest*

SERIOUS INQUIRIES into Mexican-American history are few and far between; some of the best date back to the 1930s, while some of the worst are being ground out by publishers hoping to cash in on a trend of the 1970s. There have been a surfeit of sociological analyses and a dearth of serious historical investigations.

This presentation concentrates in the main upon the recrossing of the United States-Mexican border by Mexican *repatriados* during the years of the Great Depression, 1929–39. It spotlights the federal and local bureaucratic procedures by which more than four hundred thousand people made the trip in a six-year period. While the emphasis here is upon Southern California, repatriation was a national phenomenon; detailed studies of repatriation from Texas, Arizona, or the many other states in which Mexican immigrants lived still await investigation.

American historians traditionally have approached the study of immigration from a European orientation and have almost totally ignored immigration from the Western Hemisphere. If Mexican immigration has received little enough notice from historians, Mexican repatriation studies have been practically nonexistent. That a movement of such significance previously has been omitted from our history books is a forceful indictment of the neglect given to the historical presence of the Mexican-American people.

The idea for this book originated in a graduate seminar at UCLA, conducted by Professor Theodore Saloutos, himself the author of a pioneering work on Greek repatriation. Professor John W. Caughey supervised this study at the dissertation stage, and I am indebted to him for a most generous grant from the John and LaRee Caughey Foundation, which allowed me to follow the course of repatriation through the labyrinthine stacks of the National Archives.

As the research and writing grew, so did the debts of gratitude to many persons; I hope none have been overlooked. Those who assisted me in my research included Miss Dora Holman and Miss Riva Bresler of the Los Angeles Public Library; my brother, Jerry Hoffman, who aided me in digging into obscure files at the Los Angeles Hall of Administration; former Supervisor John Anson Ford, who provided insights into the attitudes of the Los Angeles County Board of Supervisors during the depression; Al Vener of the Roosevelt High School Alumni Association; Paul S. Taylor, Professor Emeritus at the University of California, for the use of his maps; and David Aguilar, Ignacio Estrada, Mrs. Lupe Mesa, and Mrs. Lupe Tellez, who shared their experiences with me.

A condensed version of the events in chapters 3 and 4 appeared in the May 1973 issue of *Pacific Historical Review;* I am indebted to Professor Norris Hundley for his editorial guidance. "Mexican Repatriation Statistics: Some Suggested Alternatives to Carey McWilliams," *Western Historical Quarterly* 3 (October 1972): 391–404, reproduced statistical material which appears in part in the appendixes C and D; my thanks to S. George Ellsworth, managing editor of the quarterly, for his advice and assistance.

Ambassador Rafael de la Colina and Professors Arrell M. Gibson and Harwood P. Hinton expressed enthusiasm and encouragement. Professors Arthur Corwin and Donald J. Zelman, and Edward J. Kaufman joined in the frustrating search for extant photographs, while Mrs. Jan Gattis did her best to restore what was located. Photographs appear by courtesy of Ignacio Lozano, Jr., editor of *La Opinión* (Los Angeles), Archivo de la Secretaría de Relaciones Exteriores, Mexico, D.F., and the Hayden Library, Arizona State University. The maps of repatriation departure points and destinations were originally published by the University of California Press and have been reprinted herein by permission of The Regents of the University of California.

The University of Arizona Press and Stephanie Chase, my editor, offered me a post-graduate course on the differences between a book and a dissertation, and I am deeply grateful for the lessons learned. The Faculty Research Fund of the University of Oklahoma provided the means for the purchase of photocopies of source material and for the typing of an important draft of the manuscript, ably performed by Carole Pence.

For preparation of the index and for their continuing advice and encouragement, my thanks to Mr. and Mrs. Everett G. Hager. Finally, I must express my deep appreciation to Judi Hoffman.

A. H.

1.
The Border Is That Way

THE OLD MAN ENTERED the circular park, looked around, and sat
down on one of the many benches placed there for the use of the
town's citizens. Several hundred people, mostly men, were also in
the park, enjoying the afternoon sun. Sitting in the park enabled the
old man to forget the reason that had brought him there. The
deepening economic depression had cost him his job, and work was
hard to find.

A sudden commotion startled the old man out of his reverie.
Without warning, uniformed policemen surrounded the park, block-
ing all exits. A voice filled with authority ordered everyone to remain
where he was. While the policemen guarded the exits, government
agents methodically quizzed each of the frightened people, demanding identification papers, documents, or passports. With shaking
hands the old man produced a dog-eared, yellowed visa. Only the
other day, he had considered throwing it away. After all, he had
entered the country so long ago. . . .

The agent inspected the papers and barked several questions at
the old man. Haltingly, he answered as best he could, for despite his
years of residence in the country he had learned the language only
imperfectly. With a nod of approval, the officer returned the papers.
The old man sat down again; a sense of relief washed over him.

The agents continued their interrogation, and after about an
hour everyone in the park had been checked and cleared. Or almost
everyone. Seventeen men were placed in cars and taken away. The
inspection over, the policemen left the park to the people. Few

cared to remain, however, and in a few moments the place was deserted.

*   *   *

The time was 1931; the place, Los Angeles, California, in the city's downtown plaza. The government agents were officers in the Department of Labor's Bureau of Immigration, assisted by local policemen. Their goal was the apprehension of aliens who had entered the United States illegally.*

Unlike many post-World War II aliens who knowingly entered in violation of immigration laws, immigrants prior to the Great Depression entered the United States at a time when the government's views on immigration were in flux, moving from unrestricted entry to severe restriction. Many aliens found themselves confused by the tightening noose of regulations; one immigrant might enter with one law in effect, but his younger brother, coming to the country a few years later, might find new rules — or new interpretations of old rules — impeding his entrance.

With the onset of the depression, pressure mounted to remove aliens from the relief rolls and, almost paradoxically, from the jobs they were said to hold at the expense of American citizens. In the Southwest, immigration service officers searched for Mexican immigrants, while local welfare agencies sought to lighten their relief load by urging Mexican indigents to volunteer for repatriation. The most ambitious of these repatriation programs was organized in Los Angeles County, an area with the largest concentration of Mexicans outside of Mexico, D.F.

Not all of the repatriates, however, departed solely under pressure from the Anglos. Many Mexicans who had achieved varying degrees of financial success decided on their own to return to Mexico, taking with them the automobiles, clothing, radios, and other material possessions they had accumulated. The Mexican government, vacillating between the desire to lure these people home and the fear that their arrival would add to an already existing labor surplus, sporadically launched land reform programs designed for *repatriados*. Between 1929 and 1939 approximately half a million Mexicans left the United States. Many of the departing families included American-born children to whom Mexico, not the United States, was the foreign land.

*In June 1933 the bureau's name was changed to the Immigration and Naturalization Service, and in 1940, the service was shifted to the Department of Justice.

The peak month in which Mexicans recrossed the border was November 1931, and in all subsequent months the figures generally declined. Yet it was after this date that the number of cities shipping out Mexican families increased. Even after the massive federal relief programs of the New Deal were begun in 1933, cities such as Los Angeles, Chicago, and Detroit still attempted to persuade indigent Mexicans to leave.

With the start of World War II, Mexican immigration was renewed, when the United States and Mexico concluded an agreement to permit *braceros* to enter the United States. A system of permits and visas for varying periods testifies to the evolution of border regulations; their abuse and misuse bear witness to the difficulties of making such a system coherent. Later problems of Mexicans and Mexican Americans — exploitation by agribusiness employers, wetback migrations, prejudice and discrimination, efforts at unionization of agricultural workers, and wholesale deportations of hundreds of thousands of wetbacks in the 1950s — are beyond the scope of this study, as are the many contributions of Mexican Americans to American society in areas unrelated to migratory labor. The contiguous border itself exists as an ongoing problem to be solved by the immigration services of both countries. The illegal alien problem, bigger than ever, still plagues the United States. Between July 1969 and June 1970 the Immigration and Naturalization Service deported 277,377 Mexican aliens illegally in the country. The immigration service has blamed the rise of illegal entries on the termination in 1964 of the Mexican Agricultural Act, which had provided for the *bracero* program.

Numbers, of course, are misleading; the population of the United States today is larger by many millions than it was in the 1930s. The nature of the problem has also changed. Illegal aliens in the years following World War II were breaking already existing laws. But *ex post facto* procedures placed in jeopardy those Mexican immigrants who had come to the United States before those laws were passed.

No other locality matched the county of Los Angeles in its ambitious efforts to rid itself of the Mexican immigrant during the depression years. By defining people along cultural instead of national lines, county officials deprived American children of Mexican descent of rights guaranteed them by the Constitution. On the federal level, no other region in the country received as much attention from immigration officials as Southern California. Because of the tremendous growth of this region after World War II, Southern California's service as a locus for deportation and repatriation of Mexican immigrants is little remembered. To the Mexican-American community, however, repatriation is a painful memory.

To the young the depression is history, but events of the seventies jar one into recognition that the system still has its imperfections. A 1970 example was in the form of the impatience of the Immigration and Naturalization Service to understand the unique problems of an eighteen-year-old boy. The boy looked Mexican, spoke Spanish, and in a slow, curious way referred to his home in Mexico. So the immigration officers, assuming the boy to be an illegal alien, transported him from Van Nuys, California, to Tijuana. It proved to be a mistake. The boy was a Mexican American, born in California, a mentally retarded outpatient at a county hospital, and on medication. A week after his mother reported him missing he was found near Mexico City, begging for food. While immigration officials confessed to a "tragic error," the American consulate gave the boy the proper medicine and bus transportation back to his home. The deputy regional commissioner, according to the *Los Angeles Times* of 9 April 1970, stated that the case was the first he had ever experienced in which a native American had been deported as an illegal alien, and placed the blame on the youth's mental condition and on "inexperienced officers transferred here to help round up aliens in the area."

Such incidents, as well as the raids of immigration agents undertaken in 1971 against illegal Mexican aliens, have a precedent dating back over four decades. This book is a reminder that such current actions have a long and disturbing history.

2.

Mexican Movements Into the United States

THE SOUTHWESTERN SECTION of the North American continent is crisscrossed with political boundary lines. These lines pay little attention to the realities of geography and, with the exception of the Rio Grande, proceed across the land along surveyed meridians, parallels, and diagonals. Almost all of Arizona, New Mexico, and Nevada are so outlined, and the border between California and Baja California is an arbitrary one decided upon after a one-sided war fought over a hundred years ago. North of El Paso, the Rio Grande ends its service as a natural boundary; and there is little difference geographically between southern Arizona and northern Sonora.

There is, of course, a world of difference politically. Since 1848, the location of one's home on either side of this long boundary running from California to Texas determined whether one lived under one of the two different, but neighboring, governments. The fact that one spoke Spanish or was of Mexican lineage had nothing to do with which side of the border he called home. A twist of fate decreed early in the twentieth century that the economic growth of the region north of the border would far exceed that of the southern side, and that thousands of citizens of Mexico would look to the United States for their means of livelihood.

Historical irony abounds in this region. New Mexico's Spanish-speaking population dates back to the beginning of the seventeenth century, and the roots of the Spanish-Mexican people, and of the Indians who were there before all others, are deeply planted in the land. Cities, rivers, states, and mountains bear Spanish and Indian

[5]

names. Several thousand Mexicans who remained in the area ceded by Mexico in 1848 automatically became American citizens. Yet a sharp break exists between the heritage embraced by all residents of the region and the actuality of contemporary society. The English-speaking American, who sees many Spanish-speaking people living in poverty, hears of high dropout rates, and finds few Mexican Americans in the professions, frequently considers them only in terms of tired stereotypes — the mañana personality, the siesta-taker resting against the cactus, or the devoted follower of the quaint Catholic custom of blessing the animals.[1]

Many Americans who read their history carelessly or not at all believe that Mexicans have always lived in great numbers north of the Rio Grande and that the people they see today in Los Angeles, for example, have antecedents dating back to 1781. The generalists may say that since so many of these Mexicans are lacking in skills, wealth, and education, it must follow that there is something congenitally wrong with them as a people, with so little progress having been made by them after almost two hundred years. The fallacy behind such logic becomes obvious when the history of the past eighty years or so is surveyed.

Increased Immigration After 1880

Until the 1880s relatively few Mexican immigrants crossed the Rio Grande to join the Spanish-speaking people already present in the United States. From that time until the beginning of the First World War, Mexican immigration increased. Around 1908 it came to the attention of the federal government, which then began to keep track of the immigrants somewhat more accurately.

Sociologist Ernesto Galarza has suggested a reason for this gradual increase of Mexicans in the United States. In his book, *Merchants of Labor,* he noted that the obstacle to travel presented by the harshness of the Sonoran Desert had been overcome by extensive railroad construction, with capital provided to Mexico by foreign investment. By 1910 almost fifteen thousand miles of railroad track had been laid, enabling Mexicans from the central plateau region of Mexico to head north without much difficulty.[2]

The Mexican people who emigrated to the United States during the era of Porfirio Díaz were often recruited to work on the construction and maintenance of American railroads. Many of the early enclaves of Mexicans in cities such as Chicago and Kansas City originated as labor camps for the railroads. In *North from Mexico,* Carey McWilliams cites the period 1900–1912 as the peak of the railroads' recruitment of Mexicans. However, the contribution of Mexicans in keeping the railroads running increased in percentage during the first third of the twentieth century. Nine western railroads listed 5,972 workers, or 17.1 percent, as Mexicans in 1909; twenty years later these railroads employed 22,824 Mexicans, or 59.5 percent of their common labor force.[3]

Mexicans who found the economy of their country stagnating under the regime of Porfirio Díaz looked to the United States as a way out of the *hacendado* control of lands and the chronic poverty of Mexican rural life. The railroads offered an opportunity for escape which was taken by thousands of Mexicans. Once in the United States, however, many Mexicans felt little obligation to remain with the railroads that had recruited them at the wage of a dollar a day. The railroads constantly contended with losing labor to other industries. Opportunities for unskilled labor were favorable in a rapidly industrializing America. Steel mills, mines, meat-packing plants, brickyards, canneries, and other industries offered employment, and with the new century came the need for workers to pave city streets, construct new buildings, and erect dams and bridges.

The primary impetus which proved so significant for Mexican immigration in the twentieth century came from the tremendous agricultural expansion which occurred in the southwestern United States. The Imperial Valley of California, when irrigated, was transformed from arid desert to fertile farmland, and a large variety of fruits and vegetables thrived in the California climate. Similarly, opportunities for crop picking abounded in California's San Joaquin Valley, the Salt River Valley of Arizona, the Lower Rio Grande Valley of Texas, and in sugar beet fields which could be found in Michigan, Minnesota, and Colorado.

The common denominator for this agricultural employment, as well as for much of the industrial work, was that it was seasonal in nature, rising dramatically from low to high peaks of employment and back again. In the years preceding the First World War, American agricultural employers looked for a source that could easily provide them with the needed hundreds, or even thousands, of workers. That source was Mexico.

Revolution as a Catalyst

As long as the population of Mexico lived under a stable regime, little likelihood existed that any mass migration to the agricultural fields of the southwestern United States would take place. Prior to 1910 American agriculture had accepted Japanese, Filipino, Negro, and Hindu workers, as well as Mexicans. Not long after the beginning of the Mexican Revolution, however, the population of much of Mexico found itself in the midst of power struggles and political ferment which were to be the vision and curse of Mexico's awakening for a generation. One Mexican American recalled a story told by his grandfather of hearing a knock on the door in the middle of the night, and of the fear of not knowing which faction demanded entry. To identify oneself incorrectly — that is, to give the wrong pledge of political allegiance — was to invite instant death.

The Mexican people's fear of uncertainty and dislocation is little known by citizens of the United States. The American's image of the Mexican Revolution is that of the unshaven *bandido* wearing crossed bandoliers, brandishing an old rifle, and carelessly providing himself as an easy target for those very enemies he has sworn to avenge. From this view the Anglo American inevitably concludes that a people unable to govern themselves must be innately inferior.

He just as frequently fails to acknowledge the tremendous obstacle to unity posed by the divergent races, cultures, and geography found in Mexico. Writing in the 1 May 1924 issue of *Survey,* Manuel Gamio stated that:

The Mexican people is a conglomeration of several native races of half-breeds and whites all too little known to each other and divergent in their innate characteristics, their geographical conditions, living in different climates, to which they have become accustomed, surrounded by different botanical and zoological species and using different cultural and linguistic backgrounds.[4]

Anglo Americans might more profitably learn of Mexico's economic exploitation by foreign business interests, the domination of the land by a few *hacendados,* and the vicious repression of political and civil liberties in the decades preceding 1911.[5]

A coincidence of timing, therefore, brought the American agricultural employer and the dislocated Mexican together. This Mexican, frequently from a rural area, usually with a degree of Indian blood in his ancestry, found in the employment opportunities of United States agriculture a chance to regain his economic equilibrium. While the cost of living in Mexico had risen greatly, wages had remained the same since 1900. Mexican currency had also declined in purchasing power. Farmers in Mexico found the cost of living had risen 70 percent during the revolutionary period; by 1926 the Mexican worker was earning only one-fourteenth of the purchasing power of a laborer doing corresponding work in the United States.[6] "When we consider wages as compared with the cost of living in Mexico," wrote one observer of the northbound traffic across the border, "we can see why the trend of migration is still northward to the U.S."[7]

Wartime Labor Demands

World War I may at first have been a remote affair to the American grower of fruits and vegetables, or to the owners of western railroads, mines, or other industries which required a force of un-skilled labor, but a combination of factors led them to draw on the Mexican population to meet their labor demands. The cutting of immigration from Europe prevented any chance of raw immigrant help coming to work in the fields. Another potential source of labor, the southern Negro, preferred migrating to large northern cities rather than to other agricultural areas. The Immigration Act of 1917 established a literacy test and head tax, but these theoretical restrictions on entry did not apply to Mexican immigration. Upon demand from representatives of growers' associations and industrial companies, the Department of Labor granted exemptions from these regulations to recruits for the beet fields, railroad gangs, and other contracted labor.[8] These exemptions, which were granted each year from 1917 to 1920, allowed over fifty thousand Mexicans to enter the United States.[9]

Stereotypes of Mexican Labor

During the decade of the 1920s spokesmen for agriculture and industry welcomed the ever-increasing numbers of Mexican immigrants. The people utilizing Mexican labor for the most part viewed their workers with stereotyped approval. "To put it quite simply," stated a writer for *Century Magazine* in 1926, "he comes to us because he wants to come, and also because we want him to come." The Mexican was extolled as "the preferred of all the cheap labor available to the Southwest."[10]

Growers came to believe that the work of harvesting was not the kind of work that a white man would do, and they reiterated this claim frequently. In a statement on agricultural labor in California to William Butterworth, president of the U.S. Chamber of Commerce, Arthur G. Arnoll, general manager of the Los Angeles Chamber of Commerce, frankly claimed, "The American white is not physically capable to undertake many tasks in either the fruit or truck crop industry as well as cotton-picking." Arnoll went on to observe that the high temperatures and the practice of being paid on a piecework basis prevented the white man from performing a day's work for a decent wage. The white man was "entirely unfitted for labor which requires bending, crouching, or elasticity." The Mexican's willingness to do this kind of work was accepted as part of the nature of things.

Arnoll's pronouncements were echoed publicly by Dr. George P. Clements, one of the most important spokesmen for the use of Mexican labor in the United States. Clements managed the Los Angeles Chamber of Commerce's agricultural department from the time he helped organize it, in 1917, until his retirement in 1939. Throughout this period Clements conducted the affairs of his office with consistent energy. He spoke often before civic and religious groups on Mexican immigration, migratory labor problems, and other related topics, and turned out numerous memos, mimeographed broadsides, speeches, and articles.

His influence as a lobbyist for unrestricted Mexican immigration extended to the halls of Congress, where eventually some of the activities of the Los Angeles Chamber of Commerce, particularly in agriculture, came under the scrutiny of the Senate Subcommittee on Violations of Free Speech and Rights of Labor, also known as the La Follette Committee. Through it all he exhibited a positive attitude about his work, never letting his affection for the Mexican people interfere with his opinions of them, which he carried with firm conviction. The Mexicans he dealt with as agents of various chambers of commerce or of the government of Mexico were of one class; the Mexican laborers in the fields were another breed entirely.

Clements believed that the tasks of agriculture were those "to which the oriental and Mexican due to their crouching and bending habits are fully adapted, while the white is physically unable to adapt himself to them."[11] The influence of Clements and similar spokesmen for the unrestricted entry of Mexican laborers should not be underestimated. For most of the 1920s, even as quota barriers were erected for Europe and exclusion declared for Asia, proponents of unrestricted Mexican immigration kept the "back door" open.

Border Crossings

Throughout this period of triumph for American employers of Mexican labor, thousands of Mexican people abandoned the vicissitudes of life in Mexico for the hope of better opportunities north of the border. The chief border crossing stations were at El Paso, Texas; Nogales, Arizona; and Calexico, California, though mention also should be made of the crossing points at Brownsville and Laredo, Texas, and Douglas, Arizona. The available facilities were easily overtaxed by the large numbers of Mexicans seeking entry, and sympathetic observers noted the patience of the immigrants as they endured the lack of drinking fountains, inadequate sanitary facilities, and endless waiting in line.

Other Mexicans, not so patient, entered the United States illegally, either by smuggling themselves across the border or having someone help them. No harsh penalties for illegal entry existed until 1929. A Mexican caught crossing the border illegally was told that if he wished to enter the United States, he had to do so at a regular station and pay the fees.

Widespread Mexican Communities

Once in the United States, Mexican immigrants found that while employment opportunities existed, the range of jobs was severely limited. Emphasis, therefore, on Mexicans in agriculture is not misplaced. The nomadic nature of the migrant work, however, soon introduced Mexicans to many places in the United States where the Spanish language had not previously been heard.

The Bethlehem Steel Company, in need of immediate labor in 1923, recruited approximately one thousand Mexican nationals from San Antonio, Texas, for its plant in Bethlehem, Pennsylvania. The Mexican consul at San Antonio approved the wage and employment provisions and signed the contract. After their arrival in Bethlehem, the Mexicans began to look for better jobs than those with the steel company. By 1930 only forty-six of the original group were left. Bethlehem's entire Mexican community, including Mexican Americans, totaled less than one hundred and fifty that year.[12]

By the mid-twenties most large American cities had their enclaves of Mexican nationals, with such businesses as barber shops, grocery stores, and rooming houses operated by Mexicans. In 1924, Omaha, Nebraska, contained a community of some one thousand Mexicans, employed by packing houses, stockyards, railroads, and farms.[13] The Ford Motor Company's reputation for good wages attracted Mexicans to Michigan, though they found other automobile companies also offered inducements. The colony in Detroit fluctuated in size due to the work offered in the sugar beet fields and the changes in employment needs of the companies. In the late 1920s the Detroit colony reached a peak of some fifteen thousand, up from five thousand in 1926.[14] Significant numbers of Mexicans could also be found in Chicago, Kansas City, and New Orleans, as well as in other cities. By far, the vast majority of Mexicans was concentrated in the five southwestern states of California, Arizona, Colorado, New Mexico, and Texas, the latter having the largest number.

The children of these Mexican nationals born on American soil were automatically American citizens under the Fourteenth Amendment, which provides that "All persons born or naturalized in the United States, and subject to the jurisdiction thereof, are citizens of the United States and of the State wherein they reside." However, even a sociologist of the stature of Emory S. Bogardus referred to Americans whose grandparents had been the original immigrants as "third generation Mexicans."[15]

Professor Max Handman of the University of Texas classified the state's Spanish-speaking residents into three groups — political refugees, Texas Mexicans (born in the United States), and "a large number of casual laborers who have drifted in or have been attracted to Texas as a result of the recent changes in the American labor market."[16] The 1930 census, which lumped Mexican aliens and their children together, counted 683,681 in Texas.[17]

Confused Census Classifications

New Mexico's Spanish-speaking population included many residents who could trace their ancestry in New Mexico back many generations. However, the 1930 census figure of 59,340 was wildly inaccurate; the truth of the matter was that over half of the population of New Mexico in 1930 spoke Spanish. Attempts to separate old-line residents from recent immigrants were hopelessly confused by American census-takers.[18] As for other states, the census recorded 368,013 Mexicans in California, 114,173 in Arizona, and 57,676 in Colorado.[19]

Because many thousands of Mexicans in the United States were already on the move by the time the Fifteenth Census was taken, the figures cited above have an artificiality about them that belies the authority of numbers in print. Prior to 1910 Mexican immigration was uncounted, and in the years before the adoption of the 1924 Quota Act the techniques of enumerating immigrants from Mexico left much to be desired. Illegal immigration went untallied, and differentiations between "immigrant" and "nonimmigrant" Mexican aliens became meaningless, if the former returned to Mexico before six months had elapsed, or the latter stayed longer.[20]

Those concerned with figures made what they could of them, and studies of Mexican immigration usually included a comment on the unreliability of the statistics being used. In 1930 an impartial survey conducted by California Governor C. C. Young's Mexican Fact-Finding Committee reported, "In the case of Mexican immigration there is a sharp distinction between the number of *reported* immigrants and the *actual* numbers admitted." The report added that the commissioner general of immigration used only the legal figure. In *Mexican Labor in the United States,* Paul S. Taylor, who spent several years compiling a massive amount of data on Mexican labor in the United States, could only conclude at one point that his figures on immigration were "very conservative." Manuel Gamio, a Mexican anthropologist, observed in his book, *Mexican Immigration to the United States,* "that statistics compiled by the Bureau of Immigration are of little value toward correcting the earlier numerical estimates of the census, since a great number of Mexican immigrants enter into or leave the United States without the knowledge of the immigration offices."

Immigration figures of the Mexican government failed to match United States emigration figures because a Mexican reentering Mexico was subject to penalties if he did not register at a border station. Calculating the illegal entries was impossible. Penalties for such entries were not written into law until almost the end of the 1920s, and smugglers known as "coyotes" found the business of "bootlegging" aliens into the United States to be a lucrative one.

The inadequate figures and incomplete data frustrate any attempt to decide upon some definite figure. The 1930 census declared that there were 1,422,533 Mexicans in the United States, but this number was rendered obsolete by the repatriation then under way. It was also inaccurate since there was an unknown quantity of aliens who had entered illegally and avoided the census. Finally, it was unfair because it attempted to define "Mexicans" as a race, and by doing so it eliminated thousands of Spanish-speaking people of Mexican origin from the count.

Prevailing conceptions of what constituted a "Mexican" were revealed in the instructions for the taking of the census. While the 1920 census had included Mexicans as part of the white population, the 1930 census attempted to set up the Mexican as a race unto itself. Even though a person born in the United States was an American citizen, if his parents were born in Mexico he was counted as a Mexican. For all its deficiencies, however, the enumeration of Mexicans in the United States in 1930 did show that the Spanish-speaking population had increased over 103 percent during the decade.[21]

The Anglo Viewpoint

If the method of counting Mexicans (and Mexican Americans and, in the case of many residents of New Mexico, Spanish Americans) left much to be desired, the acceptance of the Mexican into American society was even more conditioned by preconceived ideas and stereotypes. Most Mexican immigrants came from backgrounds of illiteracy, poverty, and harsh existence, but their opportunities for employment and advancement were also seriously narrowed by the limited view held by Anglo Americans towards them.

Conceding that "Mexicans have proved to be efficient laborers and . . . have afforded a cheap and elastic labor supply for the southwestern United States," Samuel Bryan, writing in the 7 September 1912 issue of *Survey,* condemned their arrival because "the evils to the community at large which their presence in large numbers almost invariably brings may more than over-balance their desirable qualities." Bryan found nothing of social value in the mind and body of the Mexican immigrant. "Their low standards of living and of morals, their illiteracy, their utter lack of proper political interest, the retarding effect of their employment upon the wage scale of the more progressive races, and finally their tendency to colonize in urban centers, with evil results, combine to stamp them as a rather undesirable class of residents."

Even writers who wrote sympathetically of Mexican adjustment to American life allowed subjective attitudes to creep into their studies. "The one trait of his nature which is foreign to our temperament is his submission to existing conditions," stated a writer who was evidently unaware of the discontent that had culminated in the Mexican Revolution. The writer further noted, "He is childlike and can generally be directed into constructive activities for his advancement."[22]

Of course a statement such as this, extracted from a long-forgotten article, does not with others of the same type necessarily add up to a valid generalization. Nevertheless, the trenchant comments of Carey McWilliams on the phenomenon of "the Mexican problem" highlight the fact that sociological writings of the 1920s emphasized negative characteristics and actually created "problems" out of consequences rather than causes.[23]

Sociological studies seemed to concentrate on Mexicans who were "laborers" or of a "lower class" than other Mexicans, but Mexican immigrants found that whatever their background was, Anglo Americans almost invariably made little effort to distinguish between Mexicans of different socioeconomic status, education, or ability. Ernestine M. Alvarado wrote in 1920 that "The Mexicans who come to the United States are of three types, namely the aristocracy or leisure class . . . the middle class . . . and the peon or laboring class. . . ." She confined her study to the laboring class as did the 1927 study by Emory S. Bogardus, in which he stated that "the Mexican immigrant can hardly be called a typical Mexican. He represents the lower rather than the better culture levels. . . . This paper does not deal with the higher class Mexicans but rather with the uneducated labor types."

Katherine K. Murray assigned similar classifications in her 1933 study of the Mexican school children in Southern California, whom she said were "far from representative of the higher class of Mexico, or even of the middle classes, but rather of the lowliest type." Few studies were made of Mexican immigrants who were not of the laborer class. A good example of sociological writing which did recognize that Mexicans were individuals and not a collective mass was Charles A. Thomson's "Mexicans — An Interpretation," published by the National Conference of Social Work in 1928.[24]

The wage differential mentioned earlier may have contributed to making laborers out of Mexicans who found their skills unwanted and unneeded. Coming from a country in the midst of a great social revolution, Mexican immigrants and their children were also subjected to and measured by Anglo American standards of education, health, and color.

The difficulties that the Mexican immigrant faced in adjusting to American life were perhaps traceable to the singular method of his arrival. Although many Mexicans crossed the border leaving their families behind, the families were never far behind. The proximity of the Mexican's homeland enabled him to travel or live as a family unit with relatively little difficulty, unlike other immigrant groups which had to cross thousands of miles of ocean. Since most of the almost two thousand miles of contiguous border between the United States and Mexico is either an artificial boundary or an often shallow river, a Mexican could leave the United States and reenter Mexico with relative ease, often playing havoc with the twentieth century preoccupation with statistical accuracy.

When a Mexican arrived in the United States, whether he was contracted by a large-scale grower, railroad, or industrial company, or paid his own fees, or used the services of a *coyote* to bootleg him across, the new immigrant found that all his employers required was his strength, not his enterprise. Employers conceived of the Mexican as a mote in the mass of cheap labor, a view held and espoused by the very businesses which gave the Mexican his initial employment. Denial of the opportunity for advancement plus continued exploitation by employers, who encouraged a continuous stream of immigrants to insure a cheap labor supply, left the Mexican immigrant the victim of stereotypes almost impossible to overcome.

The chief stereotype, as has been mentioned, was the view of the Mexican as an agricultural laborer. Since most Mexican immigrants possessed rural backgrounds, there was some validity to the view that Mexicans were familiar with agricultural work. Related to the idea of the Mexican as an agricultural laborer was his usefulness in large-scale industrial employment, chiefly on railroads, but also in places such as automobile factories and meat-packing plants, invariably in the status of laborer.

Many Mexicans resisted the idea of remaining as laborers when there was the opportunity to develop skills in other endeavors. The California Mexican Fact-Finding Committee's report disclosed that eleven out of every hundred Mexicans worked in manufacturing industries, and that Mexicans in nonagricultural occupations ranged from less than 3 to over 66 percent, depending on the industry. These jobs ranged from employment as machinists, mechanics, and upholsterers to bakers, painters, and a number of other semiskilled and skilled types of work.[25]

A second stereotype centered around the reputed docility of the Mexican as a worker who worked hard for long hours at low wages without complaint. This viewpoint was often stressed by large-scale growers who had little time for labor disputes during a harvest. Actually, by 1928 the Mexican farm workers in California's Imperial Valley had already waged a strike against the cantaloupe growers, and shortly Mexicans in other areas, as well, began their persistent struggle for better wages and improved working conditions — a struggle that has still not ended.

The idea of a docile agricultural worker was promoted throughout the 1920s, and needed only a third aspect to render the stereotype complete. Growers provided this aspect when they asserted that Mexican immigrants experienced a "cycle of migration." This was the idea that the Mexican, on completing a season's work in the fields of American agriculture, then went home to Mexico and spent his newly earned wealth there, thus bringing economic benefits to both the United States and Mexico. Although there was a significant southward movement of Mexicans during the 1920s, the huge increase in the Mexican population in the United States, as revealed by the 1930 census, suggests that the growers' assertions of a migratory cycle needed to be heavily qualified. There was, to be sure, a migratory cycle, but this cycle took place within the United States as well as over the border. The idea of a migratory cycle also failed to consider those Mexicans who left agricultural work and took on nonagricultural occupations.[26]

The Immigrant's Handicaps

Apart from the stereotypes held of them, Mexicans had to endure the additional handicaps they shared in common with other immigrant groups. These included the language barrier, new laws and customs, finding adequate housing, and securing a job that paid enough to take care of family needs. Like other nationalities, Mexicans congregated together in their *colonias,* their neighborhoods, and patronized merchants who were either Mexicans or Mexican Americans themselves, or else were enterprising enough to hire Spanish-speaking employees.

Manuel Gamio observed that many Mexican immigrants abandoned the religion of their homeland, Catholicism. He attributed this to the hostility to Mexican immigration publicly proclaimed by some Catholic clergymen in the United States. Protestant sects found Mexican immigrants a fertile group for conversion, and many of the social services extended to Mexican immigrants came from Protestant agencies.[27]

Legal Restrictions

Along with other immigrants, Mexicans encountered legal restrictions wherever they might go in the United States. These restrictions could affect opportunity for employment, as in the case of local public works projects, and require circumspection in social conduct. Discriminatory laws out of proportion to the alien population could be detected in states which had received large numbers of aliens. For example, in order to be a lawyer, attainment of full citizenship or possession of first papers was required in Michigan, California, Arizona, and Colorado. Accountants had to have similar qualifications in Arizona, California, Colorado, New Mexico, and Michigan, as did teachers in California, Michigan, and Texas. Full citizenship was required for employment on certain public works projects in Arizona, California, and Illinois. Texas preferred citizens to work on its highways. In order to obtain a hunting license, Arizona, Colorado, and New Mexico required full citizenship, while Arizona and California demanded full citizenship for a fishing license. Michigan insisted on full citizenship for promoters of boxing and wrestling matches; California did the same for licensing private detectives. In 1923 Pennsylvania passed a law demanding full citizenship for owners of dogs. Only American citizens could stake a mining claim in Nevada, and South Dakota required full citizenship of people who sold poison (though not, apparently, of those who purchased it).

Amid the welter of seemingly frivolous laws, antialien patterns can be detected which, asserted a writer on the problem, were "but indices of the attitude which has prompted such legislation in part." The actual end of many antialien laws was the denial of employment on public works projects and participation in relief programs.[28]

Reluctance to Seek Citizenship

Whether a Mexican alien working in Bethlehem, Pennsylvania, was ever arrested for owning a dog is immaterial; what is important is to realize that Mexicans, and other aliens as well, lived their lives in the United States in a shadow of uncertainty. One way in which Mexicans protected themselves was, paradoxically, *not* to become American citizens. This reluctance to become a full-fledged member of his adopted homeland was due to several reasons. First, many Mexicans did not consider the United States as an adopted homeland, but still thought of themselves as Mexicans, citizens of Mexico, to where they would one day return. Second, living in close proximity in a *colonia,* Mexicans felt a group pressure not to apply for citizenship. One Mexican expressed his situation dramatically by asserting that "if I should become an American citizen my neighbors would cut my throat."[29]

Anglo Americans who believed every immigrant's dream was to become an American citizen overlooked the fact that the Mexican immigrant was crossing over to work on soil that had once belonged to Mexico. Mexicans who crossed their northern border were looking for a better life, but not necessarily a better citizenship. As with many immigrants from European countries who came to America, the Mexican immigrant held the ideal of making enough money to return to the homeland and living out his days in a comfortable, if not wealthy manner.[30] The greater the length of time spent in the United States, of course, the greater the possibility that if such a return did occur the habits acquired in the United States, particularly those of a material nature, would bring about a sense of disappointment. While he lived and worked in the United States, however, the Mexican immigrant could cherish his dream of eventual return.

The fact that Mexicans were not applying for American citizenship distressed those agencies which equated citizenship with social progress. The Mexican Fact-Finding Committee reported that only 2 percent — less than 300 out of 13,165 aliens in California — who filed first papers were Mexicans, although the ratio of Mexicans among the foreign-born in California was on the increase.[31] The Methodist Church, which did much to aid the Mexican immigrant, believed that Mexicans could make good American citizens. Reverend Vernon M. McCombs, Superintendent of the Methodist Latin

American Missions in Southern California, commented, "They hold fine possibilities of citizenship, being sturdy, independent, and filled with racial pride." He cautioned, however, that certain beliefs held by Mexicans would have to be overcome, as "the only government of which they have any knowledge is one of license and misrule." He also felt that the unlettered immigrant served as ready prey for the machinations of Industrial Workers of the World agitators.[32] As McWilliams has noted, sometimes the most sympathetic people were the most condescending.[33]

The most logical reason for the Mexican's hesitation in applying for citizenship was also a realistic one: the privileges of American citizenship offered little of substance to the Mexican national who knew that if he became a citizen he would still be, in the eyes of Anglos, a Mexican. Professor Emory S. Bogardus of the University of Southern California commented on this problem in an article he wrote in 1930 on Mexican immigration:

By remaining a citizen of Mexico and by calling on the Mexican Consul for assistance, the Mexican immigrant often can secure justice, whereas if he becomes an American citizen, he feels helpless. He does not understand our courts and is not able to secure as adequate a hearing as if he remains a Mexican citizen.[34]

Bogardus compared the Mexican immigrant's situation to that of an American in Mexico who, if he obtained Mexican citizenship, might still be treated as an American, though without the support of the United States government's consular services. As will be seen later in this study, the work of Mexican consuls in providing for the welfare of their conationals was a key factor in providing a link between the Mexican immigrant and his homeland.

Attempts to Understand

The late 1920s witnessed a desire by many people — growers, social workers, and scholars included — to understand the problems faced by the Mexicans coming to the United States. Their origins, occupations, eating habits, income and expenses, how they saved or spent their wages, crime rate — and the most important questions of all, how many of them were here and how many more were coming — provoked research to examine these topics. Much of the literature produced was of the type that McWilliams later condemned in *North from Mexico* as a "depressing mass of social data" which "proved" Mexicans were deficient in leadership ability, thrift, and ambition, and that their children were "retarded." Several studies were conducted, however, which are of enduring value to anyone who wishes basic information on Mexicans in the United States.

Of prime importance was the work of Paul S. Taylor, professor of economics at the University of California, who presented valuable insights into the life of the Mexican immigrant, concentrating on the Mexican as a farm laborer. He contributed a number of monographic studies and articles between 1928 and 1934.[35]

Another major study was undertaken by Manuel Gamio, who had been a student of Franz Boas at Columbia University, and who by 1930 was acclaimed as a top-ranking Latin American anthropologist. With the sponsorship of the Social Science Research Council in 1926, Gamio spent several years doing research into Mexican immigration, utilizing such ideas as the recording of Mexican presence in a given area by charting the number of postal money orders sent back to Mexico. His two major works were to be used by many later writers as a basic source of statistics and description of Mexican immigration.[36]

The state of California also made an effort to understand and enumerate the contribution of Mexicans to the social and economic development of the state. Governor Clement C. Young called a meeting of his governor's council early in 1928 to discuss Mexican problems, and appointed a committee "to prepare a report of a fact-finding nature and non-controversial in character, a report designed to show the actual existing conditions as to the Mexican population in California."[37]

Investigators from the state departments of industrial relations, agriculture, and social welfare, aided by the University of California, compiled the report, which was published in 1930. *Mexicans in California* presented a detailed account of Mexicans in agricultural and nonagricultural occupations, and statistics on wage rates, migration, health, relief, and delinquency. It was widely circulated and provided interested Californians with a body of facts to support whatever arguments their interests reflected.

There were a number of other studies, varying in quality from Roy L. Garis's *Immigration Restriction* of 1927[38] to the polemical arguments in magazines such as *Saturday Evening Post* and *Independent*. At the University of Southern California, Professor Emory S. Bogardus sponsored a number of Master's theses in sociology, dealing with Mexican themes, and welcomed articles to the pages of

Sociology and Social Research, the journal he edited. At the same
time he authored several books and numerous articles on Mexicans
in the United States. While the American Federation of Labor
annually vented its hostility by passing resolutions calling for restrictions on Mexican immigration, the United States Chamber of Commerce, as well as religious and civic groups, held conferences to
discuss the subject.[39]

Mexican immigration to the United States had drawn attention
to itself to such a degree that by the late 1920s the subject was
generating considerable controversy. The cessation of unrestricted
European immigration helped sharpen the focus and generated a
flood of proposals to restrict Mexican immigration. In the midst
of this controversy, the Mexican immigrant was less an actor than
one who was acted upon. The bloody upheavals which had intensified during the period of World War I and following had not
abated in Mexico; in the Mexican presidential election of 1928 *all*
of the candidates, including the winner, had been assassinated or
eliminated, and the Cristero Revolt had sent additional thousands
of refugees to the United States.

Refuting the Stereotype

Although the Mexican presence in the United States was fully
acknowledged by social workers, growers, politicians, labor unions,
and scholars, the position of the Mexican himself was seldom articu-
lated. That he did have something to say was shown by the even-
tempered observations of Ernesto Galarza, a Mexican immigrant
who had worked his way through Occidental College, Stanford, and
Columbia by laboring in the California fields, orchards, and canneries. Galarza provided a point-by-point refutation of the much-
publicized stereotypes. To the charge that the Mexican was content
to labor for low wages, low enough to keep him in beans and a
blanket, Galarza replied, "The Mexican is not innately married to
an animal standard of living." To the view that Mexicans were
improvident, Galarza suggested that "something should be known
of the high-pressure salesmanship to which he is practically always
a victim."[40]

Galarza's picture of the Mexican migrant worker bore little
resemblance to the one painted by the growers. He showed migrant
work for what it was — long on hope and short on income. Dis-

crimination in education was made obvious as the heritage of the homeland was deprecated by the public schools. Prejudice perpetuated the image of the Mexican as "unclean, improvident, indolent, and innately dull."

Farsighted Proposals

Galarza suggested possible solutions to the "Mexican Problem" which foreshadowed future developments. He proposed governmental regulations for the supply of migrant labor, a bilateral agreement with the Mexican government to solve the immigration question, use of Mexican Americans in social service agencies in contact with immigrants, and scientific and objective gathering of statistics to inform rather than mislead. And as a last point, Galarza asked "for recognition of the Mexican's contribution to the agricultural and industrial expansion of the western United States." He did not desire rhetoric in which the brawn of the Mexican in pouring cement, harvesting crops, and laying rails was acknowledged, but instead asked for an admission that the Mexican, in spite of his contributions, had been treated as a permanent foreigner in the land that had once been claimed by his ancestors.

Even as Galarza's words were being printed in the National Conference of Social Work's *Proceedings,* the question of the foreignness of the Mexican was being answered by the government of the United States, local private and public welfare agencies, and the Mexican immigrants themselves. Mexican repatriation, which during the 1920s had been publicized as part of the cycle of migration in which Mexicans would return from the United States after a season's work, took on a new meaning. With the beginning of the Great Depression, Mexicans were going home to stay.

3.
Closing America's Back Door

THROUGHOUT AMERICAN history there are many examples of people who moved or were moved from one place to another, either on a voluntary basis or under compulsion. In the eighteenth century the Acadians were forcibly removed from Port Royal by the British; after the American Revolution, Tory sympathizers lost possessions and property. As settlers moved across the North American continent, dozens of Indian tribes lost their lands and were placed on reservations often far removed from the land their ancestors had known. Negroes who experienced the beneficence of the American Colonization Society "returned" to Africa to found the nation of Liberia. Mormons who endured the hostility of their neighbors were finally compelled to seek refuge in a Zion to the West. As part of the post–Civil War movement which brought thousands of people across the continent, displaced veterans left bankrupt farms and plantations in their search for new opportunities.

Events in our recent past show that population movements, involuntary or voluntary in their causation, still occur. The most notorious involuntary movement in recent years was the relocation of the Japanese-American population of the United States during World War II. On the other hand, voluntary movements are much more subtle and less sensational than blatant violations of constitutional rights. An example of the voluntary type of movement is repatriation.

Repatriation means a return to one's homeland — more than a return — a sending back. Repatriations carried out at different times have had different meanings, tailored for the occasion. This is especially true when applied to immigrants from Mexico who returned to their homeland. Writers dealing with Mexican repatriation have sometimes found it necessary to precede the word with "voluntary" or "forced," with quotation marks to distinguish the catalyst.[1] (The various semantic differences are discussed in appendix A.)

Mexicans were not the only immigrant ethnic group to undergo repatriation. Although little has been written on the subject, other immigrants volunteered to return to their countries of origin to a degree that can be surprising to anyone who assumes that immigration to the United States was the culmination of a one-way dream. As many as four million immigrants, chiefly Englishmen, Germans, Greeks, Italians, and Poles, indicated their intention of going back to their homelands in the first two decades of the twentieth century. Between 1908 and 1922, 3,416,735 people classified as "aliens whose permanent residence has been in the United States who intend to reside permanently abroad" left the country.[2]

Inducements to Repatriate

Many aspects of the movement of Mexicans southward matched the return of European immigrants in motivation and circumstance, though with additional factors that should be noted. The closeness of the Mexican border, the convenience of railroad connections, and the nomadic nature of employment offered to Mexicans, promoted a two-way traffic across the border, as did the Mexican government's periodic announcements of agrarian reform programs. The chance to return to Mexico with relative ease to demonstrate the skills acquired and the possessions obtained, or to spend or invest the wealth earned, all contributed to a significant flow of Mexicans back to Mexico in the years preceding the depression.

Prominent agriculturists publicized the return of Mexicans to Mexico as part of the "cycle of migration" that occurred in a time of prosperity. Organized labor and opponents of unrestricted immigration, who noted the growth of the immigrant Mexican population in the United States, contested this viewpoint. The challenge of restrictionists affected the cycle of migration for Mexicans entering as well as leaving the United States. The fact that emigration from Mexico was abruptly reduced *before* the failure of the stock market deserves notice. Before the advent of the depression in 1929, attempts had been made to limit the number of Mexicans, particularly those classified as laborers, who were entering the United States.

Restrictionist Debates

Several recent studies have placed the movement for immigration restriction into historical perspective. Although the issue of a quota for Mexican immigration has been studied, it has not been described in any great detail. John Higham's *Strangers in the Land,* a study of American nativism from 1860 to 1925, presented a highly discerning examination of immigration and its restriction, but his book was concerned chiefly with immigration from Europe. Other books that included sections on immigration restriction for Mexico concentrated for the most part on congressional debates.[3] Nevertheless, a rich literature exists beyond 1924 that carries the argument on restriction to new heights (or depths) of polemical conviction, directed towards Mexicans.

Restrictionists included small farmers, progressives, labor unions, eugenicists, and racists, while large-scale growers of sugar beets, cotton, and vegetables, allied with railroads, chambers of commerce, and business associations generally favored unrestricted immigration. Both factions were prolific in their writings and verbose in their speeches, and both factions had politicians in their camps.

Passage of the Quota Act of 1924 had sealed off immigration from sections of Europe and Asia, but immigration from countries in the Western Hemisphere was not included in the law. With Mexico as the primary target, the American Federation of Labor, local governments with aliens on their relief rolls, and small farmers who felt they could not compete with growers who hired cheap Mexican labor, clamored to plug the hole in the law. They found a spokesman for their viewpoint in the House of Representatives, where John C. Box, a Democrat from east Texas, introduced one bill after another in successive sessions seeking to amend the Quota Act, only to see them die repeatedly in committee.

Box's initial effort was aired before the House Committee on Immigration and Naturalization during January and February 1926, but his bill ran into heavy opposition. Typical of the lobbyists who opposed immigration restriction was Samuel Parker Frisselle, a farmer owning five thousand acres of land in California. Frisselle's credentials included membership in the Fresno Chamber of Commerce, the California Development Association, and the California Federated Farm Bureau, all opposed to restriction. Frisselle declared that if the Box bill became law it would mean the end of agricultural development in the West. Crops grown there required large numbers of laborers to harvest them; white men would not or could not do the work, and the only source of labor came from Mexico.

Frisselle denied the existence of any established Mexican population in the San Joaquin Valley, believed the schools sufficient for the Mexican children, and, to questions regarding figures or statistics about the numbers of Mexicans, pleaded ignorance except to repeat that the Mexicans were "a transient population." He insisted, "We must have labor; the Mexican seems to be the only available source of supply, and we appeal to you to help us in the matter, imposing upon California the least possible burden."[4]

Other men took the stand to plead for unrestricted immigrant labor: farmers from Minnesota, Arizona, Texas, and other states asserted the lack of desire by white men to do farm laborer work, and their dependence upon the Mexican. In addition, by drafting the bill to apply to all countries in the Western Hemisphere, the bill's authors invited even more arguments against its passage. Box's first attempt never got out of committee.

At his earliest opportunity Congressman Box reintroduced the bill, amid speculation on the chances of the bill's being passed, or even heard. The first hearing date was set for 1 February 1928, in the Senate committee, and the first House date was three weeks after that.

Long before this, however, lobbyists favoring unrestricted Mexican immigration laid plans to meet the challenge. On 5 October 1927, some three dozen men met in Los Angeles under the auspices of the Los Angeles Chamber of Commerce. Many members of southwestern business communities, representing agriculture, railroads, and industry, were present. So were Senator Samuel Shortridge and Congressman Joe Crail of California. Unanimous in their opposition to the latest Box bill, the group voted its sentiments into writing: "The agricultural interests through the border and mountain states are a unit opposing this bill, realizing that it will interrupt and embarrass agricultural production throughout these states." The men pledged that their "whole endeavor, therefore, should be to kill it if possible." A conference of businessmen at El Paso held in November strongly upheld this position.

Agitation on both sides developed as the hearing dates neared. George P. Clements, manager of the chamber's department of agriculture, busily drafted publicity, sending mimeographed copies of antirestriction propaganda to congressmen and senators. He stressed the point that since the Mexican was an alien he could be deported, whereas Negroes, Filipinos, and Puerto Ricans, if brought into the Southwest to do agricultural work, would be there to stay.

The proponents of restriction also made their preparations. The *Saturday Evening Post,* a strong partisan of restriction, timed a series of articles by novelist Kenneth L. Roberts to appear in January, February, and March of 1928, during the hearings in Washington. Roberts reviewed not only the recent history of immigration but also the rise of southwestern agriculture, and questioned whether "the economic value in the Southwest's proposal to provide hypothetical profits for some farmers and manufacturers in 1928" was worth "the expense of saddling all future Americans with a dismal and distressing race problem." The *Post* also strongly editorialized on 7 January 1928, that "Every consideration of prudence and sound policy indicates that Mexican immigration must be put under quota restrictions."

Meanwhile in Washington, the Senate opened its Hearings on Restriction of Western Hemisphere Immigration on 1 February 1928, with Congressman Box's counterpart, Senator William J. Harris of Georgia, introducing S. 1437, "A Bill to Subject Certain Immigrants, Born in Countries of the Western Hemisphere, to the Quota under the Immigration Laws," and several related bills.

Lobbyists representing agricultural interests in California, Arizona, Texas, New Mexico, Idaho, Wyoming, and Colorado, in addition to lobbyists from the railroad, cattle, and mining interests, were present. Only the Department of Labor favored the bill; the Departments of State, Agriculture, and Interior all presented spokesmen against it. Chester B. Moore of the Vegetable Growers of Imperial Valley and Ralph H. Taylor, executive secretary of the Agricultural Legislative Committee of California, representing, as Moore later put it, "practically every producing Cooperative Association in California and representing about 175,000 farmers, orchardists, grape growers, milk and poultry producers," led the campaign against restriction.

The opposition to the bills proved more than the restrictionists could handle. Although both Moore and Taylor were interrupted any number of times by House or Senate committee members, their testimony and the statements of the other lobbyists carried the day. In 1928 the bills again did not get out of committee. On 2 April 1928, lobbyist Moore wrote back to the Imperial Valley growers, expressing his jubilation at the victory:

We were informed on our arrival in Washington that our efforts to stop legislation at this session of Congress would prove useless, and we felt the Immigration Committees were going to vote the bills out. Due to the splendid cooperation of the various states and industries interested in opposition to such legislation, we were able to make considerable impression on the Committees.

The controversy continued as proponents and opponents of restricting Mexican immigration delivered speeches, wrote articles, and petitioned their representatives in state and federal government. Before such groups as the Pasadena Women's Civic League and later the Interdenominational Council in Spanish Speaking Work, meeting at Pomona College in November 1928, Clements warned of the dangers inherent in importing the "Porto Rican Negro" for field work, preferring the "man who had no idea of becoming a citizen or a menace," the Mexican. "Should the immigration quota be applied to Mexico?" he asked his audience, and followed it with his emphatic answer: "Most assuredly NOT!"

Each side filled magazines with articles that upheld its position while denouncing the other.[5] In the war of print the restrictionists predominated, as more articles favoring restriction appeared than did those which opposed it. The *Saturday Evening Post,* with its huge circulation totalling over 2.7 million, frequently editorialized against Mexican immigration. "Readers in the Southwest continue to bombard us with requests that we redouble our efforts to make Congress see the imperative necessity for putting Mexican immigration upon a quota basis, or for restricting it sharply by other means," went a typical example in the 22 June 1929 issue.

Some reasons for restrictions were ingenious. One professor at the University of California, S. J. Holmes, wrote in the May 1929 issue of *North American Review* that he believed the present *illegal* migration sufficient to meet American labor needs and reason enough why the legal entries should be restricted. Other writers continued to warn of the dangers of miscegenation, or of an inundation of people who could not be assimilated.[6] Still others repeated economic arguments and debated the relative need for and benefit from Mexican labor.[7] The American Federation of Labor, on the state and national level, annually passed resolutions calling for restriction of Mexican immigration, since Mexican workers so often proceeded from agricultural to nonagricultural occupations, and were sometimes employed as strikebreakers, as had happened during the 1919 steel strike.

The advent of the depression brought a new urgency to both factions. In May 1930, during the second session of the Seventy-first Congress, Box again entered his proposals, this time in two bills. And again, they failed to come to the House floor. A joint resolution issued in the third session proposed a total restriction on *all* immigrants for two years. This resolution passed the House but failed to clear the Senate.[8]

Renewed Enforcement

Further attempts at restriction through legislation were rendered superfluous by an important new development: Mexican laborers were no longer entering the United States. The victory that proponents of restriction finally achieved did not come to them by act of Congress. While restrictionist attempts to secure a quota for Mexico were defeated, a partial success was achieved when consular officers, on orders from the U.S. State Department, began enforcing provisions of the Immigration Act of 1917 which in effect denied entry to most Mexicans who applied for visas. At the same time, Congress passed a law making illegal entry a punishable crime.

President Hoover had endorsed these measures as a way of solving the problem without the passage of restriction legislation that might be insulting to the government of Mexico. These moves indicated that the years of lax enforcement of the immigration laws on the United States' southern border were coming to an end.

The 1917 Immigration Act had excluded illiterates and had required payment of an eight-dollar head tax. Companies and agriculturists had once evaded these requirements by securing exemptions, but by the late 1920s the reception for Mexican immigrants at the border stations had changed considerably. Lax enforcement had allowed thousands of Mexicans to enter illegally. Mexicans who had lacked the eight dollars — and after 1924, eighteen dollars, with the imposition of a ten dollar visa fee — or for one reason or another had entered without applying through standard procedures, constituted a sizable if unknown quantity of Mexicans in the

United States. There were also Mexicans living north of the border whose residence dated back to a time that preceded any regulations on border crossing procedure. "It is difficult, in fact impossible," stated the commissioner general of immigration in 1923, "to measure the illegal influx of Mexicans over the border, but everyone agrees that it is quite large."[9]

Besides the illegal entry of Mexicans, the Bureau of Immigration had to contend with the smuggling of Chinese, Japanese, and European aliens over the Mexican border, and French Canadians over the northern border. At this time of heavy border traffic, "bootlegging" came to refer to the smuggling of aliens as well as liquor.

The Border Patrol

No force existed to combat the widespread illegal entry until 1925, when Congress appropriated a million dollars for the creation of the Border Patrol. Handicapped at first by lack of uniforms, inadequate and unqualified personnel, and a high turnover rate, the Border Patrol, nevertheless, soon developed high standards of efficiency and morale. At first the patrol lacked sufficient officers and equipment; areas which required attention twenty-four hours a day were covered for eight at the most, if at all.

In 1926, with 472 men in the Border Patrol, Commissioner General of Immigration Harry E. Hull requested a force of 660; in 1927, with the force grown to 632 employees, he asked for at least 1,000. By mid–1928 the Border Patrol numbered 781 employees, of whom 700 were patrol inspectors. The service attracted veterans and men with a sense of dedication. By 1930 the Border Patrol had achieved a reputation for integrity and efficiency, with both its personnel and its appropriation almost double their original size.[10]

The work was dangerous. In the seven years following its creation, the Border Patrol captured over one hundred thousand illegal aliens, and over twenty-six hundred smugglers who had attempted to bring the aliens over the border. Of fifteen men killed while serving the Border Patrol, twelve met their deaths along the Mexican Border.[11] Despite the impressive record that was created in so short a time, the Border Patrol probably deterred few aliens from crossing illegally during the period when it lacked funds and personnel. Yet the rapidly expanding operations of the patrol helped serve notice that the United States intended to maintain the integrity of its borders.

Visa Refusals

A second key factor in the administrative restriction of Mexican immigration lay in the instructions issued to United States consular officers. Unlike the lax enforcement of earlier years, consular officers beginning in August 1928 denied visas to most Mexicans desiring entry into the United States. Three basic reasons were used as standards for rejection. The first was illiteracy; the second, a rigid interpretation of the "LPC" — the liable to become a public charge provision of the 1917 Immigration Act. If the consul decided that a visa applicant might become indigent in the United States the visa was refused, even if the applicant possessed funds at the time of his interview with the consul. The third reason for refusal centered on the issue of contract labor and placed the applicant in a dilemma. If he indicated an advance commitment for employment in the United States, his visa could be denied on the grounds that the commitment violated the provision forbidding the entry of contract labor (though following American entry into World War I this rule had often been waived); if he kept such a commitment a secret, his application might be denied anyway, with the consul invoking the LPC provision.

The effect of this new policy on legal entries was striking, as shown by Vice Consul E. F. Drumwright's report submitted to the State Department on 4 September 1931. Between 1923 and 1929 an average of 62,000 Mexicans a year had legally entered the United States. In the year the new visa policy was put into effect, the figure dropped to 40,013; and for the fiscal year ending 30 June 1930, the number had been cut to 11,801. Between 1 July 1930, and 30 June 1931, only 2,457 Mexican immigrants were granted visas, a reduction of 94 percent from the 1929 figure.

More significantly, after March 1930 no visas at all were issued to Mexicans who were common laborers, unless they had resided previously in the United States; and 40 percent of the visas granted went to Mexicans who did not represent new immigration, but included people who were regularizing an illegal status or had lived in the United States previously as a legally entered alien.

Thus a border patrol increasing in size and efficiency, coupled with a strict policy on visa applications, provided a double deterrence to Mexicans who sought employment in the United States. Further-more, according to the Act of 4 March 1929, aliens who entered the United States by illegal means subsequent to that date were guilty of a misdemeanor punishable by a year in prison or a fine up to one thousand dollars. Under the same act, the attempted return of a previously deported alien was a felony charge.[12]

As a result of these changes in policy, there was a brief period before the stock market crash during which Mexican labor was in short supply. Mexican migrant workers in California's Imperial Valley conducted a brief but unsuccessful strike for better working conditions and wages in May 1928. Texas, having served for years as a huge labor reservoir for other states to draw upon, in 1929 passed a law which placed a tax on companies which sought to recruit workers from within her boundaries.

The Great Depression

The public debate over a quota for Mexico reached its zenith at the end of the decade. As consular officers asserted that their scrutiny of visa applications had curtailed immigration, the Border Patrol continued to guard the boundaries with horses and auto-mobiles. While Congressman Box and the restrictionists pursued their goal of a quota for Western Hemisphere countries, the stock market began its downward spiral in the autumn of 1929. The United States, accompanied by the rest of the world, entered the Great Depression.

Mexican workers in the United States were among the first to be dismissed from their jobs. During the first year of the depression, thousands of Mexicans were compelled to evaluate the position, achievements, and status they had attained by living and working in the United States. The limited employment opportunities, and the nature of the work offered to Mexicans, have already been noted. Working in the fields, Mexicans performed backbreaking tasks for their American employers. The seasonal nature of agricul-tural work made earning an adequate income an uncertain possibility. Growers expected Mexicans to answer their calls for labor and to put in a ten-hour day. Even in nonagricultural occupations, Mexi-cans earned low pay for long hours of work, in the face of the enmity of labor unions and small farmers.

Yet the differential in purchasing power made the sacrifices worthwhile. Tied to Mexico with bonds of birth, blood, and loyalty,

Mexican families waiting at a remote Arizona depot for a Mexico-bound train

many Mexicans spent years in the United States, periodically sending money back to their families and relatives in Mexico. In 1920, almost $9 million in postal money orders were remitted to Mexico; even during the agricultural depression of 1921, $4.5 million were sent. In 1928, before the depression, over $14 million in money orders were mailed back to Mexico. Individual amounts varied; some Mexicans remitted the full amount allowed by the post office, a limit of 207.25 pesos. Others might send as little as half a peso; still others sent nothing. Although some restrictionists claimed these remittances constituted a net loss to the United States, it was also pointed out that American industry and agriculture had benefited greatly from the labor which the Mexicans performed for their earnings.[13]

Even as the Mexican immigrant had made his way to work in

sugar beet fields and steel mills, his presence had provoked argument and hostility. In an age when neither the United States nor Mexico provided any meaningful supervision for laborers recruited by large companies, the Mexican worker might find himself stranded in a town whose mines had closed, or laid off during a slack period in railroad maintenance or harvesting. When this occurred, Anglo Americans were quick to complain about the presence of Mexicans on local relief rolls.

Where the English-speaking community on occasion offered active assistance, a lack of mutual understanding could occur. For example, in the spring of 1921, a period of unemployment in Fort Worth, Texas, the local Red Cross chapter noticed a large number of Mexican men in the bread lines. Anxious to do the right thing, the Red Cross offered beans to the Mexicans; unfortunately, since the Mexicans were mostly young single men, they were unable and unwilling to cook the beans, which had been given to them raw. The "bean line" was discontinued.

Some injustices and unfair practices were too much for a "docile Mexican" to tolerate. Occasionally remedies were available. California's State Commission of Immigration and Housing heard complaints from Mexicans regarding violations of contracts, fraud, interpretation of immigration laws, and wage disputes. The commission's complaint department reported that Mexicans more than any other nationality used its services, possibly because its clients could not afford to hire an attorney.

Mexico Beckons

The thought of returning to the homeland was apparently never far from the minds of most first generation Mexican immigrants. A return home prior to the depression meant short-term residents leaving after a season or two, or Mexicans who had been in the United States for years returning with material possessions and savings.

While the Mexican government endorsed a policy of repatriation from the time of Alvaro Obregón through the 1930s, the problems of Mexican politics prevented any organized program of repatriation from becoming fully implemented. Progress was made, however, in creating irrigation projects and constructing reservoirs. Projects in the states of Coahuila, Aguascalientes, Durango, Hidalgo,

Chihuahua, Sonora, and elsewhere promised a revitalization of Mexican agriculture in the late 1920s and early 1930s.

Mexicans living in the United States were frequently invited to take part in the development of farmland in these projects. Announcements of both private and government-owned lands in Mexico being opened for purposes of agricultural development were made known to Mexicans in the United States through their local consulates. Although mention was occasionally made of donating land to destitute Mexicans who returned from the United States, most land offers required capital either for purchase or rental. An investment in seed, tools, and other necessities for farming meant that only Mexicans who were financially prepared to do so could accept the Mexican land offers of the 1920s.

Too often, however, American welfare agencies accepted these offers of land and employment at more than their face value. The idea that Mexicans were leaving the United States to partake of Mexico's offers of land became a rationale in which the departure was a positive act rather than one of possible embarrassment for welfare officials.

The movement of Mexicans southward was greatly accelerated by the depression. The first repatriates to return to Mexico during the winter 1929–1930 were not generally destitute, as can be seen by the many reports of *repatriados* returning with material possessions such as automobiles and furniture. Word of possible location on an agricultural colony established for repatriates by the Mexican government, desire to see family and relatives, the prospect of purchasing land in the homeland with money earned in the United States, and the Mexican government's periodic offer to indigents of free railroad transportation from the border to the interior were all factors in a Mexican immigrant's decision to return to Mexico.

The increased traffic southward was duly noted by the American consuls in the months following the crash and ensuing depression. Consul General William Dawson reported to the State Department in February 1930 that "over five thousand Mexicans, most of them possessed of some means," were gathered around San Antonio, Texas, and "preparing to return." The consul at Ciudad Juárez, W. P. Blocker, learned in August 1930 that the Mexican Migration Service had announced that a special train would deliver two thousand people at a time from the border to the interior of Mexico. This was the second such train in ten months, and it relieved Ciudad Juárez of an excess of population.

A year after the beginning of the depression, the numbers passing through the border stations were still on the increase. Robert Frazer, Dawson's successor as consul general, estimated that almost twenty-seven hundred repatriates had crossed through Nuevo Laredo in the first fifteen days of December 1930. With the start of 1931, consular dispatches continued to describe a torrent of people passing through their border stations, an amalgam of *repatriado* and deportee, with a growing percentage of them penniless and hungry. Ciudad Juárez's municipal government was feeding two hundred people a day. On a single day, 9 January 1931, eight hundred repatriates were counted entering Mexico through the ports of Nogales and Nuevo Laredo, divided among some two hundred automobiles.[14] Mexican border stations were swamped, and where an occasional special train had been sent to Ciudad Juárez or Nogales, the Mexican government now found it necessary to provide transportation on at least a weekly basis.

The American consul at Nuevo Laredo, R. F. Boyce, made a detailed analysis of the repatriates passing through his station and submitted his report to the State Department on 8 January 1931. He found Mexicans returning from a wide area in the United States, with Mexicans from Texas predominating, as might be expected from his location. Few of the repatriates were recording their departure with the American authorities, leading the consul to believe that "at least half and perhaps more of these repatriates were illegally in the United States." It may also have been that the repatriates did not expect to return, but planned on remaining in Mexico longer than six months. The consul observed that many *repatriados* were leaving "after many years residence in the United States. Nothing but an acute unemployment crisis could have forced them out of the United States. Nearly all have been without employment for several months and have come to Mexico because they see no indication of better conditions in the near future."

In fact, conditions were about to worsen considerably for the many thousands of Mexican immigrants who had not yet considered the idea of repatriation. Viewing the large number of aliens in the United States in a time of depression, the United States government commenced an active drive on aliens living illegally in the United States. While the federal government aimed its campaign at aliens in general, Mexican aliens — those in the country legally as well as those who were deportable — were to find themselves prime targets for the Department of Labor's Bureau of Immigration.

4.
Focus on Los Angeles

DISAPPOINTED IN THEIR HOPES of earning adequate wages, thousands of Mexicans had recrossed the border of their own volition as the first year of the depression ended. Their departure for the most part was unsensational, lacking the fanfare of headlines, and was only routinely reported in the dispatches of consular officials. Then, in 1931, there occurred a series of events which resulted in a movement of Mexicans back to Mexico in unprecedented numbers. The impetus for the movement came on two levels: first, the repatriation programs organized by local public and private welfare agencies, representing an intensification of an earlier effort; and second, the federal government's campaign of threatened deportation.

The deportation of aliens could hardly be considered a new governmental practice, since the return of undesirable persons to their countries of origin was provided for by law and the policy's enforcement was a routine job of the Bureau of Immigration. Robert K. Murray's account of the 1919 deportation mania, *Red Scare: A Study in National Hysteria, 1919–1920,* indicates the extremes to which deportation policy could go. At the height of the Red Scare, newspapers warned of the impending downfall of the country at the hands of Communist agitators. The actual amount of radical activity was greatly exaggerated, and thousands of aliens, many of them completely innocent, were deported from the United States.

Although Mexican aliens in the United States received considerable attention in the early months of 1931, policies determining deportation came from the national level, with a general application to all alien groups. Defenders of civil liberties criticized harsh use of the immigration laws for their general application rather than their direction at any specific ethnic group.[1] President Hoover made his position regarding these laws and their enforcement quite clear. Believing that aliens were holding down jobs that could have been held by native-born Americans, Hoover endorsed a strenuous effort to curtail both legal and illegal entries and to expel undesirable aliens. This policy led to events often unrelated to the goal of reducing unemployment. Misinformation on legal procedures, "voluntary" deportation, and contradictory pronouncements by officials created a controversy which aroused criticism and anger in the United States and provoked the government and the press of Mexico.

Doak's Plan for Unemployment

Much of Hoover's problem resulted from his appointment of William N. Doak as secretary of labor to replace James J. Davis, who had been elected to the Senate. Doak promised to seek ways to solve the national unemployment problem. Soon after taking office on 9 December 1930, the new labor secretary proclaimed his solution. Doak proposed that one way to provide work for unemployed Americans was to oust any alien holding a job and to deport him. Announcing that there were four hundred thousand illegal aliens in the United States, Doak calculated that under the provisions of the immigration laws one hundred thousand of these aliens could be deported. During the first nine months of 1931, Doak sensationalized what had hitherto been a routine bureaucratic procedure of the Labor Department's Bureau of Immigration, and turned it into what one writer denounced as a "gladiatorial spectacle." This routine procedure was the process of arresting aliens who were suspected of being liable for deportation.[2]

Doak's immigration agents carried out the order to intensify their hunt for deportable aliens with dedicated zeal. They raided private homes and public places in a search that extended from New York City to Los Angeles. In doing so, they encountered heavy adverse criticism from liberal journals such as *Nation* and *New Republic,* which carried on a continuing editorial campaign against the arbitrary arrests and semisecret procedures allegedly practiced by the Bureau of Immigration.

Doak also vociferously protested against the findings of the National Commission on Law Observance and Enforcement, popularly known as the Wickersham Commission, which adopted a report highly critical of the Hoover administration's immigration policies. Although late in the year Doak did receive some critical correspondence from concerned citizens, most letters to the labor secretary came from private citizens and patriotic organizations, who favored his deportation campaign.

Immigration officers preferred to accomplish their work without the interference of the public or the noise of publicity. In fact, the dedication of the federal officials to the enforcement of the rules and regulations established by acts of Congress probably cannot be faulted. As the commissioner general of immigration observed in his *Annual Report* of 1931:

It is the purpose of the Department of Labor ... to foster, promote, and develop the welfare of the wage earners of the United States, to improve their working conditions, and to advance their opportunities for profitable employment; and it is a mere corollary of this duty and purpose to spare no reasonable effort to remove the menace of unfair competition which actually exists in the vast number of aliens who have in one way or another, principally by surreptitious entries, violated our immigration laws ... The force and effect of these provisions would be largely defeated if they were not accompanied by provisions for the deportation of those found in the country as having entered in violation of these restrictions.[3]

The idea that aliens were holding down jobs and that by giving those jobs to Americans, the depression could be cured, runs through the depression years as a cure-all with little foundation in fact.* Even while newspapers editorialized against the job-holding illegal alien, thousands of destitute, unemployed Mexican nationals were leaving the United States.

While Doak's agents carried on their hunt, the rationale for their work suffered from an obvious contradiction: although Doak asserted that deportation of aliens was essential for reducing unemployment, many of his targets were jobless and on relief. Doak's disregard of this distinction was further blurred by the Bureau of Immigration's intimidation of aliens who held outspoken, and

---

*This idea was sarcastically commented upon by the director of the Los Angeles immigration district in a report to the commissioner general of immigration on 17 June 1931, in which he explained his position in the events of the first six months of that year. Record Group 85, 55739/674, National Archives.

usually radical, political views. Yet despite the outcry against radical aliens and "Reds," at its peak the campaign resulted in the deportation of only eighteen aliens for advocating the overthrow of the government by violence.[4]

In cases where Mexicans were the illegal aliens, however, the immigration officials seldom bothered themselves with questions either of politics or economic status. As events proved, Mexican nationals illegally in the country were to be arrested not necessarily for political views, but more often for having violated provisions in the immigration laws pertaining to illegal entry and destitution.[5] Doak's deportation campaign reached aliens belonging to a number of ethnic groups, but the group most affected numerically was the Mexican alien in the United States.[6] The Bureau of Immigration's roundup of Mexican aliens during the Doak campaign concentrated on Southern California and the reason for the focus upon this area can be traced to a succession of moves by Los Angeles civic officials who had been concerned with unemployment relief.

Organizing in Los Angeles

With unemployment running high in Los Angeles, tentative efforts had been initiated toward alleviating the problem as the winter of 1930 approached. City and county officials, in conjunction with business leaders, concerned citizens, and the Los Angeles Chamber of Commerce, attempted to create a coordinating committee to work with charitable agencies such as the Red Cross and the Community Chest. The committee's chief goal was the creation of jobs through public works projects and offers of private businesses. Each relief agency, however, was to continue its own particular tasks as well. This bringing together of local relief efforts coalesced during October and November 1930 and was finally placed on firm ground towards the end of the following month. The delay was apparently due to the rivalry among the people involved. Mayor John C. Porter held out for a separate Los Angeles city coordinating committee, while others wanted one committee for all agencies and organizations in the county.[7]

Meanwhile, President Hoover had appointed Colonel Arthur Woods as national coordinator of the President's Emergency Committee for Employment (known as the PECE), and this organization began writing dozens of letters to cities throughout the country, offering encouragement, giving advice, and requesting information on individual local relief efforts so that the PECE could act as a clearing house.[8] Los Angeles, still in the process of organizing its relief committee, nonetheless received praise from the PECE for having "tackled the problem of unemployment in an affirmative way." Having been informed that much of the initiative had been undertaken by the Los Angeles Chamber of Commerce, the PECE suggested the creation of "a general city committee representative of local officials and the various social agencies."

Finally (and appropriately enough, on Christmas Eve), the organization of a local coordinating committee was completed — or rather, two committees, one for the city of Los Angeles, the other for the rest of Los Angeles County. Mayor Porter's unhappiness at not being made head of the county committee had resulted in a failure to achieve total unity. The county committee was to handle all unemployed people not residents of the city of Los Angeles, but the two committees did plan to work together. Harvey C. Fremming, a labor official from Long Beach, received the appointment of director of the county committee, while the same assignment for the city committee fell to Charles P. Visel.

Members of the Los Angeles Citizens Committee on Coordination of Unemployment Relief, the city committee's official title, represented a cross section of Los Angeles civic leadership. They included Mayor Porter, County Supervisor Frank L. Shaw, *Los Angeles Times* publisher Harry Chandler, Los Angeles Chamber of Commerce President John C. Austin, and various city officials and business executives. A city appropriation guaranteed the life of the committee until at least the following April. Coordinator Visel presented a plan to the committee, which approved his outline, and he began work immediately.

In its 25 and 27 December issues, the *Illustrated Daily News* reported on Visel's plan which called for contacting "all government, industrial and private sources of labor with a view toward creation of employment. Through a central clearing house, the applicants for jobs will be introduced to the available jobs most fitted for them." It was understood that preference in job placement would be given to longtime residents of the city. Office space for Visel was provided in the Los Angeles City Hall.

Visel's Scare Tactics

Visel soon placed a curious interpretation on his responsibilities. On 29 December he informed John B. Blandford of the PECE that he would "use existing agencies only and there will be no publicity," and that he would be "coordinating all existing agencies as far as possible to the standardization of applicant data, and creating all activity possible for job increase through . . . existing agencies." But Visel soon became interested in other ways of relieving the unemployment problem. Learning in early January 1931 of Doak's proclamation against the four hundred thousand illegal aliens, Visel sent a telegram to Colonel Woods, national coordinator of the PECE. In this astonishing telegram, Visel proposed a scheme through which illegal aliens living in Southern California might be induced either to remove themselves or to be removed. The telegram read:

We note press notices this morning. Figure four hundred thousand deportable aliens United States. Estimate five per cent in this district. We can pick them all up through police and sheriff channels. Local United States Department of Emigration [*sic*] personnel not sufficient to handle. You advise please as to method of getting rid. We need their jobs for needy citizens.

Visel received a reply from Woods on 8 January, in which the national coordinator asked him to contact Secretary Doak, and to state definitely how far the local law enforcement authorities would go in cooperating with the federal immigration officials. "There is every willingness at this end of the line," stated Woods, "to act thoroughly and promptly." Woods also urged Visel to use whatever influence he could muster in urging California's congressional representatives to support Doak's request for emergency appropriations.

Visel promptly wired Doak and urged the labor secretary to send agents from several other cities to create a "psychological gesture." It was not Visel's intention to press the Bureau of Immigration into conducting an indefinite number of deportation hearings, but rather to establish an environment hostile enough to alarm aliens. "This apparent activity," Visel's telegram promised Doak, "will have tendency to scare many thousand alien deportables out of this district which is the result desired." Doak responded quickly to Visel's telegram and thanked him for his efforts.

The plan of Coordinator Visel to scare aliens into leaving Southern California was built along simple lines. First, there would be publicity releases announcing the deportation campaign and stressing that help from adjoining districts would be given the local office of the Bureau of Immigration. Then a few arrests would be made, "with all publicity possible and pictures." Both police and deputy sheriffs would assist. It was hoped that some aliens would be frightened into leaving and that others would steer clear of Los Angeles.

A few days after the exchange of telegrams, Visel sent Woods a copy of the publicity release he intended to give "all newspapers of Los Angeles, including especially foreign language newspapers," for publication on Monday, 26 January. Visel also requested that the Labor Department send "a very strong wire" which might be used in a follow-up story later in the week. He informed Woods, "It is the opinion of the Immigration authorities here that these articles will have the effect of scareheading many thousand deportable aliens. This is an urgent plea for definite positive aggressive cooperation on a principal unemployment relief measure." * (See appendix B for a verbatim reprint of Visel's publicity release.)

Visel evidently based the endorsement of his plan by the local immigration bureau office on his interview with Walter E. Carr, the Los Angeles district director of immigration. According to Visel's version of the interview, which he sent to Colonel Woods, Carr had stated "that there are undoubtedly many thousand aliens illegally in this section (mostly Mexicans and Japs [sic])," and "that the machinery set up for deportation would be entirely inadequate on a large scale." Carr allegedly went on to say, however, "that with a little deportation publicity, a large number of these aliens, actuated by guilty self-consciousness, would move south and over the line of their own accord, particularly if stimulated by a few arrests under the Deportation Act."

Although Visel's correspondence with Woods and Doak suggests a particularly close-knit organization on the part of government bureaucracy in rooting out aliens, in actuality the interdepartmental lines were very tenuous. The President's Emergency Committee for Employment, which Colonel Woods headed, was an agency of the Department of Commerce, whereas Doak's domain lay in the Department of Labor. The local citizens' relief committees organized

---

*The word "scareheading" was coined by Visel and used frequently by him.

throughout the country by cities and counties (with relative success) were not the foundation stones of a hierarchical structure. The PECE's relative degree of accomplishment came from the coordinating of activities engaged in by hundreds of these local committees, some of which were well organized and active, while many others were but names on paper.

Visel's contribution from the city of Los Angeles to the PECE, apart from setting up a job bureau and contacting employers who might have job openings, was to suggest that unemployment relief could be obtained by the city's taking part in Doak's deportation campaign — an idea to which neither Woods nor Doak raised any objection, qualification, or disagreement.

In evaluating the conflicting statements, which later were made when the federal government and officials such as Carr strongly denied making any endorsements of a deportation policy aimed specifically at one ethnic group, it would seem that Visel set down in print what he had wanted to hear rather than what he had heard. Visel sent his letter and news release to Woods on 19 January, and followed it up with an impatiently worded telegram on the twenty-third, stating: "RE-LETTER NINETEENTH REPLY URGENTLY NEEDED HERE PLEASE WIRE QUICKLY THANKS."

Woods should have given Visel's news release a more careful reading and considered how it might be interpreted in a city that contained within its population the largest number of Mexican nationals outside of Mexico, D.F., plus Mexican Americans. Instead, the national coordinator tried to reach Doak, who was visiting Ellis Island. Contact was made, and Doak authorized the sending of a special officer and several agents to Los Angeles to investigate the presence of illegal aliens there. (The records of the correspondence of Woods and Visel now held in the National Archives offer no evidence that Secretary of Labor Doak ever saw Visel's news release.)

Impact of Publicity

Visel's publicity release was published in the Los Angeles newspapers on Monday, 26 January. For an alien deportation campaign, this proved to be a most portentous week. On the previous Saturday night a man, identified in one newspaper headline as a "Mexican," in another as an "alien," and in the text of the articles as both, shot and mortally wounded a police officer. The officer took until Wednesday to die; his fight for life was followed closely in the newspapers, as were the funeral proceedings. Meanwhile, the progress of the trial of two Mexicans accused of committing an attack of double rape provided daily diversion for Los Angeles readers.*

While it would be an exaggeration to describe the Los Angeles of 1931 as a wide-open town, during the depression years this city fully deserved the national reputation it had acquired for odd doings. One former district attorney was serving time in prison, another would be indicted by the grand jury in the near future, and Mayor Porter would face a recall election in 1932. A county supervisor was caught stealing funds while settling a flood control contract. Supervisor Frank Shaw replaced Porter and was himself recalled in 1938 amid charges of widespread corruption in his administration.

The Los Angeles *Record,* the only consistently liberal newspaper in an open-shop town, continuously castigated the police force as "cossacks," and the day-to-day newspaper stories made a dreary montage of crime, death, police brutality, civic corruption, and the sexual foibles of movie stars. Reverend Bob Shuler, a rival of Aimee Semple McPherson and a prototype of Father Coughlin, mixed religion and local politics in a strange combination of the spiritual and the temporal.[9]

News coverage of efforts to provide jobs for the jobless and relief for the helpless was less concerned with humanitarian issues than with the political aspects of who was at fault for doing the least amount of cooperating. In the latter part of January, the Communist party endorsed a plan of "hunger marches" on the Los Angeles City Hall. Several hundred people participated in one such march on 19 January and were met with tear gas; the city hall required a guard detail when a bomb threat was made.[10]

---

*These events can be followed in the issues of the *Los Angeles Times,* 25 Jan. 1931: POLICEMAN SHOT IN KIDNAP FIGHT; *Los Angeles Examiner,* 26 Jan. 1931: DETECTIVE SHOT BY ALIEN FIGHTS FOR HIS LIFE; *Examiner,* 27 Jan. 1931: BECK SHOOTING SUSPECT HELD; *Times,* 28 Jan. 1931: OFFICER LOSING FIGHT FOR LIFE; *Times,* 29 Jan. 1931: SLAIN OFFICER TO BE HONORED; *Illustrated Daily News,* 31 Jan. 1931: MEXICAN TO FACE TRIAL IN SHOOTING. For the rape case, see the *Los Angeles Examiner,* 26 Jan. 1931.

In the months preceding the publication of Visel's publicity release, various elements in Los Angeles had indicated support for the idea of restricting jobs on public works projects to American citizens. Motions were presented and passed by the Los Angeles city council and the county board of supervisors, while the Independent Order of Veterans of Los Angeles called for the deportation of illegal aliens as a means of aiding jobless relief.[11]

The board of supervisors went so far as to endorse legislation pending in Congress and in the state legislature, which would bar aliens who had entered the country illegally from "establishing a residence, holding a position, or engaging in any form of business." Supervisor John R. Quinn believed that such legislation would provide a sort of cure-all for all problems generated by illegal aliens, whom he believed numbered "between 200,000 and 400,-000 in California alone." Said Quinn in two remarkably all-inclusive sentences:

If we were rid of the aliens who have entered this country illegally since 1931 . . . our present unemployment problem would shrink to the proportions of a relatively unimportant flat spot in business. In ridding ourselves of the criminally undesirable alien we will put an end to a large part of our crime and law enforcement problem, probably saving many good American lives and certainly millions of dollars for law enforcement against people who have no business in this country.

Quinn also believed the "Red problem" would disappear with the deportation of these aliens.[12]

It was in this atmosphere that Visel's release was published by the Los Angeles newspapers. Each newspaper printed the text as it saw fit, so that while one newspaper printed sections of it verbatim, another summarized and paraphrased. Certain embellishments were added. "Aliens who are deportable will save themselves trouble and expense," suggested the Los Angeles *Illustrated Daily News* on 26 January 1931, "by arranging their departure at once." On that same day, the *Examiner,* a Hearst paper, announced, without going into any qualifying details, that "Deportable aliens include Mexicans, Japanese, Chinese, and others."

As the days passed, follow-up stories and editorials kept the public aware of the project. The *Express* two days later editorially endorsed restrictionist legislation and called for compulsory alien registration. On 29 January the *Times* quoted Visel, who urged "all nondeportable aliens who are without credentials or who have not registered to register at once, as those having papers will save themselves a great deal of annoyance and trouble in the very near future. This is a constructive suggestion." The impending arrival of the special agents from Washington, D.C., and other immigration districts was made known, the word being given by Visel to the newspapers.

La Opinión, the leading Spanish-language newspaper in Los Angeles, published an extensive article on Thursday, 29 January. With a major headline spread across page one, the newspaper quoted from Visel's release and from the versions of it given by the *Times* and the *Illustrated Daily News. La Opinión's* article pointedly stressed that the deportation campaign was being aimed primarily at those of Mexican nationality.

Mexican Government Investigates

By the end of the week, it became apparent that the announcements of an impending deportation campaign were attracting the attention of more than just the readership of the Los Angeles newspapers. The Mexican government, observing the movement of repatriates southward from the United States for some time, received word of the announcements in Los Angeles.[13] Its Foreign Relations Department contacted Rafael de la Colina, the Mexican consul in Los Angeles, and instructed him to send a report describing the possibility of a large number of Mexicans resident in Los Angeles being deported. The consul had been working with Los Angeles authorities on the idea of repatriating destitute Mexicans to Mexico, and also assisting the Mexican community in raising donations for that purpose. But a plan to deport de la Colina's compatriots in great numbers was something else again. Contacting the Los Angeles Chamber of Commerce's George P. Clements, a strong advocate of Mexican labor in the United States, de la Colina asked him to urge all persons involved in the publicity to restate and clarify their intentions in the newspapers.[14]

The involvement of the Los Angeles Chamber of Commerce in the deportation campaign came from that organization's relief efforts in the latter months of 1930. Visel had been keeping the chamber informed of his relief plans, including the deportation scare idea. As early as 8 January 1931, Arthur G. Arnoll, the chamber's general manager, had cautioned Visel to keep his publicity "from upsetting the whole Mexican population by wholesale raids which are misunderstood by the Mexican," and which might also disturb the communities that served California's agricultural labor needs.

On de la Colina's request, Clements went to the consulate, where he "found the Mexican Consul's office very much wrought up." The consul had the definite impression that the deportation campaign in Los Angeles was to be aimed specifically at the Mexican community. Clements "assured them that there must be some error." Then, as Clements later reported to Arnoll, the morning edition of the *Express* and an unidentified Spanish-language newspaper were delivered, "both of which virtually stated that all Mexicans were to be deported. Also while I was in the office dispatches were received from Mexico City ordering Mr. Colina to make a careful investigation and report." Clements, positive that Visel's publicity had not emphasized the Mexicans "any more than Scotland or Germany," promised Consul de la Colina that he would check with Visel at city hall, as well as look over the publicity releases the relief coordinator had written.

Without delay, Clements went to Visel. Either the coordinator recognized the misinterpretation possible in his publicity, or else Clements made him aware of its potential. At any rate, the two men then confronted Walter E. Carr, the district director of immigration, who agreed that a statement denying the intention of a general deportation campaign which focused on Mexican aliens should be published as quickly as possible. He hastily drafted such a statement and sent it to the local newspapers.

Later that day, Clements met again with Mexican Consul de la Colina to report that a news release had been issued assuring that the deportation campaign was aimed at no particular group.

Media Misinterpretations

But the manner in which the Los Angeles press treated Carr's statement failed to clarify the intentions of the immigration service. If anything, the bureau's motives were confused and misinterpreted all the more. On 30 January, the *Evening Herald* quoted Carr's release at length, the *Evening Express* somewhat less so, and the following day the *Times* and the *Illustrated Daily News* simply ran brief summaries. Wide publication did not abate Clements' concern for the press's interpretation of the release, and on 31 January, he sent a memo to Arnoll, expressing his dislike for the *Express* in particular and saying that "they have always been Mexican baiters."

La Opinión on 31 January 1931 ran a major front-page article, assuring its readers that the intention of the federal government was to prosecute aliens with criminal records. This interpretation of the deportation drive was the one Carr had given to all the newspapers. He had stated, "It has never been the policy of the State Department [*sic*] to direct its forces against any one race. We are treating the Mexicans on exactly the same basis as we treat the Canadians, neither of whom are under quota provisions."

He was also quoted as saying, "If we have aliens who have committed crimes we are going to spend all available funds, if necessary, to deport them before we deport honest laboring people who may be in this country illegally because of some technicality," thus indicating his awareness that many Mexicans, because of the changes wrought by the evolution of the United States immigration laws, had entered the country under irregular circumstances.*

In view of who was held for investigation, arrested, deported, or induced to undergo voluntary departure, the summaries of what Carr had stated were at best misleading, at worst wildly inaccurate. On 31 January the *Times* said, "[T]he Immigration Bureau in this district is confining most of its efforts to aggravated cases, especially where an alien has been convicted of a crime, and does not devote much attention to laboring men who technically may be illegally in this country." The same day, the *Illustrated Daily News* condensed it even further: "[T]he local immigration department is concentrating on aliens with criminal records." When undertaken, the actual campaign proceeded on plans rather divergent from the direction promised by the newspapers.

Federal Agents Arrive

On Saturday, 31 January, the day following the issuance of Carr's statement, Supervisor William F. Watkins of the Bureau

---

*Entry under irregular circumstances is suggested as entry during the periods prior to 1929 when it was not a misdemeanor, prior to 1924 when there was no visa fee, prior to 1917 when there was no head tax or literacy test, and prior to 1908 when there was no accurate enumeration at all. It cannot be reasonably expected that Mexicans coming to the United States for whatever reasons impelled them to make the move would be aware of all the new changes and requirements in these periods of transition.

On the attitude of people living alongside both sides of the border towards the artificiality of the laws imposed upon a natural geographic region, see Dean Williams, "Some Political and Economic Aspects of Mexican Immigration" (Master's thesis, University of California, Los Angeles, 1950), chap. 1.

of Immigration arrived in Los Angeles, largely unaware of the fanfare of publicity which had preceded him. A meeting was called at the district immigration office, where Watkins met Visel, Sheriff William Traeger, Chief of Police Roy E. Steckel, and Carr. Visel restated his reasons for requesting federal aid in deporting illegal aliens from Los Angeles. There were, he alleged, twenty thousand of Doak's four hundred thousand aliens in the Southern California area, and he assured Watkins that the police and sheriff's offices would assist in apprehending deportable aliens.

Watkins pointed out that Doak, while maintaining that there were four hundred thousand aliens illegally in the United States, had qualified his remark by stating a figure of one hundred thousand eligible for deportation under current immigration laws. Since Visel could give no source for his estimate, Watkins had to conclude "that there can not be five per cent of the total number of the deportable aliens in the United States situated in this locality." The vagueness which underlay Visel's reasoning in bringing Watkins three thousand miles across the continent plainly disturbed the immigration agent. "It serves," said Watkins, "to illustrate the viewpoint and attitude of Mr. Visel toward this matter in general."

Continuing his presentation, Visel explained that his original idea had been to have the Department of Labor send a few men to Los Angeles and, by means of extensive newspaper publicity about their activities, to "scarehead" aliens, for the most part Mexicans, out of the United States without the bother of formal deportation hearings. About this idea Watkins later parenthetically remarked in his report to Assistant Secretary of Labor Robe Carl White:

The success of such idea is. of course, open to question, as doubtless many aliens who have wilfully and knowingly entered the United States in violation of law would not choose to so easily forfeit their improperly acquired privileges here, and would more likely move further from the border rather than toward it, as a result of these deportation activities.

Appraising Chief Steckel and Sheriff Traeger as "apparently conservative, practical men," Watkins noted that while the two law enforcement officers offered "the full cooperation and assistance of their men in this work," they nevertheless "did not appear to share Mr. Visel's view as to the method of apprehending aliens for deportation." A second conference was scheduled for the following Friday, 6 February, and the meeting ended.

Visel, who, on the arrival of Watkins and his eighteen agents, had promised the supervisor office space and facilities for the deportation work, found after making several inquiries that no one could supply the immigration agents with satisfactory accommodations. Carr then offered to double up, and the local office succeeded in renting an additional room on the same floor as the district immigration headquarters. "No additional furniture is available for our needs," reported Watkins, "but arrangements are being made to rent some second-hand equipment for this purpose." He also obtained a truck and two automobiles from the Border Patrol, plus three drivers, and the promise of another vehicle from the office at San Pedro.

Unwelcome Press Coverage

Watkins had hoped to avoid contact with newspaper reporters, "but in view of the policy of publicity already indulged in by Mr. Visel, it has not been possible to prevent in every instance word of our plans reaching the papers." This was an understatement; at a meeting in Chief Steckel's office on the following Monday evening, 2 February, to map out procedures (without Visel present), they were confronted by reporters "ready to take photographs of those present apparently with the object of featuring a story."

No doubt exasperated at this point by the practices of Los Angeles journalism, Watkins insisted that no pictures be taken of his agents. The story appeared anyway in Tuesday morning's *Examiner* on the first page of the paper's local news section, under the headline, U.S. AND CITY JOIN IN DRIVE ON L.A. ALIENS, misprinting Watkins' initials and quoting several statements by Chief Steckel which were quite at variance with the moderating tone of other papers of a few days earlier: MEXICANS BEING TREATED LIKE OTHER ALIENS;[15] DRIVE AIMED AT NO ONE RACE, SAYS OFFICIAL;[16] DENY PLAN TO DEPORT MANY MEXICANS.[17] Said Steckel, "When an arrest is made, attention will be paid not only to the person under arrest, but to all members of his family." In addition to this remarkable statement, Steckel continued:

Most of our crime problems are caused by aliens without respect for the laws of the country. Many of them are open to deportation. Now, with the full cooperation of the Government, we will give particular attention to their status as citizens. In cases where there is doubt the Government will be immediately notified and will have ample time to investigate.[18]

Noting that the information supplied by the *Examiner* article was copied in the local foreign language press, "including several Japanese, Mexican, Italian and other periodicals,"* Watkins expressed the belief that all the publicity had suggested to any deportable aliens that they make themselves scarce. Nevertheless, Watkins decided that there must be fire behind all the smoke, and he planned to go ahead with the rounding up of suspected illegal aliens. On 8 February 1931, he wrote to Assistant Labor Secretary White:

I am not overly sanguine of our ability to pick up contraband aliens in large numbers or groups (much less in the volume represented in Mr. Visel's first correspondence), but I do believe from what I have observed since arriving here that there are many aliens hereabouts amenable to the immigration laws. In my opinion the situation will ultimately resolve itself into one involving relentless and diligent effort on the part of our officers to locate and apprehend the class of aliens sought.

Apprehending the Deportables

Commencing Tuesday, 3 February, Watkins and his men, with the assistance of police and deputies, began ferreting out aliens. By Saturday thirty-five deportable aliens had been apprehended.[19] Of this number, eight were immediately returned to Mexico by the "voluntary departure" method, while an additional number chose to take the same procedure in preference to undergoing a formal hearing. Several aliens were held for formal deportation on charges of violating the criminal, immoral, or undesirable class provisions of the immigration laws. Five additional immigration inspectors arrived to provide assistance, and five more were shortly expected. On Friday, 6 February, Watkins held the second conference, and the work undertaken so far was evaluated.

Evidently dissatisfied with the degree of help given him by the local authorities, Watkins made it plain "that the Department of Labor had been informed that the forces of the Chief of Police and Sheriff would apprehend and deliver to the immigration authorities for deportation those contraband aliens located in this vicinity," and he now requested Steckel and Traeger to indicate definitely if this was to be done.

---

*In 1931 about a dozen ethnic newspapers, most of them with small circulations, were published in Los Angeles. *La Opinión* was the leading Spanish-language paper, with a daily circulation in 1931 of over fourteen thousand.

The two law enforcement officers then expressed, in Watkins' words, "their inability to undertake any such campaign, and . . . for them to attempt such a drastic move, involving indiscriminate apprehension of aliens by their officers who are admittedly unqualified to determine the question of deportability of aliens, and the delivery of aliens wholesale merely on the suspicion that they might be illegally in the United States in order that they shall be examined by immigration officers to ascertain deportability, following which they would be released or held, as the facts warranted, would not only have no justification in law but [would] render them liable to numerous damage suits for false arrests, etc." Following these hedgings on the officers' promised assistance, Watkins turned to Visel, who "replied that he had no experience in police work and did not consider himself qualified to formulate a plan of action."

Watkins, seeing that now even Visel recognized the impracticality of the scheme originally proposed to the Labor Department, proceeded to lay out a plan in which the most feasible means of apprehending aliens could be organized, with the immigration officers taking the initiative away from the local authorities. Steckel and Traeger promised to assign officers to work with the immigration agents in whatever parts of Southern California were likely hiding places for deportable aliens. They were to check aliens and refer any suspects to the immigration officers for further examination.

At this point Supervisor Watkins committed an error: he decided to go through with a roundup of aliens despite the obvious facts that misrepresentations had been made to the Department of Labor concerning the numbers of aliens and the promise of active prosecution by local authorities, and that the semisecret nature of the work involved in detecting illegal aliens had been seriously compromised by all the publicity. In his 8 February 1931 report to White, Watkins wrote:

Though the representations made to the Secretary concerning the alien situation here be discounted, it is my opinion that a very fertile field exists hereabouts for energetic and intelligent activity on the part of the immigration service toward accomplishing the expulsion of deportable aliens. The force regularly attached to this office appears to be too small to adequately care for the deportation work which I believe can be developed. It is my belief that several months [sic] effort on the part of the augmented force will be necessary to accomplish the desired results in connection with the deportation of aliens hereabouts. We will, of course, devote our best efforts to that end.

Watkins had already run into the situation in which some suspected aliens stopped by his men presented head tax receipts or some other proof of entry, as if they anticipated examination. Had Watkins been aware of Visel's comments as quoted in the *Los Angeles Times* of 29 January, he would perhaps have better understood why the aliens were so prepared. Though he did brand the idea of picking up large numbers of contraband aliens at will as a "fantasy" of Los Angeles officials, his decision to stop and investigate large numbers of people in the hopes of capturing a few deportable aliens served to aggravate an already tense situation.

Unaware of the propensity of the Los Angeles press to write headlines before all the facts were in, and uninformed on particular problems of ethnic minorities in Los Angeles, Watkins nonetheless decided to press the investigation. In doing so, he showed a surprising lack of awareness as to why Mexicans had been crossing the border, the length of time they had been crossing it, and the unique problems so many of them had. "After our inspectors become more familiar with local conditions," he promised White, "and form contacts through which valuable information may be obtained as to the identity and whereabouts of contrabands, I think we can expect some very satisfactory results."

If Watkins thought that Visel had been discouraged by the more realistic attitude presented by the immigration agents at the two meetings, the impression would have been a mistaken one. Visel was pleased at the arrival of the outside inspectors, for Watkins and his men proceeded to do just what Visel's plans had called for.

On 3 February 1931, Visel notified Colonel Woods, national coordinator for the PECE, that "thanks to Secretary of Labor Doak's cooperation and the arrival of his special representative, Mr. Watkins," he could "report considerable activity on our alien deportable [*sic*] problem." Though at this point Watkins was just beginning his investigations, said Visel, "There is an aggressive campaign under way right now with, so far, gratifying results."

For about twelve days after the launching of the drive on illegal aliens, Watkins and his men managed to do their work without hindrance from the newspapers, though the *Express* continued its interest in the problem with an editorial on 13 February 1931 entitled SEND THEM HOME. While Watkins was at first successful in apprehending a number of deportable aliens, the number captured decreased shortly; the searches were also hampered by a series of rainstorms which drenched Southern California during February.

El Monte Raid

Then, on Friday the thirteenth, with the assistance of thirteen sheriff's deputies led by Captain William J. Bright of the sheriff's homicide detail, the immigration agents staged a raid in the El Monte area. This action was given prominence in the Sunday editions of the *Times* and the *Examiner*. Watkins wrote White that such coverage was "unfortunate from our standpoint," because the impression was given by the articles that every district in Los Angeles County known to have aliens living there would be investigated. "Our attitude in regard to publicity was made known to the authorities working with us in this matter," Watkins complained, "but somehow the information found its way into the papers."

Considering Carr's previous announcements that no ethnic group was being singled out and that only aliens with criminal records were the primary interest of the Bureau of Immigration, the aliens captured in the Friday the thirteenth raid could only have made the Mexican community wary of official statements. Three hundred people were stopped and questioned: from this number, the immigration agents jailed thirteen, and twelve of them were Mexicans. The *Examiner* conveniently supplied the public with the names, ages, occupations, birth places, years in the United States, and years or months in Los Angeles County, while the *Times* was content just to supply the names.[20]

While generalizations are impossible about the people stopped, questioned, and occasionally detained, the assertions that all the aliens either were people holding jobs (that only could be held by citizens) or were criminals in the county did not apply to these arrested suspects. Of the twelve Mexicans arrested, the most recent arrival in the United States had come eight months earlier, while three had been in the United States at least seven years, one for thirteen years, and another was classified as an "American-born Mexican," a term which carried no clear meaning, inasmuch as the charge against the suspects was illegal entry. Eleven of the twelve gave their occupation as laborer; the twelfth said he was a waiter.

Aliens In Hiding

As Watkins pursued the search for deportable aliens, he observed that the job became progressively difficult:

After the first few roundups of aliens . . . there was noticeable falling off in the number of contrabands apprehended. The newspaper publicity which attended our efforts and the word which passed between the alien groups undoubtedly caused great numbers of them to seek concealment.

After several forays into East Los Angeles, the agents found the streets deserted, with local merchants complaining that the investigations were bad for business. In the rural sections of the county surveyed by Watkins' men, whole families disappeared from sight. Watkins also began to appreciate the extent of Southern California's residential sprawl. He observed that the Belvedere section, according to the 1930 census, might hold as many as sixty thousand Mexicans.

Watkins had more direct success in his searches when he assigned several inspectors to check for possible aliens held in jail for other crimes. "In 200 alien investigations at the County Jail, 19 have been found to be deportable, against whom proceedings have been instituted," Watkins reported. Here he was able to quiz suspects charged with crimes like prostitution, procuring, and fraud.

Several Thousand Questioned

In a three-week period the immigration agents had checked and questioned several thousand people at various places throughout the county (most of the investigating officers spoke Spanish). By 21 February some 225 aliens subject to deportation had been apprehended. Sixty-four of them agreed to depart voluntarily and were taken to the Mexican border by truck, while the rest were held for formal warrant proceedings. The latter category, of course, held a number of Chinese, Japanese, and Caucasians, but in Watkins' words, it was "the Mexican element which predominates."

Coordinator Visel, extremely satisfied with the way the work was being conducted, wrote a letter of appreciation to Colonel Woods on 21 February:

You will recall our request for a "gesture" and help from Secretary Doak on the deportable alien problem.

We are very gratified to report to you that the special activity along this line, set up by the Department of Labor, Immigration Department, is functioning 100% efficiently, quietly, with what we feel is probably the maximum of result.

There is no question in the writer's mind but that the aliens, mostly deportable, who have already left this vicinity, have released many hundreds of jobs, which of course will automatically go to those legally in the country and help our situation just that much.

Mexicans Air Complaints

The Mexican and other ethnic communities were not about to take the investigations passively. *La Opinión* railed at officials for the raids, while ethnic brotherhood associations gave advice and assistance. A meeting of over one hundred Mexican and Mexican-American businessmen on the evening of 16 February resulted in the organization of the Mexican Chamber of Commerce in Los Angeles, and a pledge to carry their complaints about the treatment of Mexican nationals to both Mexico, D.F., and Washington, D.C. Mexican merchants in Los Angeles, who catered to the trade of their ethnic group, felt that their business had been adversely affected, since Mexicans living in outlying areas now hesitated to present themselves in Los Angeles for possible harassment. Sheriff Traeger's deputies in particular were criticized for rounding up Mexicans in large groups and taking them to jail without checking whether anyone in the group had a passport or proof of entry.

Consul de la Colina appeared at the 16 February meeting as an invited guest, and he promised to uphold the rights of his compatriots before the pressures of immigration officials who acted in so arbitrary a manner.[21] De la Colina had been working tirelessly on behalf of destitute Mexicans in need of aid or desiring repatriation. Much of his time was occupied with meeting immigration officials who kept assuring him that the Mexicans were not being singled out for deportation. He also warned against unscrupulous individuals who were taking advantage of Mexican nationals by soliciting funds for charity and issuing bogus affidavits to Mexicans who had lost their papers.[22]

The Japanese community also expressed its hostility to the immigration officials. When several agents stopped to investigate some suspected Japanese aliens, the owner of the ranch employing the aliens threatened to shoot the inspector "if he had a gun." Japanese people obstinately refused to answer any questions, and

Watkins believed that an attorney had been retained by the Japanese for the purpose of circumventing the immigration laws.

Despite the adverse reaction to and public knowledge of the drive on aliens, Watkins persisted. "I am fully convinced that there is an extensive field here for deportation work and as we can gradually absorb same it is expected [*sic*] to ask for additional help," he stated. Responding to the charges of dragnet methods, he notified his superiors in Washington:

I have tried to be extremely careful to avoid the holding of aliens by or for this Service who are not deportable and to this end it is our endeavor to immediately release at the local point of investigation any alien who is not found to be deportable as soon as his examination is completed.

The tension cooled briefly as the immigration officials held off making further raids for a few days, and Carr and Watkins again issued a statement giving assurance that they intended no persecution of a particular ethnic group, and that only aliens illegally in the country were to be deported.[23] This statement may be contrasted with the one released to the papers by Carr on 30 January. The Spanish-speaking community must have found the contradictions baffling, as official pronouncements of fair treatment alternated with intensive prosecutions. This uncertainty was reflected in *La Opinión,* which announced a raid on 15 February, a promise of amity four days later, another raid on 22 February, another promise three days later, and still another raid on 27 February.

Even the *Los Angeles Evening Express* (which had changed owners in mid-February) presented an editorial on 19 February 1931 regretting the current impression "among Mexican residents of Los Angeles that they are the particular object of search of Federal and local officials, and that irrespective of the manner of their entrance into the country they are liable to deportation."

City Plaza Raid

Watkins renewed the controversy on 26 February when his agents, assisted by over two dozen Los Angeles policemen, surrounded the downtown plaza at three o'clock in the afternoon. About four hundred people were detained within the grounds of the small circular park for over an hour.

As this raid was not covered by the Los Angeles metropolitan newspapers, the details concerning it must come from two obviously

Reproduced from newspaper clipping

On 27 February 1931, *La Opinión,* Los Angeles Mexican daily, carried this front-page photo with the following caption: "The *La Opinión* photographer took this photograph yesterday while the police surrounded the Plaza detaining all Mexicans and other foreigners who were found there. Immigration agents, dressed in plain clothes, examined some of the prisoners asking them for facts about their legal or illegal residency in the United States, while others detained wait their turn patiently. Uniformed municipal police collaborated in the raid. At the rear can be seen part of the crowd that observed the arrests."

personally interested sources: the report of W. F. Watkins and the account given in *La Opinión* on 27 February 1931. According to the Spanish-language newspaper, eleven Mexicans, five Chinese, and a Japanese were singled out of the people found in the plaza and taken into custody. A crowd of onlookers gathered to watch the proceedings. One of the spectators, a young man named Moisés González who, *La Opinión* asserted, had entered the United States legally and had never left the country since, happened to cross the siege line while the questioning was in progress. He was immediately detained for questioning, and said he happened to be at the plaza because his place of employment, J. J. Newberry's, had been destroyed by the $450,000 fire that swept portions of the downtown business district the day before. He produced the passport given him back in 1923 when he had entered at El Paso. Even though his brother, an official in the local Confederation of Mexican Societies, attempted to vouch for him, González was taken to the city jail. According to *La Opinión* on 28 February, the investigators questioned González with the purpose of determining whether he had Communist sympathies, but later released him.

Mexican Vice Consul Ricardo Hill also witnessed the raid. When he attempted to cross the line, he too was stopped. *La Opinión* believed that only by Hill's presentation of his consular credentials was he able to avoid a trip to the jail.

La Opinión attributed the detention of such a large number of people to the efficiency of the authorities who carried out the raid. All exits from the plaza were simultaneously covered, and the immigration officials ordered everyone to remain seated.* Then the immigration officers began questioning each of the men there, the vast majority of whom were Mexicans or Mexican Americans. According to *La Opinión* on 27 February, the dialogue went something like this:

Officer: *¿Cuando entraste a Estados Unidos?* [When did you enter the United States?]

Mexican: *Hace cinco años.* Five years ago.

Officer: *¿Por cuál puerto?* [Through what port?]

Mexican: *Por Nogales.* Through Nogales.

---

*It should be noted that the size and design of the plaza in downtown Los Angeles have undergone changes since 1931.

Officer: *¿Tienes papeles?* [Have you a passport?]

Mexican: *Los perdí.* I lost them.

Officer: *¿No tienes ni un papel que compruebe que me dices la verdad?* [Haven't you any paper with you which you can prove that you are telling me the truth?]

Mexican: *Todos los perdí.* I lost them all.

Some of the more curious spectators to the activities going on inside the plaza were invited by police officers to cross the line; two who accepted the invitation were temporarily detained. Before the interrogations ended at 4:15 P.M., Main Street was "deserted."

Although the account in *La Opinión* leaves much to be desired because of internal discrepancies,* the newspaper did provide an interesting aspect to its coverage: a *La Opinión* photographer happened to be at the plaza when the raid occurred and took a picture of the proceedings. The resulting photograph, spanning five columns across page one, showed police and people in the plaza, with the crowd of spectators in the background. The banner headline blared, 11 MEXICANOS PRESOS EN UN APARATOSO RAID A LA PLACITA (11 Mexican prisoners taken at a sudden raid at the plaza). The article also included statements allegedly made by Watkins (misnamed "Watkinson" in the article) in which the supervisor insisted that the raids he sponsored were not directed solely at Mexicans but were part of a national policy aimed at apprehending illegal aliens.

In his report to the Labor Department on 2 March, Watkins denied giving any interviews, particularly to *La Opinión,* and also pronounced any accusations of violence committed by officers as falsehoods. After further questioning, nine of the eleven Mexicans detained in the raid had been released, and Watkins decided that the idea of "conducting investigations at fixed places, which the newspapers term 'raid,' are not proving particularly successful," to an extent because "in this city large numbers of contraband aliens are not frequently found grouped in one place."

---

*At one point the article mentions eleven Mexicans detained, at another thirty; the former was the correct figure. Immigration officials are mentioned in one place as wearing uniforms, in another place as wearing civilian clothes. Four hundred seems an excessively large figure for the plaza, though such a number was possible. The organization of the story was awkward, as the reporter began retelling the story halfway through the article. A follow-up story appeared in *La Opinión* on 28 February.

After this Watkins planned to have his men work in small groups, as secretly as possible, concentrating on the county's outlying districts. His men had spent the past month devoting much overtime to the task of tracking down deportable aliens, and in many respects the job had been a difficult one: the glare of publicity, the accusations of brutality, the half-promises of Visel, and the animosity of representatives of ethnic groups hardly made Watkins' job an enviable one.[24]

Immigration Bureau Procedures

In view of the reactions to the federal antialien drive that would come from, among others, the press in Mexico, Los Angeles businessmen, the Wickersham Commission, and the Los Angeles Bar Association, some note should be taken of the procedures followed by the immigration agents in pursuing their duties. District No. 31, the region which welcomed Watkins on 31 January, extended from San Luis Obispo south to the Mexican border, and eastward from the Pacific Ocean to Yuma, Arizona. The director of this district, Walter E. Carr, had a force of about one hundred officers; his subordinate in charge of the Los Angeles city office, Inspector Judson Shaw, was in charge of thirty-five of the men. Watkins' arrival had generated considerable activity in the district, an intensification of the Bureau of Immigration's work that was part of Doak's declaration of war against deportable aliens. Besides Southern California, immigration agents had increased their activities in large urban-industrial centers across the country.

As we have seen, Supervisor Watkins' men rounded up large numbers of suspected aliens, questioned them, and held some for further interrogation. Aliens held for further questioning were subjected first to a "preliminary investigation." During this interrogation the accused person did not have benefit of counsel and until evidence had been produced verifying the legality of his status, he was detained. This detention could last until the immigration officials had obtained a statement from the suspected alien, which might not be for several days.[25]

It has already been noted that Watkins reported to his superiors in Washington that he made every effort to release innocent people as soon as possible. Watkins' analysis of passports and consular certificates was made more difficult by some unscrupulous Los

Angeles notary publics, who had been issuing unofficial affidavits to Mexican nationals who had lost their passports. These documents, as de la Colina strived to inform his conationals, were worthless.[26] In an age that preceded social security cards, draft cards, credit cards, or other identification people are now accustomed to carrying with them, and when fewer people had driver's licenses, proving self-identity was not an easy task.

If it was found that a provable case was in the offing, Watkins telegraphed Washington, D.C., requesting warrants which were used in formal deportation proceedings. By 7 March, Watkins had received 138 such warrants. Of this number, 80 were intended for Mexican aliens, 19 for Japanese (who fought back fiercely, 14 retaining attorneys), 8 for Chinese, and the remainder for "miscellaneous nationalities." In addition to these aliens, Watkins allowed 80 other aliens who were found to be deportable to leave for the Mexican border under the "voluntary departure" option, transportation courtesy of the federal government.

Noting that arrests in early March had noticeably declined "due to concealment and elopement of aliens," Watkins dispatched eleven inspectors to visit other parts of the district, and went himself to Bakersfield for further investigatory work. Soon he could report twenty-seven aliens apprehended, all of whom chose voluntary departure. With some difficulty, Watkins obtained a bus for the aliens and had them driven to Calexico. This marked the end of the intensified drive against aliens in the Los Angeles area. Meanwhile, the local immigration office continued to arrest deportable aliens as part of its routine.

Watkins' Success

On 21 February 1931, Watkins wrote to Robe Carl White, assistant labor secretary, and the following month to Charles P. Visel, coordinator of the Los Angeles Citizens Committee on Coordination of Unemployment Relief, that 230 aliens had been deported in formal proceedings, of whom 110 were Mexican nationals, and that 159 additional Mexican aliens had chosen the voluntary departure option to return to Mexico.

These figures revealed that seven out of ten persons deported in the Southern California antialien drive were Mexicans. By the supervisor's own admission, in order to capture the 389 aliens successfully prosecuted during this period, Watkins and his men had to round up and question somewhere between three thousand and four thousand people — truly a monumental task.

The effect of the drive on the Mexican community was traumatic. Many of the aliens apprehended had never regularized an illegal entry that might have been made years before. Other than that, to call them criminals is to misapply the term. The pressure on the Mexican community from the deportation campaign contributed significantly to the huge repatriation from Los Angeles that followed the antialien drive. But this seemed of little concern to the head of the Citizens Committee on Coordination of Unemployment Relief. By the third week in March, an exuberant Charles P. Visel could write to Secretary Doak:

Six weeks have elapsed since we have received . . . Mr. Watkins, in reply to our request for deportable alien relief in this district. We wish to compliment your department for his efficiency, aggressiveness, resourcefulness, and the altogether sane way in which he is endeavoring and is getting concrete results.

The exodus of aliens deportable and otherwise who have been scared out of the community has undoubtedly left many jobs which have been taken up by other persons (not deportable) and citizens of the United States and our municipality. The exodus still continues.

We are very much impressed by the methods used and the constructive results steadily being accomplished.

Our compliments to you, Sir, and to this branch of your service.

No Federal Endorsement

However much Visel's interpretation of the benefits derived from the campaign squared with reality,* the Department of Labor was no longer as eager to endorse the Los Angeles coordinator, or even to imply the existence of an endorsement. Perhaps the department feared any such reply might be converted into another publicity release. At any rate, with *Nation* and *New Republic* lambasting the department, Doak shied away from making a personal

---

*Visel's eighth report, submitted to the President's Emergency Committee for Employment, dated 16 March 1931, under the heading "Alien Deportation," reads: "Quietly efficient. Constructive results obtained. Results permanent. Saving in city and county welfare. Capture and deportation of many criminals. No harm being done to industrial or agricultural labor requirements. No publicity [sic]. Police, Sheriff and Forestry Department cooperating." The report is appended to a letter from Visel to Dr. Willard E. Hotchkiss of PECE, 19 March 1931, NA RG 73, entry 3, 620.1, PECE Papers.

reply. Visel's letter was answered by Assistant Secretary W. W. Husband, who acknowledged Visel's message and then circumspectly stated:

It is the purpose of this Department that the deportation provisions of our immigration laws shall be carried out to the fullest possible extent but the Department is equally desirous that such activities shall be carried out strictly in accordance with law.

Cooperation by local authorities was appreciated, but Husband made it clear that from the viewpoint of the federal government it was the local authority that was supposed to respond to the federal government's initiative, not the other way around. The sequence of events in Los Angeles, however, had made such a point an academic one.

5.
Reactions and Actions

ALTHOUGH THE ANTIALIEN CAMPAIGN had moved out of the Los Angeles area, it left behind a growing controversy. Articles describing the harassment of innocent people by the Bureau of Immigration appeared in the Los Angeles *Record,* the city's most politically liberal newspaper. For two weeks, between 13 and 25 March 1931, readers were made aware of the denial of civil liberties to aliens throughout the country as well as in Los Angeles. During the publication of this series Clinton J. Taft, director of the local branch of the American Civil Liberties Union, offered the assistance of his organization "to aliens in trouble." The *Record* prefaced the eleven articles with headlines that referred to "terror reign," "closed door investigations," "inquisition methods," "handcuffs instead of warrant," "deportation mania," and similar phrases.

The usual procedure of the Bureau of Immigration in determining whether an alien was deportable or not also invited criticism, and this invitation was accepted in a burst of righteous rage by civil libertarians in national magazines in 1931. "It is an outrage," exclaimed *Nation* on 19 August 1931, "that the Immigration Bureau officials should be investigators, prosecutors, judges, and a final court of appeals in deportation cases, and take their orders from men of the type of William N. Doak." *New Republic* concurred in its issue of the same date, commenting on "how immigration officials, who are frequently men of low character appointed through political pressure, use secret star-chamber proceedings to deport, sometimes in violation of the law, individuals whose political and economic views are antipathetic to the 'ragged individualism' of the Hoover administration."

Businessmen joined journalists in their concern for the course deportation procedures were taking. Representatives of the Los Angeles business community began reconsidering their role in a drive that had concentrated on Spanish-speaking people. The Los Angeles Chamber of Commerce, having indirectly been a cause of the alien drive by its participation in the establishing of the relief committee which Visel headed, now assumed a position of leadership in smoothing over what it could of the animosities that had been created.

Mexican Press Coverage

That the antialien drive in Los Angeles had extended far beyond the legendary city limits was evident when a Mexican newspaper clipping, dated 4 April 1931, from *El Democrata Sinaloa* in Mazatlán, reached the desk of Clarence H. Matson, manager of the foreign commerce and shipping department of the Los Angeles Chamber of Commerce. Matson, a longtime and sincere friend of many Mexican businessmen, was amazed to read of "a terrible crusade against the Mexican professional and commercial men, in spite of their many years' residence in the United States." Doctors, pharmacists, and engineers, Mexican or of Mexican descent, were the victims; violence had occurred against people who patronized these Mexican professional men.

The clipping had been sent to Matson by a member of the press department of the Tenth Olympiad Committee (the Olympic Games were scheduled to take place in Los Angeles in 1932). Matson was advised that, "while any such story in one paper might not be serious, it might be well for your department to check on this matter and see that similar stories are not running in other Mexican papers. Sometimes it is better to stop a thing like this at the source before they [*sic*] go too far."

Chamber of Commerce Leadership

Until this time, any concern of the chamber with the deportation-repatriation plans had been unofficial, even personal. Clements' contacts with Consul de la Colina were as an interested individual, not as a representative of his employer, and General Manager Arnoll's communications with Visel had been more advisory than official. Visel's office had been closed as of 1 April, when the funds appropriated for its existence were exhausted. Matson, recognizing the long-range possibilities of Los Angeles's having its international image tarnished by publicity of bigotry, immediately set up a meeting of the chamber's immigration subcommittee to discuss the problem. He invited the Mexican consul to attend the meeting, which was scheduled for Wednesday, 29 April, at noon, to give his viewpoint.

Matson's meeting was well attended. Consul de la Colina brought with him Enrique Mexía, the commercial attaché of Mexico in Los Angeles, and a number of representatives of the recently organized Mexican Chamber of Commerce. Also present were Clements, District Director Carr, members of the subcommittee, a representative of the *Comité Mexicano de Beneficencia* (an organization of Mexican-American merchants), and several others. Matson called the group's attention to the clipping he had received. Consul de la Colina then enlightened the assemblage by pointing out it was hardly an isolated case, since the original story had been printed in a Mexico City paper and "was even stronger in its statements than the clipping quoted."

Interestingly enough, one of the men at the meeting — Dr. Alejandro Wallace, a druggist — was named in the Mexico City story as one of those beaten. The druggist told the group that as soon as he had learned of the false statement he had telegraphed the paper in Mexico City, but apparently the story had already been published throughout Mexico. Although most of the men in the room could not have known it, news of the antialien campaign stressing the plight of the Mexican had been in the press of Mexico for some time. Since February 1931, Mexican newspapers had been printing stories of variable accuracy about the deportations from Los Angeles.[1]

The meeting's discussion then turned to the nature of the exodus of Mexicans from Southern California. The federal deportation campaign and the local repatriation program (to be discussed in the next chapter) had blurred into a mass movement of Mexicans and Mexican Americans departing from the region. Carr repeated his position that the immigration office did not intend to single out Mexicans for deportation, and de la Colina conceded that lack of employment was inducing many Mexicans on relief to leave. Clements expressed his concern that the Mexicans would be irreplaceable as a part of the Southern California agricultural and industrial labor force. Some of the businessmen at the meeting, whose trade was primarily with the Mexican colony, complained that the exodus was hurting their businesses. Matson concluded the meeting by recommending that the Los Angeles Chamber of Commerce take some kind of positive action to deal with the adverse publicity and bad feeling that had arisen in the community.

Chamber's Disclaimer

Other than Clements' attempts in a personal capacity to clarify the position of Mexican aliens with the immigration office and the citizens' relief committee several months earlier, the chamber had made no public statement. The chamber's new president, John A. H. Kerr, who had been installed on 14 January, had not been asked to issue a policy statement. On hearing the findings of the subcommittee, the chamber's board of directors recommended that such a statement be drafted. Kerr, known for his philanthropic work and a widely respected banker — no mean thing in 1931 — took quick action. He asked the chamber to notify the newspapers of his desire to treat the Mexican difficulties in a sympathetic manner, and immediately had a statement prepared for public distribution. The statement read in part:

We assume it unnecessary to call the attention of our Mexican friends to the fact that they should in no wise be influenced in leaving this section because of idle rumors that the people of Los Angeles do not entertain for them the most cordial friendship or that the Government of the United States is embarked upon any wholesale deportation plan aimed specifically at our Mexican people.

Whatever its naiveté, Kerr's statement received wide distribution; it was printed in the local newspapers and broadcast over KHJ, KMTR, KMPC, and KGFJ, the last three stations having Spanish-language programs. KMPC promised to read the statement daily for a week; on 20 May KHJ dedicated a special program to the Mexican people. The *Los Angeles Times* translated Kerr's message and printed it in its Spanish section, while *La Opinión* proclaimed the statement of amity on page one.[2]

Businessmen's Fears

The chamber of commerce's action was based only in part on humanitarian grounds, for its primary concern was the promotion of business activity. It was obvious that the departure of Mexicans who were not on relief, not to mention those who owed money and by leaving defaulted on their payments, left a market vacuum which was all the more distressing because of the worsening depression. Businessmen, worried that Mexicans who had bought items on credit would leave town, made their complaints to the chamber.

In a carefully worded letter, officials of the Bank of America called the chamber's attention to the Mexican bank deposits in the Bank of America's international branch, which had declined from ten thousand to six thousand in the past two months. And after the famous settlement house worker, Jane Addams, addressed a meeting of social workers in Pasadena and questioned "the economic soundness of deporting so many potential customers," more people began rethinking the problem.[3] The *Los Angeles Times* noted on 18 April 1931 that the departure had hurt some merchants and would hurt the growers and railroads when workers were needed in those industries.

Mexican Analysis and Action

In an effort to analyze the exodus of the Mexicans, Pablo Baca, president of the Mexican Chamber of Commerce, prepared a report reviewing the problem and sent a copy to Clarence Matson on 13 May 1931. The organization traced the migration of Mexicans into California, citing the inducements of employment in crop harvesting, railroads, and private and public construction work. The report estimated that, as of May 1931 ten thousand of the over two hundred thousand Mexicans in the Los Angeles area had left. Also, many of those who had registered with the Mexican consulate their intentions of leaving were persons who had homes and businesses. After all the harassment to their compatriots these people felt unwelcome and, if they returned to Mexico, their adverse descriptions of life in the United States might damage future business relations.

Pressures on the Spanish-speaking community in Southern

California could also be seen in the work performed by Rafael de la Colina as Mexican consul in Los Angeles. During 1931 he intervened on behalf of his government in 1,216 deportation cases, as compared with 171 such cases in El Paso, 152 in Houston, 52 in Chicago, 28 in Detroit, and 124 in Phoenix.[4] By contrast, the number of interventions in deportation cases in Los Angeles in 1932 dropped to 212.

Brawley Raid

Relations between the Mexican colony and the Southern California community were again strained when, on 29 May 1931 *La Opinión* printed a page-one story about a federal raid on aliens in Brawley, an agricultural center in the Imperial Valley. Although only seventeen persons were actually seized (the headline had claimed one hundred), this knowledge did not relax the tension in the community, nor dispel the thought that the drive in Los Angeles might be resumed.

Ariza's Goodwill Trip

Business relations with Mexico were also deteriorating, and the anti-Mexican agitation was blamed. In an attempt to cement a new foundation of friendship — and good business relations — the chamber of commerce's immigration subcommittee endorsed Carlos Ariza's goodwill trip through Mexico. Ariza was the former consul at Calexico and was currently in the employ of the Automobile Club of Southern California. Harry Chandler had persuaded the chamber also to provide Ariza with credentials.

On his trip to Mexico in early June, Ariza met with Mexican government and business leaders, calling on José Cruz y Celis, president of the Confederated Chambers of Commerce of the Republic of Mexico, and gaining an audience with Mexican President Pascual Ortiz Rubio. Ariza informally promised aid to Mexicans having difficulties in the United States, but such pledges were treated warily by the Mexican press. While he was gone the *Los Angeles Times* reported that since the beginning of 1931 at least forty thousand Mexicans and Mexican Americans had left California.[5]

By this time Arthur G. Arnoll, the chamber's general manager, was growing tired of the chamber's involvement in the problem.

He was also irritated because Matson, as manager of the chamber's foreign commerce department, had discovered his earlier qualified endorsement of Visel's plans.* "Undoubtedly in the long run," Arnoll notified Clements, "many Mexicans will be better off under the change than they would have been to stay here and starve to death, or be an added burden to the community." He suggested that the chamber remain neutral in the matter of repatriation, which was dealing in numbers far in excess of deportations.

Clements protested. He believed that because of the coming fiesta celebration, when the city would celebrate the one hundred and fiftieth anniversary of its founding on 4 September, and the 1932 Olympics, a publicity campaign was needed to counteract the embarrassing and tension-filled publicity of the past months. He was also concerned with the possibility that the decline in population of Mexican agricultural workers would spell trouble for California's agricultural development. But Arnoll seemed content to have the chamber's future commitments more along the. lines of scheduling guest speakers for the coming Mexican Independence Day celebration, and the chamber's participation in upholding the civil liberties of Mexican and other ethnic groups descended to the level of good-hearted platitudes.

Americans Criticize Policy

The adverse publicity continued, however. James H. Batten, a professor at Claremont Men's College, was executive director of the Inter-American Foundation, an organization founded in 1929 to advance cultural relations between the North and South American republics. He accused the public of "suffering from an

---

*Matson said he found Visel's correspondence "rather astonishing to me." He learned of Visel's work from Clements, the manager of the chamber's agricultural department, who had obtained Visel's papers after the citizens' relief committee had completed its work. The report of the immigration subcommittee, submitted on 3 June 1931, and now retained in the Clements Papers, clarified much of the confusion surrounding the reasons for the arrival in Los Angeles of Supervisor Watkins. A letter from Ivan Goodner in Washington, D.C., dated 8 May 1931 and now in the Clements Papers, is evidence that Arnoll was made aware that the chamber had been connected with criticism of Visel's actions. Goodner stated that Doak had shown him "numerous telegrams from people in Los Angeles and also much of his interdepartment confidential communications, all of which lays the blame for the present situation at the door of certain people in Los Angeles." District Director Carr was under the impression that the Los Angeles Chamber of Commerce was more directly involved with the citizens' relief committee than it actually was.

epidemic of hysteria against aliens which finds expression in rigid enforcement of the law governing deportations." Batten warned that American business would need Mexican labor when better times returned, but "we shall find ourselves up against a shortage in supply for agriculture, transportation and unskilled labor."

Mexicans and Mexican Americans were departing with bitter memories, and Batten predicted that unless the white American stopped his discriminatory practices, the already aroused suspicions of Latin America about United States insincerity would be confirmed. In addition to the deportation campaign, Batten cited the Harris restriction bill, the tariff on Mexican vegetables, the allocation of water from the Colorado River, and Senator Henry F. Ashurst's recent proposal to buy Baja California as examples of unsound American policy toward her neighbor. His remarks echoed as far as the pages of Mexico City's *Excelsior*.[6] On hearing Ashurst's proposal, an official in the Mexican Foreign Office declared the offer acceptable, if the United States in return would cede Texas back to Mexico.[7]

Had Batten's remarks been the only criticisms lodged by professional people against treatment of aliens, Southern California would have been credited with a pitifully inadequate response to the threats on civil liberties posed by the antialien campaign. But stringent criticism did come forth, from a group which could hardly be faulted for its membership or questioned for its loyalty. Not long after Watkins directed the search for aliens away from the Los Angeles area, the constitutional rights committee of the Los Angeles Bar Association assigned a subcommittee the task of investigating illegal practices of immigration officials in arresting and deporting aliens. The subcommittee was particularly interested in evaluating accusations of arrests without warrant, the holding of aliens incommunicado, and whether the Bureau of Immigration, in enforcing the immigration laws of the United States, violated other laws pertaining to civil liberties.[8]

The subcommittee membership included several distinguished lawyers, who took a month to investigate the charges carefully, hearing statements from both aliens and immigration officials. A careful study of fifty-five cases resulted in the committee's condemnation of the policies of Carr and the local office of the bureau. Extralegal methods were criticized as being "merely the old and indefensible excuse that the end justifies the means — a casuistry which, when urged by law enforcers as a justification for law enforcement, tends to bring the law and then its enforcement into universal disrepute and contempt." The report of the subcommittee went on to say:

> Another practice brought to our attention which to some extent at least seems to be indulged in by the immigration officials after procuring an arrest warrant is that of coupling their compliance with the law which requires them to advise the arrested accused to his right to counsel with voluntary advice to the accused that the employment of counsel is not necessary and that he would fare better if no counsel were employed by him.
>
> This, as we gather, is upon some sort of theory of protecting the suspected and arrested alien from unnecessary legal expense; but however good the motive, it seems to us entirely outside the province of the official so advising and it might tend to protect such official from a too close professional scrutiny of his or his subordinate's illegal practices.
>
> It might also tend to facilitate the deportation of ignorant aliens who are not the proper subjects of deportation. So while this is possibly not strictly within the province of our investigations, it impresses us as a rather questionable practice which should be discouraged.[9]

The entire practice of arresting aliens first and telegraphing for warrants afterward brought fierce criticism from the subcommittee. After hearing Carr's arguments that obtaining the evidence which resulted in a warrant of necessity had to precede the issuing of the warrant, the subcommittee reported, "[P]ossibly through ignorance of what has taken place, Mr. Carr was mistaken in some of his assertions." The subcommittee concluded that arrests without warrant were made for "obtaining ex parte statements from [aliens] by immigration officers while such persons are in the exclusive control of such officers and are deprived by such officers of any independent advice."[10] Refusing to limit its investigation to only those cases arising from the 1931 antialien drive, the committee soon disclosed that working-class aliens, even before 1931, had received less considerate treatment than aliens of means.[11]

Finally, the subcommittee recommended that all illegal practices be discontinued by the Bureau of Immigration "by order of the proper authority or authorities." The subcommittee's report was accepted and copies were forwarded to the attorney general of the United States, to Secretary Doak, to both California senators, and to the congressional representatives whose constituencies lay in District No. 31.[12] The report arrived too late to be included in the appropriate study then being published by the Wickersham

Commission, but the principal author of the Commission's report on deportation, Reuben Oppenheimer, later commended highly the work of the Los Angeles Bar Association.[13]

As might be expected, Carr hotly denied the charges of the subcommittee. While he conceded that his office did detain suspected aliens without a warrant, he denied that this was an illegal practice. "No warrant is required to arrest a suspected alien and detain him for questioning," he said. "This has been held repeatedly by the United States Supreme Court, and such arrests and detention are in general practice throughout the immigration service."

This was true, but the point left undiscussed was how the bureau's agents were interpreting such words as "detained" and "questioning." Carr strongly disagreed with the view of the subcommittee that aliens were held incommunicado. "Anyone that has a right to see them, can." Here again, semantics proved insurmountable as critics and officials failed to agree on terms. But Carr threw in a final punch: "The Bar Association inquiry actually was made at the instance of a certain attorney whose real objection to the immigration service policy is that it prevents him from promiscuously soliciting business among aliens."[14]

Mexican Embassy Inquiry

Whether Carr sincerely meant this last accusation is a moot point, for the march of events had brought the federal effort to oust aliens to international attention. As a result of inquiries from the Mexican Embassy and hostile newspaper articles in Mexican newspapers, Carr was asked to account for the motives and actions of his office in deporting Mexican aliens. On 7 May the State Department had received a communication from the Mexican Embassy, which diplomatically inquired if the United States might not "study a new means for avoiding the congestion of Mexicans excluded from [the United States] in places where the means of livelihood, in Mexico, does not permit of a sudden increase of the laboring population without causing an immediate local crisis."

In short, deportees from the United States were concentrating in border towns such as Mexicali and Tijuana. These towns lacked adequate roads or rail transportation to the interior of Mexico, forcing the deportees to increase, by their presence, a labor surplus in places already hard-hit by the depression. Secretary of State

Henry L. Stimson forwarded this message to Doak and asked for a suitable reply which might then be made to the Mexican Embassy.

At this time, perhaps by coincidence (the motivation is unclear), George J. Harris, the assistant commissioner general of immigration, sent off a telegram to Carr, inquiring ". . . how many aliens have been permitted voluntarily to depart from your district without resort to warrant proceedings during eighteen months ending April. . . . Include in this figure all who have so departed through auspices or cooperation of charities and other associations or instrumentalities. . . ." Harris may have heard of the Mexican Embassy's note, though it was not formally transmitted from State to Labor until 27 May. Carr, responding on 13 May, notified Harris, "There have been approximately forty thousand aliens who left this district during the last eighteen months of which probably twenty percent deportable." Carr based his figures on information he obtained from the Los Angeles Bureau of County Welfare, the Mexican consul, and several local charities. He omitted formal deportations.

The difference between the number of warrants requested from Los Angeles during the antialien drive (under four hundred) and the figure of forty thousand must have astounded the Bureau of Immigration, for not even Doak might have guessed that such a number would voluntarily depart from one district in the United States. The State Department, however, forwarded to the people at Labor a dispatch from the American Embassy in Mexico, D.F., which pointed out how the Mexicans viewed the movement southward. The dispatch enclosed a copy of an article from the *Excelsior* of 11 May 1931, which asserted that the thousands of deportees returning to Mexico presented "a pitiful and pathetic spectacle, for many of them are hollow-cheeked from hunger." The article went on to describe alleged cases of mistreatment, separation of families, and abrogation of contracts.

Assistant Commissioner General Harris gathered up the dispatch and the *Excelsior* article and sent them to Los Angeles, requesting Carr to clarify what had been going on there. "Please carefully note the several claims made which might be regarded as a reflection upon this service," stated Harris, "and advise the Bureau fully in respect thereto, submitting your report in triplicate, in order that two copies thereof may be furnished the State Department." Harris asked that special attention be given to the allegation "that thousands of Mexicans are being thrust or, rather, swept out of the United States without stopping to consider whether it is just in every case. . . ."

While Carr prepared his report, the Mexican Embassy sent a second note to the State Department, pointedly complaining of "an immoderate concentration of repatriates at points where their stay and subsistence is rendered extremely difficult," and requesting "that in the future deportation be carried out only through the border ports of Nuevo Laredo, Tamaulipas; Ciudad Juárez, Chihuahua, and Nogales, Sonora. . . . as the transportation and supply services will be more efficient at the points mentioned."

Washington's Explanation

In a memo to Secretary of State Stimson on 8 July, Assistant Labor Secretary Robe Carl White answered both of the embassy inquiries and replied to all other questions that had arisen as a result of the deportation campaign.

I believe I am safe in saying that a comparatively small proportion of the Mexican repatriates from the United States into the northern district of Southern California [*sic*] were removed under orders of deportation. The vast majority of these people left voluntarily through fears engendered by false reports circulated by unofficial agencies.

White promised the State Department that further details on the "false reports" would be supplied when District Director Carr filed his report, which was expected shortly. White went on to comment on the cooperation shown between Mexican and United States authorities in easing the movement of deportee-repatriates, for in truth several trips had been made from Mexicali to Nogales to alleviate the congestion in the former city. The United States had supplied the transportation, while the Mexican government had paid the expenses. White pointed out that such action proved that exceptions to rules could be made. While it was departmental policy to remove aliens to the nearest border port, "exceptions have been made where deportation . . . would result in leaving a helpless alien completely isolated from and without means to proceed to his responsible friends or relatives," who might be living near a border port further away. But White qualified this generosity by noting that such exceptions were usually limited to wives and children.

White concluded his letter by doubting that his department could move aliens deported from California across to border points such as Juárez, since the appropriations for such work could not stand "the imposition of such an excessive additional expense." This problem was solved, as will be seen in the next chapter, by the Los Angeles Bureau of County Welfare.

Defense of Los Angeles Activities

On 17 June 1931, Carr submitted a report to Harry Hull, commissioner general of immigration, which reflected his feelings about the Los Angeles relief efforts, after having been exposed to criticism and misrepresentation for the previous six months. Referring to the *Excelsior* clipping and others, he expressed the opinion that the newspaper articles were "based on stories which have been told by Mexicans who have been scared into leaving the United States by the various propaganda and activities over which this service had no control." With this point made, Carr then devoted several paragraphs to a description of how Congress, state, and local governments had legislated or proposed legislation against aliens. Their goal had been based on a fallacy that somehow such legislation could alleviate the depression. The depression would end if only the aliens would go away, and the movement of Mexican repatriates was part and parcel of this trend of thought.

Then Carr defended his actions in the recent deportation campaign:

The Chamber of Commerce in Los Angeles backed a movement to relieve the unemployment situation but which as it was actually handled was designed primarily to scare aliens, especially Mexicans, out of this community. This office was approached and requested to make a statement in the public press to the effect that officers from other districts would be brought here for no other purpose than to deport Mexicans and that all Mexicans illegally here would be immediately deported. This was to be merely a gesture, that is, to give the matter publicity and create the impression that such an activity was contemplated. It goes without saying that such request did not receive favorable consideration. I believe the Secretary of Labor was requested to make a similar gesture. In spite of the fact that this office absolutely refused to lend its name to any such publicity, certain articles were placed in the newspapers and copied in the foreign language papers in such a way as to carry the impression that the Mexican people were to be made the target of a deportation drive by this Service.

Carr went on to tell of the statement he had made to the newspapers, disavowing any campaign aimed solely at Mexicans.

He had insisted that the interests of his office were to attend to "any alien of any race actually subject to deportation under the immigration laws." Nevertheless, the high rate of Mexican unemployment, an increasing whispering campaign against the Mexicans, and the reports of opportunists who had swindled Mexican property owners, led the Mexican population to believe, according to Carr, "that Mexicans were not wanted in California and that all would be deported whether they were legally here or not."

As for the coming of Watkins to District No. 31, Carr blamed Visel (by mistake branding him an employee of the chamber of commerce) for misrepresentations to the Labor Department. These misrepresentations had been accepted as substantially reliable, and on arriving in Los Angeles Watkins and his men had found themselves enmeshed in a web of publicity which made it impossible to separate their work from the propaganda campaign launched by Visel. Carr was aware of the discrepancy between the numbers actually deported and the thousands who had "been literally scared out of Southern California."

He blamed much of the shadow cast on the image of the immigration service on the confusion by people of the federal efforts and the interference of the local officials. "The word 'deportable' has been used as applicable to all of those departures and when that word is used, to the ordinary mind, it spells immigration," wrote Carr. As a result, "Immigration service activity is now being looked upon as the actual cause for the repatriation of these thousands of Mexicans when the real responsible parties, if any there be, are the Los Angeles Chamber of Commerce and [local welfare organizations]."

Carr emphatically denied that federal officials had consciously attempted to separate aliens from their families. Where this had occurred, voluntary departure rather than formal deportation had been practiced, so that (theoretically at least) the alien could apply for reentry to the United States. Carr denied that such separations were "an everyday occurrence" and labeled the accusations in the *Excelsior* article as inaccurate distortions. He summed up his report by stating:

[T]he basic cause for the movement of Mexicans out of the United States has been lack of employment and this movement has been accentuated through fear created by agencies not in any way connected with the Government

service and over which the Service in this district has no actual control. . . .
Nothing of the spectacular has been injected into the work by the officers of
this Service. The only spectacular features have been the result of an effort
on the part of local authorities to substantiate claims which had been made
to our Department as to the number of aliens in this community actually
subject to deportation and what they could do to assist us in deporting them.

Carr's report made no reference to the criticisms leveled at the
bureau that its methods were arbitrary and dictatorial, nor did he
mention the bar association inquiry. By keeping the federal function
of deportation work rigidly separated in his mind from the large
numbers of departing Mexicans, he was able to rationalize that
the bureau had performed its duties in spite of a propaganda campaign whose goal was to exclude Mexicans by whatever means.

Carr failed to see that the importation of Watkins and the
presence of the extra agents served Visel's intentions to the letter,
and fulfilled all of the expectations outlined in the publicity release
Visel had sent to Woods in mid-January. Carr's statement that he
had absolutely refused to endorse Visel's plans is open to question,
for an absolute refusal would have meant a strong disavowal of
Visel's scheme before it ever got into print. Carr's insistence that
the bureau treated all aliens equally was small comfort to an area
where two hundred thousand people were considered "Mexican"
even if many of them had been born in the United States.

Hull sent copies of Carr's report to Assistant Secretary of
Labor White, who forwarded two copies to Secretary Stimson at
the State Department. By this time, midsummer 1931, the Mexican
government's wishes were being complied with by the Los Angeles
Bureau of County Welfare, whose organized program of repatriating destitute Mexican families was well under way. Since the
Southern Pacific railroad was transporting trainloads of Mexicans
from Los Angeles to Nogales and El Paso, with the county welfare
bureau paying the bill, no further notes at this time came from
the Mexican Embassy.

Publicity about Doak's deportation campaign faded away
after the summer of 1931, though the labor secretary could still
make headlines by denouncing those who protested the deportation
of aliens.[15] *Nation* and *New Republic* fought back with occasional
editorials which ridiculed the policies of the secretary of labor.
Much of the continuing debate centered not on economic consid-
erations but on political loyalties, as "alien" and "radical" con-

tinued their close semantic association. The significance of Doak's effort must lie in the general attitude towards immigration shown by the United States at this time. Barriers had been raised; immigration from other countries had been whittled down by as much as 60 percent. In this period, between June 1930 and June 1931, the federal government moved almost thirty thousand aliens out of the United States, either under voluntary departure or as deportees. Most were Mexicans.[16]

6.

Repatriation From Los Angeles

RUNNING CONCURRENTLY in Los Angeles with the federal government's deportation campaign was an organized program of repatriating destitute Mexican families. This program had few connections with the drive on aliens residing illegally in the country; Supervisor William F. Watkins of the Bureau of Immigration had referred to it several times in his reports to the Department of Labor, but neither he nor his agents were involved in it.

From 1931 on, cities and counties across the country intensified and embarked upon repatriation programs, conducted under the auspices of either local welfare bureaus or private charitable agencies. The Los Angeles county repatriation program deserves close study for the numbers of people repatriated, the expenses involved, the methods employed, and the amount of time over which the repatriations took place.

The year 1931 marked the one hundred and fiftieth anniversary of the founding of the city of Los Angeles, but the celebrations planned for this event noticeably excluded the region's Mexican and Mexican-American population. Even as a steering committee was being organized to work out details for the fiesta (a committee that failed to include Spanish surnames), plans were also being created for the voluntary return of what apologists for the repatriation movement considered an unassimilable group.[1]

Mexican nationals living in Los Angeles in the midst of an active federal deportation campaign may have wondered about the legality of their status. At least two-thirds of the Mexicans on relief were aliens, and almost that same figure had been in the United States over ten years. The federal scrutiny of old visas and head tax receipts could affect anyone. Mexicans could hardly be blamed for having entered the country on an informal basis, when the penalties for illegal entry were of very recent enactment. Moreover, destitute aliens could be legally removed from the country under provisions of the 1917 Immigration Act's Section 23.

Other pressures made Mexicans vulnerable for repatriation. County officials commented publicly on the increasing relief load the county was carrying and the possibility of lightening that load by removing aliens from the rolls.[2] On this aspect of the problem, sociologist Emory S. Bogardus commented:

> Many Mexican immigrants are returning to Mexico under a sense of pressure. They fear that all welfare aid will be withdrawn if they do not accept the offer to take them out of our country. In fact, some of them report that they are told by relief officials that if they do not accept the offer to take them to the Border no further welfare aid will be given them and that their record will be closed with the notation, "Failed to cooperate." Rumor becomes exaggerated as it passes from mouth to mouth. It takes only an insinuation from a welfare official in the United States to create widespread fear among Mexican immigrants.[3]

Faced with poverty, discrimination, and uncertainty as to their status, many Mexican families seriously considered the idea of repatriation.

From sources sympathetic to the plight of Mexicans in need there came offers of concrete sympathy. Destitute Mexicans received assistance from the Midnight Mission, the *Comité de Emergencia* (the emergency committee created by Consul de la Colina), the Catholic Welfare Bureau, and *La Sociedad de Damas Católicas* (the Society of Catholic Ladies). Most of the funds raised by these groups went for local distribution; about 10 percent was allotted for repatriation purposes. The Mexican consulate sponsored a benefit at the Philharmonic Auditorium on 18 February and raised money on this and on other occasions for destitute Mexicans.[4] Many Mexicans thus assisted were not accepting county aid, but they nonetheless required help.

Informal Arrangements

Many Mexicans had been repatriating themselves for months prior to any county-organized plan of returning indigents to Mexico. These people accepted Mexico's offer of duty-free admittance of automobiles, trucks, and agricultural implements. Those who returned by train were able to do so through the work of the Mexican consul who, with the cooperation of William H. Holland, superintendent of the county department of charities, and Southern Pacific railroad officials, obtained a charity rate to El Paso. A varying number of Mexicans, from as low as twenty to as high as a hundred or more, each week signed up with the consulate for the train trip during the winter of 1930–31. The El Paso-bound train made a connection at Juárez with a Mexican train headed for the interior, thereby preventing a pileup of newly returned immigrants at the border town.

George P. Clements of the Los Angeles Chamber of Commerce viewed this type of repatriation with a qualified approval, sympathizing with the desire of voluntary repatriates to return home without discomfiture or difficulty.

I would like to state that it is my honest belief that if the handling of this question were limited to the Mexican Consulate, our own Immigration Service and the railroads with a possible small group of economic advisors, it could be done at a minimum of inconvenience and suffering to these people. . . . If it were possible to find a group of philanthropic people who would produce a fund . . . it would unquestionably be of great assistance in taking care of that class of indigent Mexicans who desired to return to Mexico to be among their friends.[5]

Apart from the view that repatriation should be carried out by private initiative, the local government proposed a solution of its own. Local government efforts to relieve unemployment and generate new jobs had been unsuccessful. Besides launching his plan to exclude Mexicans from Southern California, Coordinator Charles P. Visel of the city's Citizens Committee on Coordination of Unemployment Relief did work energetically in promoting a job clearing house and various public works projects. But upon the closing of his office, he was compelled to report to Dr. Willard E. Hotchkiss of the President's Emergency Committee for Employment (PECE) that any achievements were negligible.[6]

On the county level, Harvey C. Fremming, the man appointed as director of the County Employment Stabilization Bureau, achieved some results in the creation of part-time and full-time jobs, though the problems were far greater than the solution, and he was handicapped by local politicking.[7] The relief load was now in excess of $2 million a year, with the number of cases rapidly increasing. Some means of reducing county expenses, removing unemployed persons from the labor surplus, and lightening the relief load was needed. Repatriation provided a partial answer to all three of these problems.

County Repatriation Program

The idea of an organized county repatriation program originated first in the mind of Frank L. Shaw, supervisor of Los Angeles County's Second District. Shaw, chairman of the board of supervisors' charities and public welfare committee, inquired early in 1931 as to the legality of a county's transporting indigent persons outside the county at its own expense. California state law, if freely interpreted, allowed a county to pass legislation to that effect.

The advantages of repatriation were arithmetically obvious, and indeed correspondence on the subject often included figures which indicated a tremendous saving to the county: when approximately ten thousand Mexican alien relief cases, averaging on the conservative side $200,000 a month, or $2.4 million a year, were eventually repatriated, the savings to county taxpayers would be enormous, inasmuch as the cost of transporting an entire family would be quickly repaid by their disappearance from the relief load. Mexican relief cases during the depression hovered between 9 and 11 percent Mexican-born; the welfare bureau distinguished between these and cases where the adult was a Mexican American.

Mexican families living on county relief were particularly susceptible to suggestions of repatriation for a variety of reasons. There was little likelihood of employment, as the economic depression progressively worsened. The offer from the board of supervisors' charities and public welfare committee contained a number of inducements, which were increased when the number of volunteers for repatriation declined. Such benefits as free transportation, food, clothing, medical aid, and the assurance of cooperation by the Mexican government and railroads, all presented strong temptations to accept repatriation. Plans for repatriation colonies in Mexico were constantly being projected and there were hints, accurate or not, that a return to the United States would be possible after an improvement in economic conditions.

The removal was planned to occur over a period of time, with periodic trains scheduled. Agencies at all levels were amenable to the plan. The Mexican consulate approved, the Southern Pacific railroad extended a low charity rate, and the Interstate Commerce Commission agreed not to question the fare prices as long as the cost was borne by a county or municipality. The Mexican government, for its part, favored the idea; new repatriation centers were planned, the National Railroad of Mexico would remove repatriates from the border to the country's interior, and duties on goods were relaxed.[8]

County-Sponsored Trains

Active preparations for the first organized shipment of repatriates were already under way when Supervisor W. F. Watkins of the Bureau of Immigration arrived in Los Angeles to commence the drive against illegal aliens. A tentative date, 18 February 1931, had been set for the departure of the first trainload. Approximately three hundred and fifty Mexicans were expected to leave, but at this stage of planning certain oversights occurred that necessitated the postponement of the departure. It was unclear, for example, how many of the repatriates were men, women, or children, whether food for the travelers would be purchased in Los Angeles or on the trip, and what the exact expenses would be.

On the motion of Supervisor Shaw, the board of supervisors authorized the sum of six thousand dollars to transport the indigents to the somewhat ambiguous "place of legal residence wherein they will be officially accepted"; the consent of the Mexican government, moreover, was still pending. Noting that the first trip had been postponed, Watkins pessimistically reported to Robe Carl White, assistant labor secretary, "In my opinion it is still a matter of conjecture whether or not this plan will really materialize."

Despite these delays, the bureau of county welfare, a branch of the county department of charities, went ahead with the proposed plan. With the final legal and political obstacles removed, the three hundred and fifty Mexicans who had signed up for the first trip, which was rescheduled for 23 March, left on that date for El Paso and its counterpart across the river, Ciudad Juárez. From there, the repatriates were transferred to the National Railroad of Mexico. Details for the first departure are sketchy, but it is clear that the county miscalculated the cost: after the second departure was carried out on 24 April, an additional ten thousand dollars had to be appropriated to meet the expenses of both trips. There was also some uncertainty as to the exact number of Mexican aliens on relief who desired repatriation, figures being cited as anywhere from three thousand to five thousand people.

It should be emphasized at this point that the county-sponsored repatriation trains did not leave Los Angeles on as casual a basis as has sometimes been described. The bureau of county welfare did not lack applicants for repatriation during the first year in which repatriations were conducted, and once the initial problems were ironed out, the departures were organized on an efficient basis.

Some confusion on the part of observers resulted, however, when the county-sponsored trains were mistakenly confused with trains departing with Mexicans who were not on relief but were being repatriated through other assistance. This was understandable, since the same train might be carrying repatriates whose fares were being paid by the county, repatriates paying their own fares, others assisted by the Mexican consulate, some undergoing the Bureau of Immigration's practice of voluntary departure, and a few deportees being removed, the last two categories being at federal government expense.

Statistics covering Mexican repatriates, depending upon the sources of information, might cover any or all of these types. For example, while the second departure, carried out on 24 April, had a total of 1,150 Mexican repatriates, approximately 800 of these had their fares paid by the county; the other 350 had made their own arrangements. The situation was further confused by the fact that Mexicans leaving without county aid were taking a weekly train, and if a large number of Mexicans departed during a particular week, it was thought by some that another repatriation at county expense was occurring. The actual county-sponsored repatriation trips, which took place with intervals of over a month or more between trips, are itemized in appendix C.[9]

The confusion about numbers of Mexicans leaving Southern California was increased when the totals given by the county, the newspapers, the chamber of commerce, or other sources failed to indicate just which figures were being totaled, and what period of time was encompassed in them. Thus the *Los Angeles Times* announced on 7 June 1931 that 40,000 Mexicans had left Southern California since the start of the year, while the county recorded only 1,350 repatriates at that time. Still another source, the Los Angeles *Record,* announced on 16 June that 29,000 Mexicans had departed.

Some confusion of terms also occurred, as repatriate and deportee were used as interchangeable words, especially in the press of Mexico. The American consul general in Mexico, D.F., Robert Frazer, reported to the Department of State on "the inability of the newspapers to differentiate between illegally admitted Mexicans who have been or are being deported, and repatriated Mexicans who were legally admitted to the United States." The impression given was "that nearly every Mexican entering Mexico from the United States has been deported, and under the most trying circumstances for the deportee." The real difficulties faced by Mexicans and Mexican Americans at this time — the adverse publicity of deportations, the stigma of poverty, the opposition of labor unions, and the condescension of social workers, press, and spokesmen for employers — would suggest that bitter Mexican feelings had valid roots.

The first few county-sponsored departures were covered by the local newspapers and even picked up by the wire services. The tone of the articles was one of "all for the best," agreeing with the announcement of A. C. Price, assistant superintendent of the county department of charities, that a large number of Mexicans had "suffered severely through unemployment and have become public charges. With the cooperation of the Mexican government and Mexican charitable agencies we are sending these needy non-citizens back to Mexico as rapidly as jobs can be provided for them there.[10]

Some Mexicans who chose repatriation found their departure made somewhat easier by sympathetic people. The Reverend Allan A. Hunter of the Mt. Hollywood Community Church appointed a committee of four to investigate the Mexican exodus, and the Good Will to Mexico Committee came into being. This committee, headed by Ernest Besig, worked with the *Comité Mexicano de Beneficencia* and the Mexican consulate in raising voluntary contributions, providing food for up to four days of travel, and donating canned milk for babies.

Since the Mexicans being assisted were those leaving on the weekly trains, not the county-sponsored trips, their numbers were often fairly small, though occasionally many might leave in a particular week. On 14 May, twenty-five *repatriados* received aid; on 28 May, twenty; and on 4 June, eighteen. Again, such figures must be qualified, since it is obvious that other Mexicans who were leaving may not have received charitable assistance, while some may have been departing with county aid. Inevitably, the departures fused in the public mind into the assumption that most repatriates were county cases.[11]

The magnitude of the repatriation movement, combining as it did elements of coercion, voluntary return, and a desire by local government to cut expenses, evoked comments from several observers. The Los Angeles Chamber of Commerce attempted to allay the fears of a Mexican community that had been exposed to federal agents questioning hundreds of people suspected as illegal aliens and to sensational newspaper publicity. Its statement, which had insisted that no deliberate pressure for removal was intended, was qualified by Arthur G. Arnoll, the general manager, who minimized any serious effects the movement might have had on the Los Angeles Mexican and Mexican-American community. "It would appear," Arnoll wrote Clements, "that all of the movement was not due to any scare which may have been thrown into the Mexican by the efforts of the government to deport the deportable ones."

Despite Clements' arguments that a sizable departure of Mexicans would present difficult problems for the future of California agriculture, Arnoll insisted that "a good many Mexicans decided it was a good time to return in any event." The chamber thus backed away from any serious analysis either of the needs of agriculture or those who sought employment in it.

A Valuable Source of Labor

The use of the Mexican as a commodity for labor rather than acceptance of him as a human being prompted criticism from James H. Batten, Claremont College professor, who in his denunciation of the federal deportation campaign also called attention to the value of Mexico's contribution to agricultural development in the United States. "That the Mexican is the most dependable common laborer of the Southwest does not admit of any debate," he said. "In depleting this supply we may be riding for a fall when normal conditions return. White men are doing work today that they will not do when other work is available."[12]

The threat of a labor shortage was echoed by growers who preferred an adequate labor supply at hand, though it should be noted that the people who underwent repatriation may not have been as closely linked to agriculture as was once thought. The assumption that Mexicans on urban relief in the winter automatically gravitated to the fields at harvest time overlooks the urban jobs which in more prosperous times gave employment to the unskilled and semiskilled: building projects, paving of roads, bridge construction, and various industrial jobs in places such as brickyards.

Ignorance of the Law

Batten also had harsh words for the idea of repatriation, accusing the bureau of county welfare of taking advantage of the Mexicans' ignorance of law, "in order to induce them to cross the border voluntarily, giving them to understand they could return at will. When they sought to return they were denied admittance, resulting in hardships to them and their families."[13] Such incidents occurred because of the stringent policy of border officials in rejecting applicants for visas whose occupations fell under the class of laborers.

Clements supplied further evidence that Mexicans were being misled by county officials. He had attended the departure of the first two county-sponsored repatriation trains, and on the third scheduled departure, on 17 August, he made the discovery that the county was issuing "departure cards" to the *repatriados.* Clements reported to Arnoll that "Most of them had been told that they could come back whenever they wanted to. I think this is a grave mistake, because it is not the truth." The face of the card was innocuous, just identifying data, but the back of the card had been stamped "LOS ANGELES COUNTY / DEPARTMENT OF CHARITIES / COUNTY WELFARE DEPT. [*sic*] / By_____." Clements noted that this stamp "makes it impossible for any of the Mexican born to return, since it shows that they have been county charities." All that the American officials had to do was invoke the "liable to become a public charge" clause of the 1917 Immigration Act and deny readmission.

Returning to Los Angeles

Carey McWilliams has remarked that most of the Mexicans who were repatriated eventually came back to Los Angeles, "having had a trip to Mexico at the expense of the county."[14] The validity of this assertion is open to question, since no statistics are available to prove that later Mexican immigrants were the same ones who

Families and friends gathering at the Los Angeles railroad station on 17 August 1931 to bid farewell to *repatriados* departing on the third county-sponsored train

left earlier. The high rejection rate among visa applicants suggests strongly that if repatriated Mexicans returned to the United States in the mid-thirties, they would have had to do so illegally.

Later, of course, with the advent of the Second World War and the call for Mexican labor going out again, Mexicans who had been exposed to life north of the border might have been the quickest to return to the United States. But this line of reasoning ignores the status of the Mexican as a human being, with the obligations of providing for the stability of his family. The fact remains that the county-sponsored repatriation trains took on family units as passengers, and many of these families had lived for years in Los Angeles.* Journeying back to Mexico to visit relatives is one thing; to assume that entire families were at the beck and call of American agriculture and industry is another matter, particularly when to answer that call meant to commit a crime by crossing the border illegally. And few Mexicans recrossed the border northward legally during the depression years.

Shipment Procedures

By the third trip, the bureau of county welfare in the county charities department had settled into a routine that would be substantially the same for all succeeding train departures. Depending upon the number of *repatriados* who signed up for the trip, as many as three Southern Pacific trains would be used. The destination, again depending upon the train and the passengers aboard it, might be Nogales or El Paso. Passengers were transferred at the border to Mexican-operated trains; the fare for the whole distance was paid for by the county.

On each train, the bureau of county welfare sent a man from the charities department to insure that county-provided food was properly distributed, that the health and safety of the repatriates was maintained, and above all, that all passengers stayed with the train until the destination was reached. Occasionally the Mexican consulate also sent someone to accompany the train to the border.

---

*A survey conducted by W. F. French, chief of the county charity department's division of accounts and collections, and submitted to Deputy Superintendent Rex Thomson on 24 April 1934, showed that of the 4,220 Mexican welfare cases interviewed in California, 62 percent had lived in the United States for more than ten years.

Accompanying the second train on 24 April, for example, were Philip J. Robinson of the charities department and Mexican Vice Consul Ricardo Hill.

The third repatriation train, which left Los Angeles on 17 August, carried the largest passenger manifest to date. One hundred fifty-five cases, comprising 899 individuals, filed a "voluntary request for return to their native country because of the acute unemployment situation here." The sum of $12,000 was requested, an amount that proved an excellent estimate, as $11,642 was actually expended to cover all costs of the shipment of repatriates. To accompany the trains, the board of supervisors authorized Robinson and Horace D. Roberts to see the repatriates safely as far as Mexico, D.F., while G. A. Elderson was to supervise the processing of the Mexicans through the border station at El Paso. Mexican Vice Consul Ricardo Hill also joined this third trip south.

Since this trip received close attention from several observers and since it was the last departure that would receive any degree of attention (as succeeding trips became matters of routine), observations made about the 17 August departure should be noted. Besides the 899 repatriates whose transportation was being paid for by the county, there were approximately 400 other Mexicans who were repatriating themselves without county aid.

Among those present to see them all off were Clements, the Reverend Robert N. McLean, welfare officials, railroad officials, policemen, some concerned citizens, and reporters and photographers for the *Evening Express,* the *Record* and *La Opinión.* Clements arrived at ten o'clock in the morning and his observations, which he reported to Arnoll, made an interesting contrast to the account which appeared the next day in the *Express,* 18 August 1931.

A Question of Citizenship

The newspaper saw the departure as an opportunity for the Mexicans to seek a better life in their homeland — though both it and the *Record* admitted that many of the repatriates being described as Mexicans were actually American citizens and that "most of them were born here." According to the *Express* article, "few of them spoke English," yet Clements reported that "the vast majority of them spoke the English language."

While the newspaper article described the children who would be "following their parents to a new land of promise, where they may play in green fields without watching out for automobiles," and even featured a photograph of four such children, Clements, in reporting to Arnoll, took a far more hardheaded view of what the *Express* accepted so casually:

No child could return, even though born in America, unless he had documentary evidence and his birth certificate and was able to substantiate this, the burden of proof being placed entirely on the individual. This means that something like 60% of these children are American citizens without very much hope of ever coming back into the United States.

The bureau of county welfare's view disagreed with Clements' appraisal of the American-born children. Its request to the county board of supervisors for the 17 August repatriation trip stated that "All of these people [apparently including children] are at present receiving aid from the County Welfare Division and none of them are American citizens." While it is obvious that the casual observations of both Clements and the *Express* reporter would be a less reliable source than the official request of a county welfare official, logic demands that *some* of the children out of the 469 officially counted minors under age twelve (the *Express* estimated 700, which included non-charity repatriates) would be American-born. This observation was reinforced all the more when Clements, reporting his having interviewed a number of the adult repatriates, said that many of the men admitted they had been in the United States at least ten years.

The underlying significance of this problem was the bureau of county welfare's belief that even though these children were American-born, culturally they were Mexican. By thus mixing nationality and culture, Los Angeles County — and many white Americans across the country, as well as in the Southwest — excluded from its mind the thought that Mexican-American children, whose parents were on relief in a period of economic depression, might some day become productive American adult citizens. This style of thinking was, and to a disturbing extent still is, characteristic of an Anglo-American population (even though the "Anglo American" might have parents from Poland, Germany, or Ireland) that has consistently stereotyped the Mexican American and his antecedents.

Besides observing the children, Clements spent the morning noticing other details about the repatriates, including the relative ages of the passengers. He interviewed as many people as he could within the available time before the trains pulled out. He believed that many men with whom he had spoken were more than just agricultural laborers, that they were "artisans or workmen, none having any criminal stigma." He also wanted to know if any of them had owned property in Los Angeles, "but it was impossible to do this in the short time that I had with any authenticity."

With this third shipment of repatriates from the Southern Pacific depot, the department of charities underwent a change of leadership. The department had been under fire by the grand jury for some time, there being suspicions of financial irregularity. As a result of this investigation, Superintendent of Charities Holland resigned on 25 August, pleading ill health. He was succeeded in the post by William R. Harriman, who had been superintendent of the county farm. Despite some criticism, Holland's assistant, A. C. Price, then became superintendent of the bureau of county welfare.[15] No change in policy in the repatriation program occurred, though the bookkeeping seemed to have improved.

The third movement of repatriates occurred just two weeks before Los Angeles celebrated its one hundred and fiftieth birthday. Throughout the year, publicity notices had been issued to the newspapers, and a program lasting several days before and after 4 September was planned. The fiesta committee seemed almost culturally schizoid as it planned the birthday celebration. While newspapers made many references to old Spanish customs, costumes, dances, and music, little attention was paid to the Mexicans living in Los Angeles. The telephone operators at city hall were instructed to greet callers with "Buenos días," as if the words were newly minted for the festivities. As a highlight of the fiesta, a queen was crowned, her identity kept a secret until the moment of glory. The recipient turned out to be the descendant of an Anglo-American pioneer who had come to California during the Gold Rush.[16]

Mexican Welfare Conference

As the events of the birthday fiesta reached their final stages of preparation, those citizens of the city who carried a consistent concern for the problems of Mexicans in California laid plans for a conference on Mexican welfare, to be held at the Los Angeles Public Library on 14 September. This conference was an outgrowth of an earlier one that had been held on 15 June, at which only a

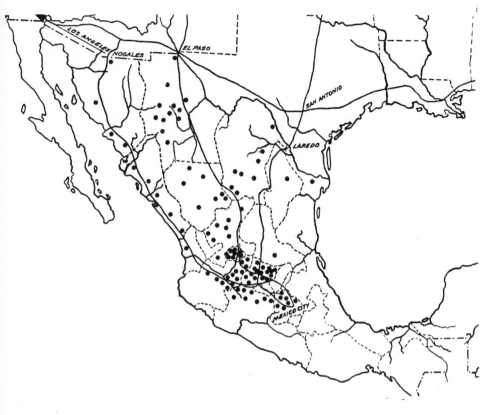

Paul S. Taylor, Mexican Labor in the United States: Migration Statistics, IV.
Destinations of Mexican repatriates from Los Angeles County, 1930–1932

few organizations had been represented. "The purpose of the Conference," read the invitation, "is particularly to learn of present conditions and problems existing in our Mexican communities, and the adoption of an intelligent future plan of action to meet the situation."

Sixty-eight people representing thirty-five organizations attended this conference. Among the people taking an active interest were Ernest Besig, who presided over the meeting; sociologist Emory Bogardus; the Reverend Robert McLean; Mexican Consul Rafael de la Colina and Vice Consul Ricardo Hill; Mr. and Mrs. John Anson Ford; and many others, representing the chamber of commerce, various churches and aid societies, community centers, the Southern Pacific railroad, schools, and the All Nations Foundation.

The ideas of a free Mexican employment bureau, the creation of public jobs, a clearing house for legal aid cases, and the need to educate the Mexicans as to their rights and duties under the law were all discussed. Unfortunately, while the people attending the conference were sincere in their interest, the meeting ended on an inconclusive note. No formal minutes were kept, and the committee appointed "to study the future plan of action" went the way of all committees charged with such a vague responsibility.*

Shipments Become Routine

During September and October the bureau of county welfare signed up new volunteers for repatriation on a fourth shipment, scheduled for 29 October. Besides this effort, approximately three hundred Mexicans under the auspices of the Mexican consulate planned to leave on 8 October. Writing to S. T. Olafson of the chamber of commerce, Ernest Besig admitted that after the Conference on Mexican Welfare he had thought that Mexican repatriation had reached its peak, "but it seems to be starting again with renewed vigour."

As autumn came to Southern California, the organized repatriations took on the polish that comes with the perfecting of a routine operation. Despite some criticisms of coercion, the bureau of county welfare did not lack repatriation volunteers for the next scheduled shipment, or those that followed.

Rafael de la Colina found nothing to criticize in the county's program, and in fact praised those who helped run it smoothly. "Allow me to express, in behalf of my Government, our sincere appreciation for the work your Welfare Department has been doing among my countrymen, in helping them return to Mexico," he informed the board of supervisors. "I wish to make special mention of the cooperation and help extended to repatriates by Messrs. Philip J. Robinson and Horace D. Roberts." The board responded in kind, as the chief clerk replied to the consul that he "was directed by the Board to express to you its appreciation of your appreciation."

The fourth repatriation shipment, on two trains — one to Nogales, and the other to El Paso — departed on 29 October with

---

*On 13 November 1931, the Los Angeles *Record* reported that Mexican repatriation was also a topic of discussion at the annual conference of the Friends of the Mexicans at Pomona College, but it, too, brought forth no action.

approximately 1,200 Mexican repatriates, of whom 1,059 were having their way paid by the county. Robinson and Roberts, by now familiar with the routine, were accompanied by Rex Thomson, a department of charities employee making his first trip with the repatriates. More than anyone else in the coming years, Thomson was to make repeated trips to Mexico, either on the repatriation trains or else to meet with Mexican officials concerning employment for the returnees or the development of repatriation colonies.

Apparently more *repatriados* were expected to depart than actually made the trip, for Superintendent Harriman of the department of charities was unsure until the last minute just how many Mexicans would be leaving. Despite such uncertainties, Supervisor Frank Shaw assured the public that the county was saving a considerable amount of money, since the price of the ticket was considerably less than what was needed to maintain the aliens on the charity list.[17]

As a point of legal nicety, Shaw proposed to the board of supervisors that the resolution of the previous 4 May, which had authorized the superintendent of charities to pay the fares of repatriates to the border, be more clearly defined and revised so that it read "to their destination or homes in Mexico," since that was, after all, the purpose of the whole program. This also absolved the county of any charges that repatriated Mexicans were being abandoned at the border. From a national viewpoint, many *repatriados* were victims of this practice, though not by Los Angeles County. Since county welfare workers were seeing the Mexicans down as far south as Mexico, D.F., the rationale for this comment had a degree of validity.

It would be quite repetitious to describe each succeeding repatriation shipment in detail, but some general comments can be made. As soon as a sizable number of Mexicans had volunteered for repatriation, the superintendent of charities wrote out a request to the board of supervisors, giving the tentative date of departure, the estimated number of people who would be leaving, and a sum of money calculated to cover the cost of food and transportation. The superintendent also requested that certain welfare officials accompany the repatriates, their expenses being figured in with the general cost of the shipment. Assistant Superintendent A. C. Price described the recurring complications to the board of supervisors:

> There are many problems that arise during the journey requiring the judgment and action of one who is familiar with the policies of this department.

Tickets are lost en route, expenditures at rural junctions are often necessary for families, there must be supervision of meals and necessary medical attention, payment of fares on tickets to rural stations, etc. require the attendance of one familiar with rules and regulations of this department.

The coming of the new year, 1932, brought no change in the routine, as the departure of 12 January, the fifth trip, was similar to the previous shipment in numbers, costs, and chaperones, as were the sixth trip on 8 March, the seventh on 29 April, the eighth on 7 July, and the ninth on 18 August. Regardless of how routine, the difficulties of calculating numbers and costs always presented themselves. With the 29 April departure, the projected number of repatriates and the cost were considerably higher than the actual number departing, as 875 instead of the projected 1,500 people boarded the trains. Later for the 7 July trip, Harriman initially estimated the cost to be $24,000, then revised it to $17,000, almost the exact cost. These trips were all characterized by a decided lack of interest by the Los Angeles newspapers, which in 1932 gave either perfunctory mention or none at all of the departures.

Departure Estimates

Estimates of the number of Mexicans who had left Southern California varied. On 7 February 1932, the special correspondent of the *New York Times* quoted a figure of 75,000 Mexicans who had left the region in 1931; later that same year, the Los Angeles *Record* on 7 March gave a similar figure of 50,000-75,000 departures. Both figures would have had to include Mexicans who had left under all varieties of repatriation, including by automobile. The official county total — those Mexicans on relief who had had their tickets bought for them by the bureau of county welfare — was 2,308 in the first four trips, comprising 877 relief cases.

Mexicans repatriated under the auspices of the Mexican consulate totaled 7,755 in 1931, plus an undetermined number aided by private charitable organizations. Not included here are Mexicans not seeking aid, who left California and returned via automobile through Arizona, New Mexico, or Texas: their numbers would contribute to the figures given for leaving the United States in general.*

---

*The *New York Times* of 8 December 1931 gave a figure of 112,407 for the entire country up to that date, while the Los Angeles *Record* of 7 March 1932 recorded a total of 150,000 repatriates. For figures of people assisted by Mexican consulates, see Secretaría de Relaciones Exteriores, *Apendice a la Memoria, 1931–1932,* table following page 984. The U.S. commissioner general of immigration

Contributing Factors

While this mass movement is traceable to a variety of factors, including the depression, persuasion by welfare agencies, homesickness, and the announced willingness of Mexico to receive her wandering sons, the passage of years has found the conclusions of Carey McWilliams the most enduring. In several of his books McWilliams discussed the Los Angeles repatriations and linked them with such problems as agricultural exploitation and antiunion activities by certain large farm interests. McWilliams deserves credit for being virtually the only writer to deal with Mexican repatriation, but his work needs to be revised in the light of documents available since his books were published.[18]

Colonies in Mexico

One particularly neglected aspect of the repatriation of Mexicans from Los Angeles was the effort by the department of charities first, to make certain that such colonies existed; second, to ascertain the success of the repatriation and colonization projects; and finally, to determine whether "jobs" really awaited the repatriates upon their return to their homeland. Although the department sought to avoid charges of dumping repatriates at the border, such inquiries were not made until over a year after the start of the repatriation program.

In the summer of 1932, shortly after the ninth repatriation shipment, Superintendent Harriman received word of a colonization project in Baja California which was willing to accept one hundred families from Los Angeles County. Vague as to the source of the offer, Harriman was somewhat reticent about endorsing the project, when he informed the board of supervisors on 26 September that:

... the conditions as described to us make it doubtful whether we should assume responsibility of sending these people back to their country without verification of the facts regarding the proposed establishment of this colony. If successful, it would relieve the County of a very considerable expenditure during the next year.

----

admitted in his *Annual Report, 1932,* (page 2) the inability of the bureau to count the number of people leaving, "but with the purpose of laying the groundwork for future readmission without expense or trouble, many of the aliens sought to impress upon our officers that they were leaving the country but temporarily. It is certain that nearly all will seek to return when employment and business conditions improve, as our country is the promised land for these people."

Harriman recommended that Rex Thomson, as a deputy superintendent, be authorized to drive down to Baja California, using a
county car and under county expense, to ascertain whether the offer
was a feasible one for the county to accept. Supervisor Shaw presented Harriman's suggestion to the board of supervisors, which
unanimously voted its approval.

Thomson, driving county car no. 750, spent several days in
Baja California checking on the validity of the offer, which had
apparently been made through unofficial sources. The proposed area
for colonization, an 8,000-acre tract known as Palm Valley, was
located some fifteen miles east of Ensenada. Thomson spoke with
the president and vice president of the Baja California Light, Water,
and Telephone Company, the region's largest utility, and learned
that the company had already made an investigation of the Palm
Valley area.

Land was indeed available for colonization. But the available
acreage was not the best land in the region, and all previous efforts
to turn a profit by agricultural endeavors had failed. Thomson
reported to the board of supervisors that company officials had told
him "that upon irrigating the major portion of the valley, the rising
water table brought the alkalies to the surface, rendering the soil
unsuitable for profitable cultivation." The company had abandoned
its plans for colonization, although about fifteen settlers were farming
on a subsistence level in the valley at the time of Thomson's trip.
Dry farming had also been attempted, although this effort too had
not proved profitable for those who had tried it.

Besides the utility company officials, Thomson interviewed
Augustín Olachea, the governor of Baja California. The governor
made it clear that he was quite opposed to indigent Mexicans being
repatriated to any part of Baja California, Palm Valley included.
Thomson reported that the governor had stated his territory "was
now overburdened with unemployed citizens and to such an extent
that he has shipped some hundreds to Mexico proper where they
could be readily assimilated, and that to allow any influx of indigents from California, would be an added burden to his people
which they could ill-afford."

On the other hand, Governor Olachea did indicate that he
would welcome Mexicans who had farming experience and the financial resources to sustain themselves "over the pioneering period without becoming a burden to the country." But Olachea warned that

earlier attempts on the best government land, including an effort by a Japanese colony, had failed to produce profitable results. Another aspect of the problem lay in Baja California's isolation; there was no market available for surplus agricultural products, and a dearth of manufactured items.

As a result of his interviews, Thomson expressed pessimism toward any plans for sending Mexican repatriates from Los Angeles county to Baja California. He had in fact been told by those to whom he had spoken that the best policy was to continue sending the repatriates to Mexico proper where, the officials assured him, "the repatriate has the opportunity of becoming self-supporting through employment offered him by industry, commerce, agriculture, mining, etc., and where he can, in addition, receive assistance from friends and relatives."

In conclusion, Thomson presented to the board of supervisors the most recent statement of the governor of Baja California, brought to him personally by a representative of Olachea. This statement, directed to the Mexicans living in Los Angeles County, recommended "that only settlers who are experienced in agriculture and financed to carry themselves for at least a six months period, will be welcomed to settle on government land in Baja California." Thus any misguided attempts at colonization by repatriates in Baja California, by Los Angeles County officials, or Mexicans themselves were stamped as clearly inadvisable.

In spite of the negative view of Governor Olachea, a number of Mexican repatriates did attempt to colonize Baja California lands. Approximately one hundred and fifty Mexicans from Santa Monica made the trip south and established themselves on a modest basis. News of this effort prompted some welfare agencies to ask that Harriman reinvestigate the prospects of settlement in Baja California. It should be noted that the Santa Monica *repatriados* had not departed from the state of California with the aid of county funds. Harriman asked that Thomson meet with Governor Olachea again. Accompanied by Mexican Vice Consul Hill, Thomson drove to Baja California on 24 March 1933.

While no formal report by Thomson was found in the county records, it is reasonable to assume, in view of the fact that the county-sponsored trains were still being directed to the towns of Nogales and El Paso, that no significant number of repatriates could realistically be sent to Baja California. The presence of repatriates there was not due to the work of Los Angeles County's department of charities, although county officials would have liked to have sent them there.[19]

Thomson's investigatory work for the board of supervisors was repeated again, several months after his return from Baja California. At the request of Juventino Espinosa, governor of the state of Nayarit on Mexico's west coast, Thomson was invited to attend "an important governmental conference" at Tepic, the capital city, 8–10 June 1933. According to Vice Consul Hill, the Nayarit government was "very anxious that this country [sic] be settled up by those indigent Mexicans now dependent on the generosity of the Americans in Los Angeles County." Hill told the board of supervisors that the Mexican consulate in Los Angeles believed a Nayarit colonization project would be of particular value to the county. Nayarit, described by Hill as "one of the most fertile states in Mexico and one possessing a climate only second to California's," was closer geographically to Los Angeles than El Paso [said Hill], and the opportunities that awaited newcomers there were very good.

The board of supervisors authorized Thomson to make the trip, and for reasons that are not known, Thomson chose to make the trip by automobile. Driving from Los Angeles to the city of Tepic in the summer of 1933 must have been quite an adventure. The trip down and back, including time spent at the conference, took twenty-seven days. Thomson's county car suffered a tire blowout, and expenses for his trip, which included lodging and automobile repairs, were almost three hundred dollars.

Upon Thomson's return, the contrast between the Mexican and Los Angeles approaches to the Nayarit proposal became evident. Under the headline, "MEXICAN EXODUS PLANNED/County Would Send 5000 Families Now on Welfare Rolls Back to Their Homeland," the *Los Angeles Times* reported on 7 July 1933 the disparity between what Mexico wanted and what Thomson could send as repatriates.

The article quoted Thomson as stating, "The Mexican government . . . wants professional men, such as doctors and lawyers, as well as tradesmen and laborers." That Thomson could supply a significant number of indigent doctors, lawyers, and tradesmen from the welfare rolls who were willing to return to Mexico was highly unlikely. Although he expressed great enthusiasm for the project, nothing came of it.

While Thomson made the three trips in 1932–33, the county-sponsored repatriations continued. Between October 1932 and April 1933 four shipments, at approximately two-month intervals, left Los Angeles. During that period 868 relief cases, totaling 3,150 men, women, and children, underwent repatriation to Mexico, as well as an uncalculated number of Mexicans who returned without the aid of the county. To say that these families "volunteered" or to charge that one way or another they were "coerced" would be to oversimplify their problems. On the one hand, there seemed to be no end to the problems of the depression, and the last-resort offer of a free ride back to relatives and old friends, plus hints of employment in Mexico, seemed tempting. On the other hand, reports of difficulty in getting back into the United States, the resistance of American-born children to leaving, and the admittance of failure, implicit in leaving while others were staying, must have made choosing or rejecting repatriation an extremely difficult problem.

L.A. County Expenses

With the inauguration of a new administration in Washington, D.C., the Los Angeles county repatriation program found itself at a financial crossroads. Financial support for people on county relief was now materially aided by federal funds, with the condition that no such funds were to be spent on transporting indigents out of the county. If the county desired to continue its repatriation program, it would have to do so with money appropriated exclusively from county funds. While the county had benefitted from this practice in preceding months, the question of whether the county would wish to continue so in the future, inasmuch as federal money was now aiding indigents, would have to be answered. Los Angeles County decided to continue appropriating welfare bureau funds for Mexican repatriation. But the number of departures abruptly declined. On 14 April, 914 *repatriados* departed.

Berry Pickers' Strike

Several months later Southern California was treated to an unusual strike when Mexican farm workers refused to pick berries for Japanese employers at the rate of nine cents an hour. The strike mushroomed into an international incident as Mexican government officials, including ex-President Plutarco Elías Calles, donated money and fired off telegrams to President Roosevelt and Governor James Rolph of California. Documents in the Clements Papers at the University of California, Los Angeles, reveal that the chamber of commerce and various agricultural employers had hoped to remove large numbers of the strikers through county repatriation.

Hiatus of Shipments

Despite this desire, only 453 people — of whom 40 were single persons and 366 were from 82 families — departed in the fourteenth repatriation shipment on 3 August. Over four months then elapsed before another departure was scheduled. In the meantime Supervisor Harry M. Baine, on a trip to Mexico, discovered that Los Angeles county had been paying a tax of 15½ percent on that part of the ticket cost which covered traveling within the Republic of Mexico. The fourteen repatriation shipments had cost the county to date, without its being aware of it, an additional eleven thousand dollars. Baine expressed his dissatisfaction over this state of affairs to Mexican government officials and, as a result of his efforts, the cost of the fare within Mexico was reduced for future county-sponsored trains.

On 12 December 1933, the fifteenth repatriation shipment left Los Angeles. Instead of the anticipated 600 volunteers for repatriation, only 412 Mexicans actually departed. Mexican repatriation was clearly on the ebb. There now followed a hiatus of repatriation shipments; not for six months was another county-sponsored departure scheduled.

Statistical Evaluation

With the close of the year 1933 there came an impulse for an evaluation of the repatriation program as it had been carried out to date. Part of this evaluation, as might be expected, was statistical: by the end of 1933, fifteen repatriation trains had transported 3,145 county relief cases, totaling 12,668 Mexicans, back to Mexico. To effect this movement of people, the bureau of county welfare had paid a total cost of $182,575. The financial savings to Los Angeles County, in the words of Supervisor Baine, "being the difference between the cost of maintenance on our welfare rolls and the gross cost of repatriation," was approximately $435,000. These figures vary according to the sources giving them, and variations even within county offices can be easily noted. Exact calculations were made difficult because certain costs refused to remain static, such as the price of railroad tickets, or the average cost per family.

County welfare officials, finding it difficult to estimate the exact numbers of expected volunteers for repatriation, often under- or over-estimated the funds necessary and the numbers of people involved. A further complication, found in calculating aggregate numbers, lay in the period of time over which the repatriations occurred; the dates for certain figures might differ, or overlap, or somehow vary, and with them the numbers as well. Common sense dictates that the figures given by the division of accounts and collections, statistical service, within the department of charities, were the most reliable of the sources offering statistical evaluations. From appendix C, based on this source, it appears that food and medical expenses were kept at a necessary minimum.

Qualitative Evaluation

Apart from statistical summaries, qualitative evaluations also appeared at this time. Reports were prepared by the department of charities and sent to the board of supervisors and the Mexican consulate, discussing the origins, procedures, success, and future of the repatriation program. Perhaps the most important observation made by the charities department centered on the abrupt decline of volunteers for repatriation. Only after an "intensive recruiting drive" was the department able to register 120 relief cases, these being the 412 individuals who had left on the fifteenth shipment. This decline was due, the department believed, to the federal relief assistance now being given to the county under a policy which insisted "that we show no preference between the alien and the citizen as regards direct relief."

The charities department complained, however, of a contradiction in the federal programs: the Federal Civil Works Administration projects provided priority for American citizens on its projects, or those who had taken out first papers.* The federal government also

----

*The Federal Civil Works Administration was created by President Roosevelt's executive order on 9 November 1933 and placed under the direction of Federal Emergency Relief Administrator Harry L. Hopkins. When its term of operation expired on 1 July 1934, part of its function was continued by the Works Progress Administration, later renamed Works Projects Administration.

raised the standard of relief for those who were not able to obtain employment on federal projects. "Therefore, we find a peculiar situation and a most unsatisfactory one," stated Earl E. Jensen, who had replaced Harriman as the department's superintendent, "where the Mexican alien's monthly budget has been increased 30% and yet we refuse to allow him to do any work in return for the same, even if he were willing to do so." The department of charities thus found itself giving additional funds to Mexicans who could not be employed on certain public projects.

In an effort to improve the unsatisfactory state of affairs, the department made several proposals. The first of these — that Mexican federal and state governments provide further inducements for repatriation through additional land grants, home building loans, and new public works projects that gave preference to repatriates — was undercut by Superintendent Jensen's admission to the board of supervisors of the difficulties involved in Mexico's carrying out such ideas:

It has become increasingly embarrassing on the part of Mexican Federal and State Governments to sanction, sponsor or encourage our repatriation activities, due to the fact that the taxpayers resent their Government's encouraging this County to burden their communities with increased numbers of destitute people who, for some time after their arrival, must, naturally, take the status of public charges.

In spite of this, the charities department recommended that the repatriation program be resumed, with certain revisions. Food and medical attention, minimally provided by the county throughout the trip, were to be discontinued on crossing the Mexican border, as were additional expenses that had been provided to see a repatriate to his final destination. Instead, each repatriate was to be given the illusion of possessing his own financial resources. A repatriate would receive a financial allotment covering himself and his family; 25 percent of this was to be paid to the repatriate at the branch of the Bank of Mexico of his choice, either in Nogales or Juárez. This would permit the repatriate to cash the check at a rate of exchange favorable to him. It was then presumed that the repatriate would use this money to obtain the services that previously had been provided by the county, a point assured by the continuing accompaniment of county officials such as Thomson and Robinson on the repatriation trains. The repatriate received the remaining 75 percent of the allotment when he disembarked from the train, so that he did not automatically arrive as a public charge. The average amount per family of the cash allowance was ninety pesos.

These new procedures were put into practice with the next repatriation shipment. This departure, the sixteenth in the series, took place on 19 April 1934, and included 172 relief cases, totaling 664 individuals.[20] A. C. Price, heading the bureau of county welfare, estimated the net savings to the county at over $32,000 for the coming year. Warrants were given to the repatriates at the border, and a bank draft at their point of debarkation, as per the new policies. Rex Thomson and two other county officials escorted the repatriation train, distributing the travel allowances at the appropriate places.

County Negotiations With Mexico

No sooner had Thomson returned from the repatriation shipment, when the board of supervisors sent him back to Mexico to attend further conferences on the settlement of repatriates in colonization projects. This latest effort came at the behest of Miguel E. Bracho, a Mexican government official delegated to work with repatriation from Los Angeles County. Bracho had been working energetically to provide Thomson with concrete outlines for repatriation colonies. Besides government agencies, he had contacted chambers of commerce on the idea of bringing back *repatriados* to colonize the west coast states of Mexico. Bracho had set up a series of meetings with official and semiofficial agencies, and he urged Thomson not to miss the scheduled Mexico City conferences.

Thomson's return to Mexico City and his interviews with officials there represent in some ways the high point of the repatriation program he had worked so loyally in developing; but this high point was to prove a climax rather than a beginning. He gained audiences with a number of prominent Mexicans, including Manuel Gamio, who was at the time serving in the Department of Agriculture and Public Works. On 4 May 1934, Thomson submitted a detailed report to Francisco S. Elías, the department's secretary. This report described the history, rationale, and future hopes of the Los Angeles County repatriation program. Having noted the possible uniqueness of an official of a local government in one country reporting to a federal official in another, Thomson wrote Elías that:

Even though it may seem egotistical on the part of officials of Los Angeles County to organize and send out Mexican citizens who have contributed so much to the development of the State, the reasons for this voluntary exodus are quite just and fundamentally economic. If our community cannot furnish employment to its own citizens, there is little possibility that it may be able to provide employment for foreigners.

Thomson made no mention of the fact that many of the "foreigners" he so described had lived and worked in the United States for years and were raising children who were American-born citizens. The thrust of his report strongly suggested that Los Angeles county harbored a wellspring of Mexican aliens who were either passively ready to be returned to Mexico or were actively seeking repatriation.

Thomson's report contained a half dozen recommendations designed to assure the success of future repatriations. In essence, Los Angeles County asked the Mexican government to subsidize repatriated colonists for the amount of time necessary for *repatriado* farmers to be able to sustain themselves, and also requested that Mexican officials working with the repatriates "possess a knowledge of American speech and laws and of our methods." The county further recommended that the Department of Agriculture and Public Works have exclusive control of all repatriation projects, and that this department, in addition to accepting these plans for consideration, also appoint "a competent person with a knowledge of the English language that he may immediately cooperate in Los Angeles with our Department toward the organization of those groups of repatriates in accord with instructions and the respective regulations of your Division of Colonization."

Thomson noted that his ideas had been warmly greeted by the businessmen and chamber of commerce members with whom he had conferred, as well as officials of the Southern Pacific Railroad of Mexico. With the approval of the plans, Thomson predicted "that in time not only will the individual repatriates have benefitted but the Country in general as well." The country Thomson referred to was unclear, but he was no doubt referring to Mexico. He concluded, "Such benefits will, in turn, result in the mutual commercial exchange between the two countries [*sic*] as well as social and political comprehension between our respective peoples."

Secretary Elías replied to Thomson's report in a brief but graciously written note several days later:

This department has given full consideration and thought to yours of the 4th instant. It is aware of the far reaching influence that the solution of the repatriation of the Mexican aliens, who now reside in Los Angeles County, will have not only on the citizens of the United States but on the government of this country as well, therefore this department has issued orders to proceed with the formulation of a plan along practical and rapid lines to arrive at the solution sought; taking into consideration suggestions offered in your letter. We shall be pleased to advise you later as to the procedure of our plan.

Thomson's presence in Mexico, D.F., and the reasons for his being there, were noted in the Mexican press.[21] He also paid a visit to the U.S. Consulate General in the city, and there spoke with Vice Consul John S. Littell, who reported to the State Department on 7 and 11 May 1934, that Thomson's diplomatic position was rather interesting: since Thomson was a representative of a local rather than a federal government, the negotiations were not being "made an international question." According to Littell, this meant that "any difficulties which may later arise will not be attributed to the United States Federal Government."

Thomson explained the county repatriation program to Littell and outlined his proposals for future repatriations. The vice consul, favorably impressed with Thomson's sincerity and dedication to the success of his county's repatriation program, expressed in his report the belief that should the program become operative, benefits to both countries might result. These benefits included a lightening of the relief load "from the almost unbearable burden of supporting thousands of unassimilable aliens" (apparently Littell did not know that Mexicans considered eligible for repatriation composed at the most 12 percent of the relief load); the return to Mexico of people who had become acquainted "with a higher standard of living"; an increase in commercial relations as a result of the tastes acquired by repatriates for material items; and "further strengthening of the good-will between the two countries resulting from close and effective cooperation."

His trip also came to the attention of the U.S. State Department through inquiries from the Mexican Embassy in Washington, which was apparently unaware of Thomson's meeting with Elías. The State Department investigated the actions of Los Angeles County in Mexico and reported, to the satisfaction of the Mexican Embassy, that Thomson's efforts had been open and aboveboard.

Following Thomson's visit, the Mexican government set up the National Repatriation Board, headed by Elías. But whatever benefits Mexico was supposed to obtain from absorbing additional thousands of people at a time when that country was also experiencing an overabundance of workers and a high rate of unemployment, the fact remains that by 1935 Mexicans in Southern California no longer wished to be repatriated, nor had they had such a desire for some time.

Despite Thomson's high hopes for the success of his plan, the proposed alliance whereby Mexicans from Los Angeles County would be directly integrated into colonization projects supervised by the Mexican government did not become a reality. Thomson's proposals followed rather than preceded the peak of repatriation and proved to be a climax to the program.

Repatriation on the Wane

The last attempt at repatriation on a grand scale, and in fact, the only attempt following Thomson's return from Mexico, was scheduled for 20 March 1935. When the board of supervisors referred the proposal back to the superintendent of charities to see if the repatriation could be performed with state emergency relief administration funds, the plan became bogged down in red tape.

Confusion on the part of the county at the beginning of 1935 was evident when the board of supervisors went on record as *opposing* legislation stopping state aid to aliens after a six-month period. The Mexican Community Organization, a group supported by friends of the Mexican-American neighborhood of Belvedere, filed a strong letter of protest against the legislation with the board of supervisors. This legislation had been prepared by the Los Angeles County counsel's office, the idea for it possibly coming from Rex Thomson, who had recently been named superintendent of the department of charities.

These developments must have been a disappointment to Thomson. For several years he had been the head of a quasi-official division of rehabilitation within the bureau of county welfare, and repatriation had come to be his special field. Although a continuation of the program was approved, intensive recruitment of prospective repatriates was expressly forbidden by a policy stating that no coercive measures were to be directly or indirectly used on any alien in order to obtain his consent to being returned to Mexico.

After 1934 Mexican nationals on relief in Southern California were unresponsive to the invitation from the bureau of county welfare to continue the movement "back to the homeland." The movement had ended because of several factors. The relief programs of the New Deal permitted a higher relief allotment and eased the financial burden placed on local welfare programs. The depression years were a time of municipal and county construction in Southern California, and many of the viaducts, tunnels, and flood control projects in the region were built in the decade of the 1930s. Such projects and the prospect of employment on them would have helped reduce the temptation to travel hundreds of miles just for similar work. While programs under the Civil Works Administration and later the Works Progress Administration gave first preference to American citizens, those citizens, by being so employed, lightened the relief loads.

Thomson's belief that Mexicans eligible for repatriation were unassimilable foreigners rested on faulty assumptions. Many Mexican families had American-born children who in their home and school environments shared the experiences of the second generation of other immigrant groups. These children attended American schools, spoke English as well as Spanish, watched motion pictures, and listened to radio programs. It would have been impossible to find a Mexican family eligible for county relief that was so insulated as not to have been exposed to various aspects of Anglo-American culture, positive as well as negative.

Los Angeles County's bureau of welfare had initiated its repatriation program when the depression was but fifteen months old and continued it over a period of four years. During that time economic conditions worsened. To claim, as Thomson did, that county welfare officials had "foreseen" that conditions would get worse before they improved would be to grant a local governmental agency with powers of prescience. The argument for repatriation in 1931 was based on the fact that economic conditions were bad enough, and to continue having Mexicans on relief would present the county with an intolerable welfare burden.

But the county's own figures, released three years later, stated that Mexican aliens on relief constituted at the most 12 percent of the total number of cases, and this percentage fluctuated at different times of the year; it was as low as 9 percent at times. Of the 112,500 relief cases in November 1933, the Mexicans numbered approximately 10,000. Removing this fraction would not necessarily have reduced the relief load for obvious reasons: the repatriation of Mexicans occurred on so gradual a basis that Mexicans previously not on relief took the places of those who left, so that the percentage of Mexican relief cases remained fairly constant. At best, the county succeeded in balancing any increase of Mexicans on relief by siphoning off several thousand a year through repatriation.

Saving Money

On a procedural basis, the repatriation program did operate successfully. Once the initial difficulties were ironed out, the county perfected a routine operation and did indeed save money by removing relief cases. In 1935 Thomson, reviewing the accomplishments of the program, announced that a total of 3,317 cases had been removed from the county rolls through the repatriation process. Thomson spelled out the savings in monetary terms for the board of supervisors:

According to a survey conducted during March and April, 1934, the cost per Mexican case aided averages $25.23 per month. Applying this cost to the period these cases have been removed from relief, shows that a total saving has been effected amounting to $2,187,138 to September 30, 1934.

That a sum in excess of two million dollars was actually saved by the county is debatable. Thomson's figure was based on the assumptions that the relief case would have continued through the entire period of repatriation had the family not returned to Mexico, that a case that did return was on relief at the start of 1931, and that costs were static. Actual savings to the county were much closer to the realistic estimate given by Supervisor Baine, who assessed that the county probably saved a net of around half a million dollars through its repatriation program.

Justification or Excuses?

On an ethical basis, however, Los Angeles County's welfare bureau created a theory to justify its practices. Assumptions that Canadians in Los Angeles received equivalent treatment with Mexicans; that nationality was determined by culture rather than birthplace — a convenient way of removing the American-born child along with his parents; that Mexicans were an unassimilable group;

and that they constituted a disproportionate share of county relief cases, were used as excuses for the practice of getting as many Mexicans out of the county as possible. These assumptions, current not only in Los Angeles but also across the United States, contributed to the climate of uncertainty that prompted thousands of Mexicans, in addition to the 13,332 people sent to Mexico by the county, to seek repatriation. Eventually Mexicans proved less resilient than had been assumed, and Thomson's plan for returning another 12,000 Mexicans never was put into practice.

The Los Angeles County repatriation program stands as the most ambitious of the organized plans for returning Mexicans to Mexico in the 1930s. Its uniqueness, however, stems only from the numbers involved and the duration of the program. Across the country, in the same period that Los Angeles County was repatriating part of its Mexican colony, other municipalities, counties, and states, with varying amounts of effort, organization, and success, were attempting to perform the same task.

7.

Repatriation Across the Country

MEXICANS WERE ON THE MOVE during the Great Depression, but this movement was not a new, spontaneous one. The Twenties had already witnessed Mexicans moving not only back and forth across the border, but many heading farther north in search of work in the sugar beet fields, steel mills, and automobile factories of the Great Lakes region.

With the opening of a new decade came acute unemployment, increased competition for existing jobs, and more restrictions preventing aliens from entering certain occupations. These conditions compounded by reports and rumors of free land donated by the Mexican federal and state governments sent many Mexicans southward in a movement that had already reached significant proportions by 1929.

This acceleration of the repatriation movement was distinguished from the departures of the previous decade by the belief of so many Anglos that this time it was a one-way trip, a view reinforced by consular officials' stringent observance of immigration laws. By enforcing the LPC or "liable to become a public charge" provision of the 1917 Immigration Act, they effectively ended the return of the laborer class to the United States.[1]

Los Angeles differed from other areas that undertook repatriation programs only in the degree of organization and the amount of time over which the programs were conducted. In percentage terms, some cities disposed of the Mexicans in their midst more successfully than Los Angeles, but only because there were fewer Mexicans to be rid of. While only 3.6 percent of the Mexican nationals lived in Michigan, Illinois, and Indiana, more than 10 percent of the repatriates across the country came from these three states alone.[2]

Any attempt to describe the movements of large numbers of people carries within it elusive hazards. Generalizations must be qualified and words and statistics checked for hidden subjectivity.

Questions of assimilation and citizenship could not be readily answered with one clipped explanation. Obviously many of the Mexicans who left the United States during the Great Depression had been in the country for so short a period of time that the problems of floundering between two cultures and of obtaining citizenship rights never presented themselves. In some ways, they were the prototypes of the *braceros* and other workers who came in later under government-sponsored farm labor programs. Just as obviously, many hundreds of other Mexicans had lived in the United States for many years, were no longer working in agriculture, were acquiring property or engaging in business, and were absorbing or at least observing some of the mainstream of American culture.

Conditions which made a return to Mexico desirable or preferable varied from region to region, from city to city, and might include factors of economic hardship, coercion, prejudice, discrimination, uncertainty as to legal status, homesickness, relative ability to move, and the distance to be traveled.

The nomadic nature of many of the Mexican laborers in the United States rendered demographic statistics susceptible to distortion or manipulation. Because some families undoubtedly moved from state to state seeking employment before crossing over to Mexico, Mexican repatriation figures often blended with the migration of Mexicans within the United States. Though some did bypass border stations, eventually almost all the Mexicans leaving the United States came to be tallied.

United States border officials generally conceded that statistics on departing Mexicans supplied by the Mexican Migration Service were more reliable than their own. Robert E. Frazer, the American consul general in Mexico, D.F., reported to the State Department in 1931 "that while we have consulates at seven Mexican ports of entry and departure on the border, the Mexican Migration Service has offices at twenty-six such ports, which maintain and submit regularly to the Mexican Migration Department at the capital statistics concerning migration." Throughout the early depression years, the statistics supplied to the United States Department of State were from Mexican sources.

Southwestern Enclaves

Of the Mexicans living in the United States, 90 percent of them resided within the borders of California, New Mexico, Texas, Arizona, and Colorado. Sizable Mexican enclaves also sprang up in Detroit, Chicago, and St. Paul, as well as in more limited numbers in other American cities located near regions where agriculture and industry had drawn Mexican labor.[3]

The pathways of repatriation were governed by the existing railroad trackage and highways in the United States, which funneled the travelers to the large border towns of Nogales, El Paso, and Laredo. Other towns, though smaller, attracted their share of returnees: Douglas, Arizona, faced Agua Prieta, Sonora; Brownsville, Texas, and Matamoros, Tamaulipas, were on opposite sides of the Rio Grande, as were Eagle Pass, Texas, and Piedras Negras, Coahuila. Mexicans undergoing repatriation from California who wished to return to the interior of Mexico proceeded through Arizona to Nogales, or went on to El Paso, these towns being the chief goals of the Los Angeles repatriation trains. Because of the geographical isolation of the Baja California peninsula, few Mexicans headed there, though Mexicali, across from Calexico, California, was a fair-sized border town.

The "stream of migration" of Mexicans leaving the United States in the early years of the depression reveals the largest number coming from Texas and returning primarily to the northeastern Mexican states. Most Mexicans of the first and second generations in Texas were concentrated in the southern half of the state, and many of them had worked for years as tenant farmers. Others worked as migrant laborers. The huge Mexican and Mexican-American population in Texas — around seven hundred thousand in 1930 — and the fact that possibly as many as one hundred thousand of this number were third-generation Texans, suggests that even though Texas led the country in repatriations, its percentage of returnees to Mexico was not large enough to reduce significantly the state's Spanish-speaking population.[4] In 1934, in his *Mexican Labor in the United States: Migration Statistics,* Paul S.

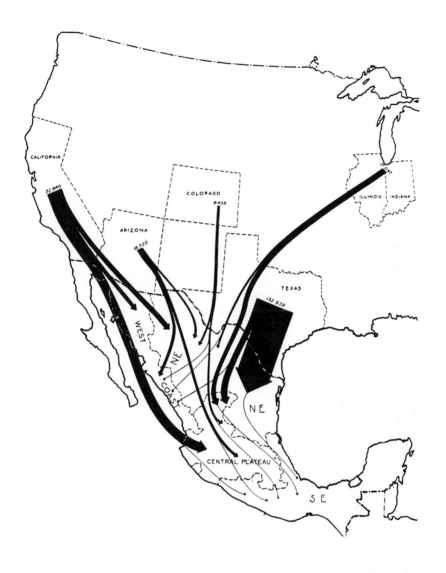

Paul S. Taylor, Mexican Labor in the United States: Migration Statistics, IV.

Regional destinations of Mexican repatriates from Texas, California, Illinois,
Indiana, Arizona, and Colorado, 1930–1932

Taylor recorded that 132,639 people of Mexican heritage departed Texas between 1930 and 1932.

Northern Enclaves

Repatriation from the northern industrial states, however, came much closer to the goal of removing the Mexican problem from relief rolls and school budgets. Based upon data from the Mexican Department of National Statistics and its successor, the Department of Economy and Statistics, the Taylor study revealed that a total of over 32,000 Mexicans departed from Illinois, Michigan, Indiana, and Ohio, between 1930 and 1932. California's figure for this period, also from the same source, was 52,946. As many of the shipments were unstructured and unpublicized, the occasional newspaper or magazine account of the repatriation movement rarely reported more than isolated incidents.

From Minnesota, where Mexicans had been attracted by employment in the sugar beet industry, St. Paul's bureau of public welfare paid the way of one hundred Mexicans on 4 November 1932, and in 1934 over three hundred more left, including American-born children.[5] In March 1934 the State of Ohio paid an average of fifteen dollars per person to repatriate about three hundred Mexicans from Lucas County.[6] Also during the depression, several thousand Mexicans left the Chicago area, where a sizable colony had developed.

At the suggestion of the East Chicago, Indiana, American Legion, the relief commission in that city established a repatriation program early in 1932, based on reasons virtually identical to those stated by Los Angeles officials the year before. This program removed some 1,800 Mexicans from East Chicago by the end of 1932, while almost 1,500 were repatriated from the city of Gary.[7]

Detroit's Mexican colony, which numbered around fifteen thousand in 1928 (an inflated figure largely arising from the influx of Mexicans due to the Cristero Revolt), experienced a drastic decline in population during the depression. Lack of employment, a problem hardly unique for any breadwinner in the depression, left the Mexican alien vulnerable. Ignacio Batiza, Detroit's Mexican consul, at first attempted to organize a relief program for destitute Mexicans, but this soon evolved into a program of repatriation. Consul Batiza noted the relatively recent arrival of many of the colony's residents, concluding that "they have not adapted themselves to the American ways and have been hit hard by the current depression."[8] Working with Detroit's department of public welfare, Batiza arranged for the voluntary repatriation of Mexicans who had arrived in Detroit after 1929, while the federal government transported repatriates to the border who had come to Detroit prior to that date.

The Michigan State Welfare Department believed "that any reduction in the relief load effective through repatriation service will be a significant factor toward the solution."[9] Detroit's department of public welfare proceeded to follow this injunction. A Mexican bureau was set up within the department, and Mexican nationals needing welfare aid, as well as naturalized or American-born Mexicans with similar problems, were interviewed by social workers who urged repatriation as a remedy for their troubles. At the end of 1932 some fifteen hundred Mexicans had been repatriated from Michigan; Consul Batiza's claim that over forty thousand Mexicans had left the state, while excessively high, was based on the assumptions of unemployment, lack of opportunity, and pressure from welfare officials.[10]

Repatriation from Michigan was searchingly evaluated by Norman D. Humphrey of Wayne State University, who weighed objectively the advantages and disadvantages in returning to Mexico. "The program of Mexican repatriates occurred . . . as an economy measure for returning to the homeland a large ethnic group," he stated, "which, with the coming of the depression, was not capable of self-support." The successes were overbalanced by the shortcomings, as Humphrey asserted:

Repatriation as a voluntary measure may well conform to the best standards of case work procedure, but actually, in the carrying out of the program, untrained case workers exerted undue pressure in some instances, and in others actually violated clients' rights. As a money-saving device the program may well have been effective, but as a case-work method involving cooperation by the worker and the agency, for the rehabilitation of a rightful segment of the American population, the program may be viewed as having been a failure.[11]

In many ways the Detroit repatriation was a small-scale duplication of the Los Angeles effort. There was the rationale of funds saved; the belief that Mexicans were unassimilable and a heavy, constant relief burden; the promises of employment, free land, and farm tools back in Mexico. After an initial enthusiasm for repatriation in the colony, resistance developed to the idea, as word of unfulfilled promises and disappointments filtered back to Detroit. Families which did not desire repatriation were pressured anyway, being advised that relief might be cut off or reduced.[12]

Arizona Migrations

While repatriation from the Great Lakes proceeded down through Texas, joining with the larger numbers departing from that state, the stream of migration traveled along other courses as well. Arizona's sizable Mexican population — over 114,000 in 1930[13] — had found employment chiefly in agriculture, the mining industry, and the railroads. Many had found work in the Salt River Valley's cotton fields. This important farming region had faced a similar repatriation problem in a depression period in the early 1920s. At that time the growers had left the Mexicans stranded.

During the 1930s the Maricopa County Board of Public Welfare, with its central offices in Phoenix, found its resources swamped by people seeking aid, including Mexican nationals who had lived and worked in the Salt River Valley cotton fields for a number of years. Exaggerated stories of huge numbers of Mexicans surreptitiously crossing the border to seek welfare aid were circulated by a few vocal groups who sought the capture and deportation of such aliens. Investigations made by border patrol officers as to whether deportable aliens were on the Phoenix welfare rolls were met with little cooperation, however, by the Maricopa County Board of Public Welfare. The welfare workers, reported an inspector, felt "that it might result in criticism on the ground that many deserving aliens would be afraid to ask for help."

Eventually an accommodation between local and federal officials was reached; welfare application forms were improved, with more data asked of the applicant, and border patrol officers were permitted to consult these forms to determine an alien's status. Despite the uproar about deportable aliens crowding relief rolls, border patrol investigators found little to substantiate such claims. "It has been found from experience," reported one inspector, "an alien who is unlawfully in the United States does not apply for relief unless he finds it absolutely necessary, through fear that he will be found and deported."

Although little in the way of organized repatriation developed in Arizona, the movement of Mexicans through that state made repatriation through its border stations significant.* Taylor found that 18,520 repatriates left the state of Arizona between 1930 and 1932.[14] Arizona also witnessed the passage of Mexican nationals in Baja California unable to get to Mexico's interior except by rail passage through United States territory. After a large amount of paper work had been performed, a series of such movements, supervised by the Bureau of Immigration, was undertaken in 1931 and 1932.

Federal Deportation

Besides Mexicans repatriating themselves, either voluntarily or under pressure to do so by local welfare officials, the federal government added to the number of Mexicans moving south. Fairly large numbers of Mexicans were deported under warrant proceedings, often for technical violations. "Without proper visa" was a common cause for deportation, though immigration officials informed the apprehended Mexican that if he left voluntarily, his chances of returning to the United States under legal status were much better than if he underwent formal deportation.[15] The low entry figures from Mexico in the 1930s, however, suggest that this point was more rhetoric than fact.

In several annual reports, the Department of Labor had admitted the inadequacies and ambiguities in the enforcement of immigration laws. Because it encouraged the practice of detaining suspects without warrants, the procedure of issuing arrest warrants by telegraph from the Labor Department in Washington had long been criticized. Joining the list of critics in 1931, the Wickersham Commission recommended the decentralization of arrest warrant issuance. But it was not until after the inauguration of Frances Perkins

---

*One of the few Arizona attempts at an organized repatriation program occurred in Douglas, a smelter town of approximately ten thousand people, adjacent to Agua Prieta, Sonora. In 1931, about one hundred and eighty Mexican families were on relief in Douglas. Hearing of the Los Angeles repatriation program, the Douglas Chamber of Commerce proposed a similar program, in an effort to lighten the burden placed on the local Red Cross chapter, which was assisting unemployed people in the town. After some discussion of the difficulties Mexicans classified as laborers were having in attempting to return to the United States, civic officials changed their minds about repatriating their Mexican families. See *Douglas Daily Dispatch,* 13 May and 21 June 1931.

as secretary of labor in 1933 that the use of telegraph warrants from Washington was discontinued.

Although handicapped by regulations which failed to conform to realities, the Bureau of Immigration stated that "the remedy lies not in a return to illegal or extra-legal methods of enforcement but in the amendment of the law." More considerate treatment was extended to aliens guilty of technical violations, and the practice of voluntary departure was rephrased to emphasize its positive rather than negative aspects.[16]

Another important procedural change within the Bureau of Immigration came with the cessation of the practice wherein a single inspector acted as investigator, judge, and jury for the same case. "Instructions have now been issued directing that the preliminary and final hearings shall not be conducted by the same man," stated the bureau in the 1934 annual report. "It has also been impressed on inspectors that their function is judicial and that they should be careful to prepare a full and fair record." In addition, district directors were urged to give their own views on each case and to note any extenuating circumstances that might be involved.[17]

In the interest of increasing bureaucratic efficiency and reducing costs, President Roosevelt issued an executive order on 10 June 1933, merging the separate bureaus of immigration and naturalization into the Immigration and Naturalization Service.[18] The quality of the personnel in the bureau was also improved, and in the spring of 1934 the bureau's officials received printed lectures on immigration and naturalization procedures, the first of these emphasizing the necessity for courtesy in dealing with the public.[19]

Mexican repatriates were only slightly affected by these improvements in federal bureaucratic procedure. For one thing, the peak of repatriation had already passed by the time the measures mentioned above were put into effect. Apart from this, it has been shown that the actual movement of thousands of Mexican nationals was not due solely to federal motivations, but was the result of a web of factors spun by acute unemployment, the threat of deportation, the urging of welfare officials, and acceptance of the repatriation idea, with its lure of colonization projects and free transportation.

Deportation and Repatriation Statistics

Figures for repatriation have varied with the authors who have listed them.[20] One of the most frequently cited writers has been Carey McWilliams, who summarized repatriation in *North from Mexico,* by stating that "in the depression years, some 65,000 Mexican immigrants were repatriated, some voluntarily, some with the aid of the Mexican government, some being summarily shipped back to Mexico by welfare agencies in this country." McWilliams gave no source for this number. Interestingly enough, in *Factories in the Field,* he gives a figure of 160,000 for the period 1928–1933, again without citing a source. Subsequent writers who have accepted the 65,000 figure have not searched very deeply for a more accurate figure.[21]

Shortcomings in the available published statistics have thus led to inaccuracies in the reporting of numbers of people repatriated. The U.S. Department of Labor figures for Mexicans, both repatriated and deported, are at considerable variance from those compiled by the Mexican Migration Service of all Mexicans returning to Mexico. The Labor Department files do not include the many numbers who were repatriated by local groups or who returned of their own volition.

The department reported that between July 1931 and June 1932, deported Mexicans numbered 7,116, while in the same period 6,350 people were sent back to Europe and 2,338 Canadians were deported. The "vast majority" of the 10,775 additional aliens who were listed in the department files and who chose voluntary departure over deportation returned to Canada or Mexico; consistency of Canadian-Mexican figures suggests that Mexicans exceeded Canadians in this category by four to one.[22] However, for this same period, the Mexican Migration Service reported that a total of 132,469 Mexicans had returned to Mexico.[23] Quite obviously many aliens repatriated never came within the Labor Department's sphere of operations.

For the fiscal year, July 1932 to June 1933, the Labor Department reported that 7,750 Mexicans were deported, while it effected the voluntary departure of 10,347 Mexicans.[24] For the same period, the Mexican Migration Service tallied 53,767 Mexicans returning.

For the following year, July 1933 to June 1934, the department counted 3,883 deportees to Mexico, with an additional 5,027 people choosing voluntary departure.[25] Again the Mexican figure for total arrivals exceeded the Labor Department count; Mexican officials reported a total of 24,228 returnees for the same period.

Summarizing the period of the fiscal years, July 1929 to June

1935, as a whole, the federal government removed from the United States, either under warrant proceedings or as voluntary departures, a total number of Mexicans in the neighborhood of 82,400.[26]

Even without considering the Mexican Migration Service's high totals, the mass removal of Mexicans by the Labor Department far outnumbered the deportation or departure of any other ethnic group from United States territory in recent American history. By the Labor Department's own admission, most of the departures had as a basis for cause not criminal or immoral offenses, but the simple fact of illegal entry, which until 1929 had not even been a punishable crime.

As for overall totals for repatriates, more accurate calculations can be made and documented by totaling the numbers supplied by the Mexican Migration Service and accepted by the American consul general in Mexico, D.F., as being the most reliable source. Analyzing the figures on a month-by-month basis reveals that between September 1930 and August 1932 the number of Mexican repatriates never descended below six thousand departures a month.

Repatriation had reached its peak between August and December 1931, when departures of Mexican nationals reached a high of over 20,000 in November alone. After August 1932 the 6,000 a month figure was never again reached, and after the start of 1933 the number of Mexicans leaving the United States descended bumpily to an average of between 2,000 and 3,000 a month for that entire year. From a peak of over 130,000 Mexicans repatriated in 1931, almost double the amount of 1930, the number dropped to less than 80,000 in 1932, approximately 33,500 in 1933, 24,000 in 1934, and around 15,400 in 1935. This figure declined even further in 1936 and 1937.

When the figures for deportation cited by the Department of Labor and the statistics submitted to the State Department are combined, a total of about half a million Mexicans leaving the United States between 1929 and 1935 results. If the deportation figure is discounted because of the possibility that deportees were counted as *repatriados* by the Mexican government, the total still remains in excess of 415,000.* Inevitably, of course, all numbers

---

*The Mexican Migration Service kept separate figures for Mexican tourists return-ing to Mexico, which are not included here, nor are its figures for holders of border permits.

must be considered as approximations. Totals for the entire period are reproduced in appendix D.

Los Repatriados

The sharp upswing of repatriation in the latter part of 1931 coincided with the aftermath of the federal deportation campaign so highly publicized in Los Angeles and elsewhere, and the beginnings of the organized repatriation programs in that county and others across the nation. It also signaled the height of the return of Mexicans by automobile, funneling towards the border towns with their families, their material possessions, and their hopes for a better life back in the homeland.

Who were these Mexicans? Were they agricultural laborers returning to Mexico in the cycle of migration postulated by the farm interests and industrial concerns? Were they an unassimilable group of immigrants who found it feasible to return home because of the proximity to Mexico, unlike European immigrants who had an ocean to cross? Or were they victims of the assumptions of those who professed to aid and understand them — welfare workers who mistook effects for causes and allowed stereotyped views to cloud their judgments? Did the Mexicans leave the United States, as some said, because of offers from the Mexican government of colonization projects and farmland? Or did they return because the hope of a better life north of the Rio Grande had proved hollow, full of discrimination and exploitation?

Few of the returning Mexicans kept a record of their travels, although some letters indicate the feelings of those who wrote them. The *repatriados* were an observed group; their movements were commented upon and reported by consular officials, welfare workers, sympathetic observers, and those glad to see them go. One observer, recalling his witnessing a repatriation shipment leaving Los Angeles in 1933, remembered the "holiday spirit that seemed to pervade the deportees" [*sic*]. He added, "Those to whom I spoke expected to return the next spring and were glad of the opportunity to visit relatives in Mexico."[27]

One of the more prolific writers, Reverend Robert N. McLean, fell into the category of a qualified sympathetic observer. In several articles published during the height of the repatriation period, McLean analyzed the movement and described the motivations of the repatriates in their decisions to return to Mexico. Much of the value of his comments came from his eyewitness descriptions of the repatriates traveling by automobile, such as this one appearing in the 1 May 1931 issue of *Survey:*

> ... I crossed the bridge from El Paso, Texas, into Juárez. On both sides of the street in front of the immigration office were parked the cars of homesick Mexicans ... most of them battered Fords, and every car carried a California license. Loaded in the cars, upon the running boards, on racks behind, on bumpers in front, and even on the tops, was a motley and ill-arranged display of every conceivable thing which a family might collect as part of a house-keeping equipment. There were beds, bedsprings, mattresses, washtubs, cooking utensils, washboards, trunks, cots, tents, tent-poles, bedding; and a-top one of the loads was a crate of live chickens.

McLean asked a Mexican stenographer at the customs house about animals brought back by the repatriates, and quoted her as replying, " 'Yes, they bring their animals!' she exclaimed, throwing up her hands in a gesture of despair. 'They bring their dogs and their cats and their chickens, and yesterday a man brought a live goat. I ask them why they bring their chickens, and they say it is so they will have something to eat by the road!' "

McLean observed that repatriates without automobiles underwent much hardship at Juárez as they waited for the Mexican government to provide railroad transportation to the interior. January 1931 was a particularly rough time, as Mexicans shivered while living outdoors, although when it rained they were allowed access to the large examination rooms in the customs house. Juárez citizens contributed to their needs with donations of food, but people were still hungry. "Women swarmed about the warehouses," observed McLean in the same *Survey* issue, "picking up one by one the beans which spilled through holes in the sacks." At the end of the month two trains provided by the government relieved the pressure by shipping twenty-seven hundred repatriates southward, and afterward several special cars were attached to southbound trains to transport the repatriates.

The reports of American consular officials usually corroborated the description of the repatriates given by McLean. "From information received here it is indicated that about twenty-five per cent of those returning," commented the American consul at Piedras Negras, "bring back with them farm implements, automobiles, trucks, farm animals, household furnishings, and a certain amount of money." The consul at Nuevo Laredo noted, "In crossing the international bridge each day one can always see a line of cars with licenses from nearly half the United States filled with household effects of Mexicans returning and waiting to make the necessary arrangements with the Mexican authorities."

"These repatriates bear tales of the extreme difficulties they have had in earning a living under present conditions in the United States," reported Saltillo's American consul. "They have been passing through Saltillo for points south in a great variety of trucks and cars and also in railway cars." The comment from Nogales was that "those coming by train have their passage paid by the States or Counties where they have been living." The chief reason given for returning was "lack of work," though "many of them who are of migratory tendencies take advantage of the offer of a free trip to Mexico."

Other observations were in the same vein. "The number composes only those of the working classes, who return to Mexico with furniture, animals, and personal effects, and not those returning to visit." The Mexican repatriates "resemble gypsies as they usually return by either wagon or broken down motor car in which children, household furniture, and domestic animals are loaded," was the description given by the consul at Matamoros. "Their return was due entirely to economic conditions in the United States and their belief that they would find a means of livelihood in their own country," observed another consul, who also noted the lack of attention paid the repatriates "either by the authorities or by charitably inclined persons or organizations" in Monterrey.

There were, inevitably, a few discrepancies. "Although many repatriates are particularly destitute, there is little evidence of hunger or want," stated the vice consul at Ciudad Juárez. Another vice consul, in a report on migratory movements in Mexico, predicted that "the arrival of many experienced farmers and other repatriates from the United States, should have a beneficial effect," evidently not considering that Mexico was also contending with economic problems, and that destitute *repatriados* might create labor surpluses and demands on existing resources.

The variety of situations and circumstances within which Mexican repatriation occurred makes such generalizations difficult to accept without serious qualifications. For example, McLean's analyses of various "types" of Mexicans who were returning to Mexico were much less exact than his personal descriptions of them. In trying to create categories of returnees, he established a number of artificial groupings. His article in the 1 May 1931 issue of *Survey* listed four groups. They included the deported Mexicans, "by far the smallest group," and the voluntary departures — those deportable aliens given a chance to leave, the alternative being formal deportation. A third group, "made up of those who are either here legally, or whose status has never come under the scrutiny of the immigration service," was obviously vague. The fourth group were the indigent Mexicans being returned by organized repatriation programs, such as those arranged by consuls or local charities departments.

A few months later, in an article in the September issue of *Mexican Life,* McLean forgot to mention the indigent group. The following year, in an article written for the 24 August 1932 issue of *Nation,* McLean listed "five classes" — deportees, voluntary departures, aliens fearful of an uncertain status, indigents, "and the fifth class is made up of those who have long been out of work, and having sacrificed their homes for a fraction of what they are worth, are using the proceeds to go back to Mexico in the hope that things may be a little better and in the conviction that they cannot be any worse."

Throughout the period, in different localities, Mexicans made their decisions as best fit their circumstances. Some decided to remain as a result of the pleas of their children, to whom Mexico was the foreign land. Others decided to return because of their fears about this very reason, worried that their children would forsake the old for the new. Last to be hired and first to be fired, with only the most menial jobs available, many Mexicans felt they could subsist better on Mexico's lower standard of living, and left; others, who were not willing to return to that standard, stayed.

In a political context, the subsiding of the antireligious campaign originated by President Plutarco Calles encouraged some to return. From the autumn of 1930 until the spring of 1932 Mexican repatriation was at its height, and within this period enthusiasm for a return to the homeland was clearly shown. Thus the picture of Mexicans repatriating themselves by driving an automobile loaded down with their worldly possessions seems accurate.[28]

After the summer of 1932, however, an increasing resistance to the idea of returning to Mexico could be detected. Welfare agencies then became more strident in their appeals to indigent aliens that

Archivo de la Secretaría de Relaciones Exteriores, México, D. F.
Automobile caravan of repatriate families assembling at Karnes City, Texas, 1931

repatriation be undertaken. But the opportunity to return to the United States after a visit to Mexico had disappeared with the rigid enforcement of immigration laws that in better times had been loosely observed. Mexicans whose economic status had fared better than others were not therefore tempted to make the move. Once the New Deal programs were inaugurated, reluctance among poor Mexican nationals to return to Mexico became more pronounced.

In the mid-thirties indigent Mexicans were coerced into leaving by threats of being cut off from relief payments, and for them acceptance of a railroad ticket thus became the lesser of two evils. Eventually local relief agencies, bolstered with federal aid that was proffered with conditions protecting aliens, dropped the practice of shipping out repatriates in carload lots after 1935. During these years Mexican repatriates far exceeded the number of Mexicans allowed to enter the United States, even though the number of repatriates dropped each year after 1931.

Still another factor affecting repatriation was the word that came up from the south concerning promises that had not been fulfilled by the Mexican government.[29] Mexico's appeal to her sons in the country to the north had been more than answered; but the overwhelming numbers of repatriates posed a dilemma to Mexico's government and people.

8.

The Dilemma in Mexico

THE RETURN OF THOUSANDS of their compatriots created serious problems for the citizens of Mexico. The influx of so many people in so short a period increased an already large labor surplus and placed added demands on relatives and friends. Mexican welfare organizations, especially in areas close to the border, found their resources stretched to the limit in caring for Mexicans who arrived without food, clothing, or money. The Mexican government, challenged by the need for providing transportation and possible employment for the repatriates, quickly involved itself in the establishment of repatriation committees and colonization projects.

As the economic depression in the United States worsened, it became increasingly obvious that the numbers of Mexicans returning home were far greater than those of the repatriations of the early 1920s. Mexican newspapers followed this trend and published frequent editorials detailing either the Mexicans' plight in the United States or the movement of repatriates southward. Harsh treatment of Mexican nationals was publicized and sometimes exaggerated, while decisions to return to the homeland were warmly applauded.

Inimical Editorials

The poor treatment of Mexicans in the United States received close scrutiny in Mexico's newspapers. This editorial policy served the interests of the newspaper editors and also the Mexican government, which sought to limit emigration of its citizens as much as the United States desired to restrict their entry. Editors quickly com-

[133]

municated word of exploitation or unfair treatment to the Mexican public. Such publicity was characteristic of the Mexican press during the depression years. It came in the form of pronouncements from Mexican government officials and labor organizations, or from the newspaper editors themselves.

Few of the editorials were friendly to the United States. "For some time past our compatriots residing in foreign countries have frequently complained to the Mexican government of the injustices of which they are the victims in the countries in which they reside," began an editorial in the capital city's *El Universal* on 22 January 1931. "More of these complaints come from the United States than from any other country." Of course, more Mexicans had emigrated to the United States than to anywhere else, but this is an unimportant detail. The article went on to make the point that consular offices in the United States required additional funds and support from the home government in order to provide adequate legal protection for the Mexicans who were "so exploited and reviled especially in the United States."

Some editorials bitterly attacked American imperialism. The first issue of the Cananea *Idea Leberal* [*sic*], which appeared on 2 November 1931, inveighed against the "persecutions, despoliations, humiliations, tasks of slaves, miserable pay, brutal and unjust treatment at the hands of unjust and domineering authorities, mass arrests and deportations with cruel and innumerable penalties" which occurred in the United States. In its 2 June 1932 edition, *Excelsior* of Mexico, D.F., vented its rage over United States treatment of Mexican nationals after reflecting upon the incredible number of Mexicans who had returned since the start of the depression:

The repatriates are fleeing from the poverty, from the "crisis" which is cruelly beating down on the great Republic of the North, emporium of wealth, the owner of more than half the gold that exists in the world, the forge of industries which reduces to insignificance the mythological one of Vulcan, the producer of cereals, and fruits of every description in quantities sufficient to supply the armies of Osiris, fertile land of ham and preserves, the country creating the "Standard" types from razors to love-making and from skyscrapers to attacks of appendicitis . . . that formidable nation with its eight million unemployed . . . practically throws out foreigners in the egoistic defense of its nationals. . . .

We agree that the United States should show preference to their own nationals over the foreigners; but we do not agree that among those foreigners, the Mexicans should be the most persecuted. . . .

Our readers will therefore see that anti-Mexican sentiment in the United States has diminished not at all, and that we are continuing almost as in those times when their Armies invaded us to the cry of "Remember the Alamo."

Mexican coverage of the difficulties of their compatriots in the United States could on occasion be inconsistent, even baffling. The papers tended to print the news as received, without inquiring as to proof of assertions. For example, the Saltillo *Diario del Norte* began receiving United Press dispatches in July 1931, which commenced with several objectively written articles on the problems of Mexican nationals living in the United States. Several months later, however, on 4 November 1931, the Saltillo newspaper reported that the United States Bureau of Immigration had ceased its policy of deportation in favor of committing illegal Mexican aliens to forced labor.

Newspapers devoted more editorial space to specific problems than to general condemnations of how Mexicans were being treated in the United States. If it was suspected that Mexican aliens were being singled out for discrimination, such issues as preferential employment for American citizens over aliens were noted. Widespread unemployment was conceded to be a fact of life, and the Mexican press pinpointed its existence in specific localities, warning Mexicans not to consider emigrating to those places.[1] On the other hand, such developments as the federal deportation campaign or reports of mistreatment might mix fact and rumor, with the Mexican press printing either or both as information was received.

The interest of the Mexican press in the welfare of Mexicans in the United States was matched by its coverage of the movements of repatriates. Both *El Universal* and *Excelsior* published numerous articles and dispatches describing the repatriation of Mexican nationals who had been unable to secure employment or had crossed the path of the Bureau of Immigration. Editorials favored governmental action to assist repatriates by providing transportation and assistance in finding accommodations and employment, while articles reported the government's moves in providing such aid.[2]

Government Assistance

Throughout the 1930s the Mexican government continued its policy of welcoming returning Mexicans to the homeland. The transformation of this policy from rhetoric to implementation was successful in some respects while a failure in others. Hindsight would indicate that most repatriates had returned not with the intention of participating in colonization projects or land purchases, but because Mexico seemed preferable to the United States in a period of depression. However, the Mexican government did take some positive measures in providing for the *repatriados*.

One key policy adopted by the Mexican government was to allow repatriates to bring back material possessions duty free. This included machinery, animals, and household appliances. In addition, fees usually charged by local consuls for such services as processing of legal papers were eliminated.[3] It is therefore understandable why so many cars were loaded with such a range of possessions in the movement of the repatriates southward.

A second active form of assistance was the free transportation provided by the government from the border to the country's interior. As congestion in the border towns increased, the government increased the number of trains and passenger cars to relieve the pressure on citizens of towns like Ciudad Juárez and Nogales who were attempting to provide relief for their indigent brethren. This assistance was particularly needed during 1931, the peak year of repatriation. At the end of that year the American consul at Ciudad Juárez reported that while over thirty-five thousand repatriates had come through the town in the preceding twelve months, only five hundred repatriates were now in the vicinity. The rest had been moved to the interior, either by motor car or rail transportation.

While these actions of the Mexican government did much to alleviate the circumstances surrounding the return of the repatriates, other policies did not work out so well. Offers of employment to *repatriados* had been seized upon by American newspapers and trumpeted as rationales for the repatriation of Mexican immigrants.[4] Even though such proposed programs as distribution of government lands, colonization projects, and highway construction sounded appealing, implementing them proved quite another matter. *El Universal,* while commending the government's work in providing adequate transportation for repatriates, cautioned on 12 February 1931 that "this is neither the most important nor the most difficult part of the repatriation problem." Two other problems, generated by the arrival of the repatriates, would have to be solved: "First, that of accommodating them during the present unemployment situation; and second, that of preventing their presence from harming those workmen who had remained in the country."

Problem Solving

To that end, the Mexican government made several efforts to solve the larger problems. The Mexican Migration Service of the

Ministry of the Interior, which had worked closely in many matters with the United States Bureau of Immigration, held several annual conferences, beginning in 1930, to discuss migration problems and propose resolutions to the government.

The 1931 meeting called attention to the paramount importance of the repatriation problem, but its chief recommendations centered on providing transportation. At the meeting the following year, the conference proposed the establishment of a colonization commission to create communal agricultural colonies for repatriates, greater coordination of programs for repatriates (to be under the supervision of the Migration Service), and a tax on private property to raise funds for the proposed colonies.

National Repatriation Committee

Of the recommendations suggested, the idea of a colonization commission to provide for the needs of repatriates captured the imagination of one official in particular. Andrés Landa y Piña, chief of the Migration Service, believed that a repatriation committee could be organized to handle the repatriates and the problems they brought with them. Landa y Piña conceived of a committee that was not, strictly speaking, a part of the government, but one that would consist of representatives of governmental departments, business groups, and charitable organizations. On 23 November 1932, Landa y Piña presided over a meeting at which just such a committee was launched. The National Repatriation Committee, as it was called, included as its members Landa y Piña, Alfredo Levy of the National Chamber of Commerce, and representatives of the Red Cross, the Department of Public Health, and the Ministry of the Interior — a curious amalgam of private and public agencies. The committee's ultimate responsibility seems to have been a tenuous one. Also active in the creation of the committee was José González Soto, a citizen of Spain who held extensive investments in Mexico. González Soto pledged one thousand pesos towards a subscription campaign to raise funds for the committee. The goal of this campaign was set at five hundred thousand pesos, which in 1932 equaled U.S. $150,000.

The National Repatriation Committee at the outset achieved instant popularity, as contributions to its campaign for funds soon indicated. After six weeks an estimated eighty-six thousand pesos had been collected, including a contribution of five thousand pesos from President Abelardo Rodríguez, and over seventeen thousand pesos from government employees and elected officials. A special bullfight program yielded an additional twenty-five thousand pesos to the fund, while Mexican radio stations XEW and XEB contributed time for solicitations. "The campaign is being kept before the public by almost daily articles," observed a vice consul at the American consulate, "coming from all parts of the country, published in the Mexico City press, and Mexico seems determined to do something in the near future for its repatriates from the United States."

Setting Goals

For all the fanfare surrounding the committee's campaign, the National Repatriation Committee still had the difficult task of deciding what its goals were. Although such ideas as establishing lunchrooms and dormitories for repatriates and the unemployed of Mexico were seriously discussed, the committee soon decided that the funds raised were to go to the development of agricultural colonies to be peopled by repatriated Mexican families. This decision was not greeted with unanimous enthusiasm.

A group of repatriates in the Federal District, noting the absence of repatriates on the National Repatriation Committee, inquired as to how the committee proposed to aid the repatriates, and when this assistance would be inaugurated. The committee informed them that no money would be directly distributed to repatriates, but instead would be channeled to the proposed colonies with the double goal of providing work for repatriates and expanding Mexican agriculture. Disappointed in their expectations, the delegation formed a "Union of Mexican Repatriates," which began urging that the policy of welcoming more returnees to Mexico be suspended until the problems of those already in the country had been solved. They also protested that the collection of the five hundred thousand pesos was proceeding too slowly.

The committee responded to the opposition of the repatriate group by issuing a statement to the press a few days after the meeting. "With reference to the idea which some persons have that repatriation must be suspended," the committee stated, "the phenomenon of repatriation has not been provoked by the will of the nation nor can it be suspended seeing that, whether we wish it or not, the current of migration will continue to sweep aside all methods of limitation which are decreed against it." The colonization projects became the chief preoccupation of the National Repatriation Committee, which began formulating plans for the creation of several colonies in the west coast region of Mexico.

Colonization Projects

Although in retrospect the idea of colonizing lands in a tropical zone seems rather hazardous, at that time the possibility of developing the fertile lands there seemed quite feasible. An inspection and surveying party left for Guerrero in the second week of February, consisting of committee members and several engineers from the Ministries of Public Health and Agriculture and Development. In the meantime, the committee granted credentials to five hundred repatriates for permission to work in the state of San Luis Potosí, and arranged for rail transportation there for the repatriates. The working wage was to be one peso a day.

The National Repatriation Committee's intentions of establishing colonies composed entirely of *repatriados* were multiple in purpose. First, as Manuel Gamio had expressed it, skills acquired in the United States were lost to the Mexican economy if the repatriates, upon their return, scattered to all parts of Mexico.[5] Second, by being sent to colonies deep in the country's interior, the repatriates would find it difficult to return to the United States, after having enjoyed free transportation and relief assistance from the Mexican government. This had happened in cases where repatriates who had been located on land near the United States–Mexican border shortly afterward had attempted to return to the United States. A third reason was that the isolation of the colonies would effectively remove the *repatriados* from competition with other Mexicans for jobs — assuming significant numbers of repatriates could be sent to the colonization projects.

By mid-April 1933 the colonization plans became a reality. Two colonies were organized, while a third was being actively planned, with others being planned for the future. The first of the colonies, designated Colony Number 1, was established at El Coloso, Guerrero. Located not far from Acapulco, the colony had quite modest beginnings. A group of about twenty *repatriados* from Detroit, Michigan, had arrived at the site as early as December 1932, but the development of this colony was mostly experimental in nature. Committee member Alfredo Levy described El Coloso as "just an experiment."

Of far greater importance was the colony established at Pinotepa Nacional, near Minizo, Oaxaca. This site, designated Colony Number 2, was selected with high expectations for its success. The Pinotepa location possessed fertile lands, a generous water supply, and a sparse population. On 19 April 1933, four hundred repatriates left Mexico, D.F., by train for Oaxaca. Two weeks later, several hundred additional *repatriados* and their families left the United States and were taken to the new colony.

Many assurances were given promising success for the colony. Anastasio García Toledo, the governor of Oaxaca, offered land with clear title. The soil was reputed to be capable of growing two crops of corn a year. The governor also indicated that the residents of Oaxaca were willing to donate or loan without charge (the exact intention is unclear) livestock and draft animals to aid the repatriates while the first crops were being grown. Parcels of land had been marked out by the committee, and houses constructed of palm trees had been built. The committee's funds, which by 18 March had been increased to 154,062 pesos, were largely earmarked for the Pinotepa colony. Lands which had to be purchased were bought by the committee and sold to *repatriados* on "easy, long time terms," according to Levy, with the colonists paying back the loans in crops. Assistance to repatriates also included tools, farm machinery, food, and sundries.

Although expectations for the success of the Pinotepa colony were considerable, the realities of colonization proved to be somewhat different from the fanfare. Upon arriving at the intended location of the colony, the *repatriados* found that the people charged with the administration of the colony had no intention of including the repatriates in policy-making decisions. While the colonists began agricultural work with enthusiasm, this turned into disillusionment when they learned that the corn they had raised was to be fed to farm animals. Supplies that had been ordered failed to arrive at the port of Acapulco. The administrators doled out food rations sparingly and practiced harsh discipline on colonists who protested. Armed men accompanied the directors as they made their rounds of the colony. Much of the abuse seemed to have arisen after the resignation of Landa y Piña in November; but *repatriados* had begun to leave almost as soon as they had arrived. Particular details as to the mismanagement and controversy during the months of the colony's existence are blurred, but the failure is clear: from a peak of between five and seven hundred repatriates in April–May 1933, by the following February only eight colonists remained, governed by fifteen administrators. The El Coloso colony, which never numbered over two dozen *repatriados,* met a similar fate.

Departing the Colonies

Many of the *repatriados* who left the Pinotepa colony departed in a body, making the journey between the Pinotepa Nacional area and Acapulco in twenty-three days, on foot, with great hardship. The erstwhile colonists then lived on the charity of the Acapulco residents, matters coming to a head when the municipal authorities requested their departure. By coincidence, Lázaro Cárdenas, running energetically as the presidential candidate, arrived in Acapulco as the repatriates were being ordered out of the city. Out of his own pocket, he paid the transportation expenses of the unfortunates back to Mexico, D.F.

The factor of health also had made the colonization project a costly one. People sickened and died in the tropical climate; sixty colonists had perished in a twenty-day period. The *jejens,* little black flies, swarmed everywhere and bit everyone; their allies, the *nihuas* — jigger fleas — dug in under the colonists' fingernails. It was impossible to go out at night. One *repatriado* reported, "You have to wear a netting over your head. There are lots of other insects, too. Very bad; they don't let you sleep at night. One kind called *pinolillo* is small like a microbe and makes you itch all over."

During the period of the colony's existence James C. Gilbert, a graduate student at the University of Southern California, was traveling throughout Mexico gathering material for his Master's thesis on repatriate readjustment in Mexico. Gilbert planned a trip to Pinotepa Nacional, but was dissuaded from making it by acquaintances familiar with the area, who warned him of the unhealthiness of the region and the risk outsiders took in living there. A repatriate who had endured the rigors of Pinotepa Nacional told Gilbert, "The people who live there are mostly Negroes and Indians. They say that outsiders never grow old there. Once one of them lived three years. That was a long time. He died too, finally." Gilbert learned that the colony was situated in an area where once Porfirio Díaz had sent political prisoners.[6]

The repatriates complained about other points as well. There was, for instance, the matter of the funds raised in the campaign to assist the repatriates in making their start. Although the goal of half a million pesos had not been reached, over 300,000 pesos had been contributed. After considerable delay, the National Repatriation Committee finally published its accounts. Of the 318,221.65 pesos raised, 216,786.32 pesos had been spent. Expenditures included transportation, food, medical aid, clothing, household items, tools, machinery, and an undetermined amount for the cost of setting up the El Coloso and Pinotepa colonies. None of these items was individually itemized. All this came to 202,777.48 pesos. For the committee's general expenses, 14,008.84 pesos more were deducted. This left a balance of 101,407.09 pesos on deposit in the Bank of Mexico, plus a few pesos on hand.[7]

National Committee Dissolved

After some fifteen months of existence, in which time the committee's support went from national praise to ignominious criticism, the National Repatriation Committee underwent a process of dissolution. In its final months the committee endured the vocal complaints of disillusioned *repatriados* and the hostility of the once-friendly press, which now publicized the committee's mismanagement and failures. The question of the 101,000 unspent pesos remained unsettled until March 1935, when President Cárdenas decreed that the money should go to colonization efforts in Baja California. In the meantime, efforts by repatriates to secure a distribution of the funds met with failure, and were in fact ridiculed by committee member José González Soto. He noted that if every claimant were to receive an equal share, then each person would receive no more than twenty-seven centavos.

The National Repatriation Committee met its official end on 14 June 1934. President Rodríguez's decree provided that the Ministry of Agriculture and Development would assume responsibility for all funds, implements, and other resources originally held by the committee. The Office of Rural Population, National Lands, and Colonization within the Ministry was specifically named as the agency to administer the funds received, and to render aid to the unfortunates who had been involved in the colonization ventures. A final point was that the dissolution of the committee did not dissolve any responsibilities incurred by committee members during the National Repatriation Committee's existence.

Thus ended a curious experiment in which officials of Mexican governmental agencies worked along with representatives of private charitable and business organizations, with everyone serving a committee that had been established with no concrete plan other than a semi-altruistic intention. Only a small fraction of the repatriates in Mexico was affected by or had participated in the colonization projects. The experiment having proved a failure, the Mexican government finally stepped in to make a greater commitment to the care of Mexicans who had returned and needed assistance in reestablishing themselves. It is in this context that the arrival in Mexico, D.F., in May 1934 of Rex Thomson of the Los Angeles County Department of Charities must be seen.

New Board Established

Thomson arrived during the interval between the formal dissolution of the National Repatriation Committee and the creation of the National Repatriation Board, which was established by presidential decree on 26 July 1934. The statements made by Thomson during his visit, concerning large numbers of potential repatriates in Los Angeles County and elsewhere in the United States, received wide coverage in the Mexico City press. There are strong indications that his claim that there were as many as fifty thousand Mexicans in California who desired repatriation influenced officials of the Rodríguez administration in deciding to set up the new board. Thomson's conferences with officials such as Secretary Francisco Elías spurred the movement towards the Mexican government's official assumption of responsibility for the repatriates.[8]

The scope of the National Repatriation Board was somewhat wider than the repatriation of Mexicans from Southern California alone, although mention of the twelve thousand Mexican families in Los Angeles allegedly awaiting repatriation was often made. The board consisted of representatives from six ministries, presided over by Secretary Elías of the Ministry of Agriculture and Development. Other ministries included Foreign Relations, National Economy, Interior, Public Health, and Labor. The National Bank of Agricultural Credit also had a representative on the board. The purpose of the board was to coordinate movement, assistance, and settlement of the anticipated resurgence of repatriation, which had been declining ever since the November 1931 peak. In addition to the work of the board, the Ministry of Agriculture and Development now undertook the responsibility of relocating the few remaining repatriate-colonists from Pinotepa Nacional and El Coloso. These people were transported to San Luis Potosí, where they were given provisions, tools, and better opportunities with which to use them. Other *repatriados* who had encountered difficulties were similarly moved. With much less fanfare than the National Repatriation Committee, the Ministry of Agriculture and Development included the repatriates from the United States in its agricultural programs and irrigation projects. No more than two or three model colonies, planned for repatriates, were to be organized. If they proved successful, others would also be established.

Realization of the plans of the National Repatriation Board never materialized. The 101,000 pesos were applied to the acquisition of land in Baja California, but few repatriates went there as colonists.[9] Thomson's plans for a renewed repatriation effort by Los Angeles County were frustrated by the resistance of the Spanish-speaking community there, which had largely abandoned repatriation as an alternative to enduring the hardships of life in an economic depression. The National Repatriation Board thus planned for a movement of people that failed to occur. In sum, the Mexican government, at first in a semiofficial capacity and then with an inter-departmental agency, attempted too little, too late in direct assistance to repatriates. The little that was done was concentrated on several projects that for various reasons proved impractical. Only about 5 percent of the Mexican repatriates became involved in colonization programs.[10]

Irrigation Projects

Far more successful, as far as both the government and people of Mexico were concerned, were those programs which were designed for the people of Mexico rather than repatriates specifically. The most publicized of these were the irrigation projects, particularly the Don Martín Dam in the states of Coahuila and Nuevo León. Following the completion of the dam in 1930, canals extending the irrigable acreage were constructed. By 1935, 60,000 *hectáreas* (148,200 acres) were under cultivation, with corn, cotton, wheat, and other crops being grown. The lands watered by the project extended into the state of Nuevo León, some fifty miles west of Laredo, Texas. The Mexican National Irrigation Commission, organized in 1926, advertised the lands for sale, and hundreds of Mexicans had accepted the offer. James C. Gilbert visited the area in November 1933 and found the project operating very successfully. He estimated that 40 percent of the colonists there had repatriated themselves since the beginning of the depression, while an undetermined number had returned to Mexico before the depression began. Approximately fifteen hundred colonists were working the land here in 1933.[11]

Repatriates who settled on irrigated lands could purchase ten, fifteen, or more *hectáreas* of land by choosing one of several methods of payment. One plan required a yearly payment of 5 percent of the land's value, while a second plan enabled the colonist to pay 10 percent after three years, with twenty-five annual installments to follow, at 4 percent interest. Delivery of 25 percent of the crop was considered equivalent to the 10 percent payment. Lands could also be rented on a share-cropper basis, but land purchase was favored by most colonists. Unlike the repatriation colonies in Oaxaca and Guerrero, tools and food were not furnished by either the government or the committee, and seed was available only on a loan basis. The colonists paid for the water and the maintenance of the irrigation system. Gilbert divided the *repatriados* he observed in the Don Martín district into two general groupings — those who had purchased land and those who were employed by others. Most in the latter group lacked the means to make an investment as a farmer.

The Don Martín Project owed its success to several key factors. The irrigation system was crossed by a railroad and a highway, and the area's proximity to the United States border facilitated commerce. Geography and climate were similar to that in Texas; Gilbert noted that "nearly all" of the repatriates had come from there, and that they found their new situation was similar to the old in many respects. Even the sharecropping system resembled the tenant farming in Texas, except that here it was the government who received payment.[12]

Although the opportunity existed for the purchase of land at the Don Martín Project or the ten other irrigation projects in Mexico at that time, many *repatriados* were unable to take advantage of the offer. The absence of quantitative data makes generalizations difficult, but it seems clear that those repatriates who were returned to Mexico during the depths of the depression in a destitute condition had much less of a chance to purchase lands in such projects, even on the easy terms provided by the Mexican government.[13]

A Difficult Adjustment

The vast majority of Mexicans who returned to Mexico during the depression did not take part in government-sponsored programs. Most repatriates simply returned to the area where they had been born and where their relatives and old friends lived. In many cases the children they brought with them looked upon Mexico, not the United States, as the foreign land.

While in most instances the reception given the repatriates was a friendly one, friction between those who had remained in Mexico and those who had left could on occasion be detected. Mexican border towns, as well as other cities in northern Mexico, were willing to assist needy repatriates entering Mexico from the United States; but they were also anxious for the travelers to be on their way. "A local charity society is providing meals for the repatriates," observed one American consul. He added, however, that there was "a very noticeable desire on the part of the municipal authorities in Saltillo to hasten their departure from this city." The same could be said for Monterrey. Since American relief agencies had expressed reluctance to continue aiding Mexican indigents, it is understandable why Mexican charitable organizations also feared a strain on their resources. Both Saltillo and Monterrey possessed "a desire to prompt the repatriates to continue their journey forthwith to other points."[14]

Observations regarding the adjustment of Mexican repatriates, once they arrived at their particular destinations, are handicapped by the paucity of sources. Gamio's studies were made just prior to the depression; other studies are limited by their narrow focus, concentrating on one place, one individual, or one person's observations. Professor Paul S. Taylor authored a monograph on one community in which he analyzed the effect of repatriation there,[15] and several articles describe in a limited way how the repatriates were received.[16]

The most intensive research, covering several regions in Mexico, was conducted by James C. Gilbert as he gathered material for his Master's thesis. Gilbert spent over seven months in Mexico, from July 1933 to February 1934, and in that time he interviewed over one hundred repatriates in some two dozen towns, from Vera Cruz to Nogales.[17] His findings, which he did not suggest were definitive in any way, nevertheless are important to one who would generalize about the repatriates four decades later.

The Mexicans who returned to Mexico either did so with some funds saved and some material possessions obtained, or else came back with nothing to show for their years in the United States. Those who came back empty-handed rejoined family and friends, and their experience in the United States became but an interlude in their lives.[18] On the other hand, repatriates who had achieved a modicum of success returned with the opportunity before them to continue their lives on an improved level. Gilbert reported meeting Mexicans who had brought automobiles back and were using them as taxicabs; others who had driven back in trucks were utilizing the vehicles in hauling produce and freight items. Some Mexicans were able to put skills acquired in the United States to good use. Gilbert saw auto mechanics and carpenters whose skills had been learned north of the border. But he also saw *repatriados* who could find no market for their abilities in villages that lacked gasoline stations for cars or electricity for motors.[19]

While some repatriates who had returned with capital made good use of it, others spent their savings until they were as poor as their neighbors, or made unfortunate investments. Many found the unemployment problem as serious in Mexico as it was in the United States, without the diversions and conveniences that even a poor family in the United States might enjoy. Repatriates who had experienced a taste of urban life were often unhappy over the monotony of life in small towns and villages; city-bred young people disliked it even more. *Repatriados* who had returned to the larger cities of Mexico seemed to Gilbert to be better adjusted to their new life than those in the villages.[20]

The effect of life in the United States could be most easily observed in its material sense. Overalls rather than white cottons, shoes rather than *guaraches,* and the presence of automobiles, trucks, tools, and machinery suggested the influences of the United States that the Mexicans had brought back with them.[21] In this sense repatriation contributed positively to Mexico's economic development during the 1930s, though the extent of this influence was subject to other factors and is difficult to measure. Over half of the 114 repatriation cases interviewed by Gilbert "were not following the same occupations in Mexico as in the United States."[22]

Even considering their lack of homogeneity as a group, the repatriates might have offered a new impetus for the advancement of Mexico's economy and industries had their newly acquired skills and approaches not been lost through the factors of their reversion to the older way of life, unemployment in both countries, and the lack of a successful, coherent plan in Mexico for putting the repatriates to the country's and their own best use. Gilbert noted that generally the repatriates were welcomed back by their compatriots with few recriminations. "With but few exceptions, observations of social situations in which there were both repatriates and non-repatriates showed no social distance between them. . . . They were all members of *la raza*. The few exceptions noted were occasions in which the non-repatriate objected to the use of English or too many expressions of dislike for the local environment and a desire to return to the United States. This latter behavior sometimes, but not always, brought forth the censure of other Mexicans."[23]

Many *repatriados,* disappointed by the lack of employment opportunities in the homeland, were also unhappy over the lower standard of living in Mexico. Luxuries to which they had become accustomed were nonexistent in many villages; the lack of running water, recreational offerings such as motion pictures, and the lack of electricity brought a sense of disillusionment to many repatriates.[24] Enough were motivated by their disappointment to come to the attention of American consular officials. The consul at Piedras Negras reported to the State Department on 16 January 1935:

This office continues to receive applications daily for immigration visas from repatriated Mexican citizens, who give as their reason for wanting to return to the United States, that their children cannot become accustomed to the mode of living in Mexico, after having been born and reared in the United States, that their children cannot find employment or earn wages that will support their families, that after having worked on farms in the United States with all modern facilities and on a profit-sharing basis, they are not willing to work on a wage basis.

Impact on Children

The inclusion of children in the repatriates' arguments for a visa to reenter the United States is indicative of the lever with which Mexican-born adults attempted to pry an opening into the country to the north. While Mexico (along with a number of other countries such as Greece and Italy) provided citizenship for the children of her nationals born in foreign lands, the United States granted citizenship to anyone born on American soil, regardless of the parents' nationalities. Thus Mexican children, apart from a few technicalities, enjoyed the privilege of dual citizenship.[25]

In reality the position of the Mexican-American children was a most unhappy one. A sense of cultural dislocation affected many American-born children who were old enough to remember what their parents had given up by undergoing repatriation. Repatriation separated families, the children in some instances remaining with friends or relatives in the United States while the parents returned to Mexico. Repatriation's impact on Mexican-American children could be capricious at times. Just before the family of eight-year-old Julian Nava was to undergo repatriation, the boy developed appendicitis. While he recovered, his parents changed their minds about returning to Mexico. Julian Nava grew up in Los Angeles, served in the navy in World War II, received a Ph.D. from Harvard, and was elected to the Los Angeles Board of Education.[26] Although it would hardly be valid to assert that repatriated Mexican-American children could have achieved similar success had they remained in the United States, the fact remains that their opportunity to make the effort to do so in American society was denied by the repatriation movement.

Consular officers interpreted the immigration regulations rigidly and were inclined to take the claims of visa applicants with a certain amount of disbelief, as shown by a report to the State Department on 1 June 1934:

Many of these Mexican repatriates have moved from place to place in Mexico, and end by claiming that they cannot accustom themselves to living in Mexico after having lived for a long period in the United States. Especially is this true of those families which include grown children born and reared in the United States. These motives, however, are rarely the true ones, as almost invariably it appears, on examination, that the children have never gone to school in the United States, many of the children of school age being unable to read or write in their native [*sic*] language.

Mexicans who had never regularized their original entry into the United States could not obtain a legal record of their departure, while legal immigrants found a plethora of red tape facing them if they wished to insure their legal return. Misunderstandings between inspector and repatriate could also result in difficulties if the repatriate decided to return to the United States. The impediments of illiteracy, of possibly having been a public charge, or of laborer status blocked the hopes of many repatriates who had changed their minds.[27]

As the consuls could only advise that for Mexican Americans to maintain a continuous residence in Mexico would be to risk loss of American citizenship, the factor of dual citizenship put many Mexican parents into a dilemma as to the future of their children. One *repatriado* expressed his anguish, in Spanish, in a letter to the Los Angeles County Board of Supervisors. He stated that all of his children "were born in the U.S. of A., they do not like the Mexican customs and wish to return to the U.S. in company with their parents. . . ." The letter continued:

> I want to arrange everything legally; I do not wish to violate the frontier Immigration law, and I want my Passport issued with the seal of an American citizen. I worked in the U.S. of A. since 1904 with different companies. I registered in the world war in Johnson, Arizona, Cochise Co. I have never given my services to the Mexican government nor to Mexican capital. I have worked all of my life, since I was 19 years of age in the U.S. of A., and that is why I wish to return to the country where I am entitled to live with my children so that they be educated in the schools of your country and not in Mexico.

The writer listed his children's names and places of birth in the United States; his two eldest children were born in Arizona, while the other four were born in California. The letter was received and filed, with no indication as to action taken.

Other families, however, were more fortunate in their attempts to return to Los Angeles County. A study made in 1939 revealed that a number of repatriated families had succeeded in returning to the United States, some as recently as the year following their repatriation. Although the county was aware that most of these families had reentered the country illegally, federal authorities were not called in, usually because of the family head's previous record of employment, his American-born children, and the degree of acculturation they had achieved. To generalize about such cases proved extremely difficult because of all the factors involved.[28]

One solution of the problem of dual citizenship was the separation of the family, split by the political boundary between the United States and Mexico. Some Mexican Americans who were old enough to be on their own returned to the United States, obtained employment, and were then able to bring their parents and near relatives back under State Department regulations.

Preventing Reentry

Even as the United States consular and immigration officials restricted the entry of Mexicans, the Mexican government pursued a policy of discouraging *repatriados* from attempting to return to the United States. Having provided free transportation and other assistance to thousands of repatriates, the Mexican government was reluctant to see the recipients of this aid depart for the United States at the first opportunity.

Since the repatriates were prevented from making legal application for visas by the stringent enforcement of the rules, an undetermined number tried to cross the border illegally. Illegal entry did occur during the depression, but it certainly did not compare in numbers with the previous informal crossings or the wetback movements of the 1940s and 1950s. The depression years encompass a period in which legal entry hovered at around thirty-five hundred people annually, a figure that included students, ministers, and professional people, not laborers. If an alien left the United States, the effort to be made in effecting a successful return was a monumental one. Regardless of how many years the alien had resided in the United States, or how many American-born children he had raised, if he left the country, his attempt to reenter was treated as if he were seeking entry for the first time.

The desire of many repatriates to return northward was communicated to Mexican communities throughout the Southwest and elsewhere in the United States. Reports of unfulfilled promises, disappointment, and disillusionment had their effect on the southward-bound repatriation movement. Numerically, repatriation declined, until by 1937 its significance as a mass movement no longer attracted the attention of scholars, businessmen, and journalists. The migrants from Oklahoma and the dust bowl, who more than replaced in agriculture the numbers lost through Mexican repatriation, presented new problems for sociologists to study and novelists to dramatize.

One last effort at repatriation remained, however. This time the incentive clearly came from Mexico; its spokesman was President Lázaro Cárdenas. Along with the agricultural reforms he advocated, Cárdenas endorsed the return of Mexico's sons to the homeland and tried to implement plans for receiving the *repatriados*. The response of the Mexicans in the United States to Mexico's overtures in the late 1930s forms a final chapter in the Mexican repatriation movement.

9.
Tapering Off

As PRESIDENT, Lázaro Cárdenas retained the interest in Mexican *repatriados* he had shown during his energetic campaign for the office. Although the National Repatriation Board had proven ineffectual and the efforts to create meaningful programs for returning Mexicans had failed, President Cárdenas still envisioned Mexico as a beckoning homeland. With nationalistic pride, he launched a drive to attract Mexicans in the United States back to their mother country. This effort was related to Cárdenas' programs of agricultural reform and expropriation of foreign investments such as the oil companies, but it has not received treatment by historians working in recent Mexican history.[1]

Cárdenas's interest marked the first time that the Mexican government exercised the initiative in calling for a repatriation program. Previous efforts were complicated by the unwillingness of Mexicans to leave the United States and the efforts of local and federal agencies to help them on their way. There had also been a tendency for the United States newspapers and spokesmen for business and labor to believe that Mexican offers of land and assistance were to be taken literally, and this had figured prominently in previous repatriation movements. The Mexican government had also paid the expenses of stranded nationals because neither the United States government nor American businesses would accept the responsibility of taking care of them.

Cárdenas, however, expressed a positive concern for the welfare of Mexicans in the United States. Although his attention was focused upon the more familiar issues of oil expropriation, reorganization of the National Revolutionary Party (PNR), and agrarian reforms, Cárdenas was also interested in insuring that Mexican nationals in the United States were not mistreated or persecuted. He strongly endorsed the proposal that Mexican consulates in the United States should retain attorneys for the express purpose of defending Mexicans accused of various crimes.[2]

First Government Plan

The Cárdenas administration proclaimed a policy of repatriation for Mexican citizens abroad. Unlike previous repatriation movements, this was the first to originate with the Mexican government. In late October 1937 the Mexican Autonomous Department of Publicity and Propaganda announced that Mexico intended to repatriate its citizens before allowing foreigners to immigrate to Mexico. The mention of foreigners stemmed from Cárdenas' offer of asylum to refugees of the Spanish civil war; opponents, particularly Sinarquistas, had objected to the proposal, pointing out that repatriates instead of Spanish refugees should be the recipients of any lands and assistance the Mexican government might give.[*]

The new offer of repatriation received its share of publicity, but in practice the proposal was stillborn, chiefly because it lacked any mention of implementation. Several months after the announcement, one Mexican consul denied any knowledge of an active repatriation program. Although no funds had been provided to transport repatriates, Mexico's consul general announced that his government would pay to move repatriates once they arrived in Mexico, but they would have to make it to the Mexican border on their own.[3]

Throughout 1938 the Autonomous Department of Publicity and Propaganda (DAPP) continued to lay the groundwork for a proposed repatriation program. Government officials journeyed to the United States in order to ascertain firsthand the conditions under which Mexicans were employed there, especially in Texas and California. One such official, Minister of Interior Ignacio García Téllez, during his tour of the border states in November, publicly expressed the belief that only Mexicans who were destitute should be repatriated from the United States; Mexican nationals

---

[*]In April 1939 the U.S. Embassy in Mexico, D.F., reported to the State Department that some eight thousand Spanish refugees desired to come to Mexico.

who were prospering there should remain and foster links of friendship between the two countries.

At the end of 1938 the problems surrounding repatriation were analyzed at a conference on population in Mexico, D.F. One controversial proposal called for the postponement of a large-scale repatriation program, based on the argument that since Mexicans were being returned to Mexico every day, either by deportation or repatriation, talk of programs and plans for additional numbers was unrealistic. Until the present returnees were integrated into Mexico's economic life, plans that called for either organized repatriation or the postponement of such an idea were simply rhetoric. Mexican cabinet officers, however, still struggled with the idealistic goal of soliciting the return of Mexican nationals.

Finally, in the spring of 1939, the Cárdenas administration announced the implementation of a repatriation program with the establishment near Matamoros, Tamaulipas, of a colony named the "18 de Marzo" after the date of the oil expropriation decree of the previous year.

Official Visits U. S. Barrios

While this colony was being organized, the Ministry of Foreign Affairs sent Under Secretary Ramón Beteta on a lengthy trip through the United States, intending that he visit the *barrios* of cities in the Southwest, from Texas to California, and speak to Mexicans and Mexican Americans on the virtues of repatriation.

Beteta's trip aroused considerable attention on the northern side of the border. An earlier trip made by Foreign Secretary Eduardo Hay had resulted in some embarrassment to the American State Department when Hay's automobile and luggage were thoroughly searched by quarantine inspectors. Such inspection was waived for Beteta. The State Department, experiencing a period of delicate diplomatic relations with President Cárdenas, desired that Beteta's trip promote friendly relations between the two countries;* in spite of the fact that the announced goal of the journey was to welcome back immigrants who had failed to achieve some part of the American dream.

---

*When State Department officials hopefully asked if he would be participating in the negotiations on the Mexican oil expropriations, Beteta replied that he had nothing to do with that problem.

On 5 April, Beteta left Mexico to inform his compatriots in the United States of the new colony at Matamoros, as well as the offering of lands for colonization and cultivation in Sinaloa and Baja California. Directing his appeal to Mexicans with agricultural rather than industrial skills, Beteta was also, according to a DAPP release, to "take a census of the persons who need and desire to return to their homeland to devote themselves to agricultural activities." He planned to sign up prospective repatriates, especially those in difficult circumstances, and came equipped with the promise that the Mexican government intended to assist repatriates in a positive manner.

Beteta's journey brought him first to Texas where he spoke to Mexican nationals and Mexican Americans alike, giving promises of payment by the Mexican government for transportation expenses. These expenses were to include, according to Beteta, whatever furniture, farm tools, automobiles, and animals the repatriates brought with them. The repatriates could choose between twenty irrigated acres or fifty unirrigated acres of land which was said to be in Tamaulipas, Sinaloa, or Baja California.[4]

By 19 April, Beteta had made his offer in San Antonio, Corpus Christi, and in towns along the Rio Grande Valley from McAllen to Brownsville, including places with large Mexican populations like Karnes City and Kenedy. Mexican consular officers accompanied the under secretary along the way. Beteta's speechmaking was reported to be generous in the extreme. Not only was he said to be making his offer to Mexican Americans as well as Mexicans, he also extended the offer to settle in Mexico to Americans who were not of Mexican descent. Forty million pesos were being provided to carry out the repatriation and, if necessary, work on public projects would be halted in order to bring the repatriates home.[5]

Beteta's appearances and speeches met with enthusiastic audiences, but it soon became apparent that the response was not going to be significant in terms of persons actually deciding to return to Mexico. In early May some one hundred families from the San Antonio area elected to return. If these people were successfully received in Mexico, then a similar number would leave the region each month.

Back in Mexico, officials disagreed over whether Beteta's trip would yield tangible results. The Ministry of the Interior believed that conditions in the American Southwest were not so terrible that Mexican nationals there would be willing to leave. Andrés Landa y Piña, again chief immigration officer of Mexico, had learned from his earlier experience with the National Repatriation Committee of the complexities involved in a repatriation program, and was openly skeptical, noting that money, plans, and much preparation were needed to make a repatriation movement successful. Despite this cautionary note, President Cárdenas said in a DAPP release on 12 April 1939 that any temporary inconveniences caused by an influx of destitute repatriates would be more than balanced by an "increase of the economic potential of the country."

The under secretary himself recognized that many Mexicans were reluctant to leave the United States. One chief fear was that once they crossed the border, Mexican aliens would lose their right of residence in the United States. Some Mexicans who owned businesses or property would be compelled to sacrifice a great deal in order to return to their homeland. Mexican-American children were also reported to be unhappy about the idea.[6]

On 20 May, Beteta met President Cárdenas on the president's train near Ciudad Juárez. Following the meeting, which lasted two hours and in which Beteta presumably briefed Cárdenas on how his journey had progressed, Beteta joined the presidential train as Cárdenas visited the west coast states of Mexico. Beteta's accomplishments were heralded in the Mexico City press, but the extent of the news coverage exaggerated the significance of the numbers. Forty-five people left San Antonio on 16 May, fifty-three more on 24 May, and smaller numbers from other Texas towns were considered newsworthy. The American consul general expressed the belief that these headlines were ammunition against Sinarquista criticism of Mexico's aid to the Spanish refugees.

Beteta resumed his trip through the United States and on 19 July met with California Governor Culbert L. Olson at his home in Los Angeles. Although their conversation was apparently innocuous, word leaked out that Beteta had allegedly commented on a bill pending in the California legislature that would bar aliens from state relief rolls — a bill Olson later vetoed. Since U.S. Embassy officials in Mexico had on occasion been criticized for making observations concerning Mexican legislation affecting American interests, the State Department made a discreet inquiry as to whether Beteta's words could be similarly criticized. Olson reported that

Beteta had discussed the problems of Mexicans in the United States in a general way, commenting on living conditions of Mexicans in California, his plans for renewed repatriation, and the possibility of employment for the repatriates in Mexico. The State Department decided that Beteta had not interfered in American internal political matters and let the matter drop.[7]

Although Beteta continued on to a number of other southwestern cities, the excitement of the idea of renewed repatriation quickly abated. Publicity had far exceeded reality.[8] The anticipated thousands of families destined for the new colonies never arrived, though several hundred families did make their homes in the Matamoros region. Conflicting stories filtered back regarding the degree of difficulty involved in making adjustments in Mexico, and these stories probably contributed to inhibiting further repatriation.

There is enough evidence to suggest that Cárdenas's pronouncements on Mexican repatriation were a way of answering Sinarquista criticism of his offer of Mexico as a haven for refugees from Spain. While this may be true to an extent, Cárdenas also seems to have had a genuine interest in having Mexicans with agricultural skills who were living in foreign lands, particularly the United States, return to their native soil. For almost a decade Mexican immigrants in the United States had weighed the hardships of life in the United States with the possible advantages of returning to the homeland. Throughout the decade, however, reports of the failure of the Mexican government to fulfill its promises reached the people who had remained north of the border. Cárdenas's invitation seemed no better than the offers of his immediate predecessors. That his invitation met with such a poor response indicates that the time for repatriation as a mass movement was over.

Los Angeles Efforts Abated

If incentives for repatriation emanating from Mexico were unsuccessful, what came of the efforts in the United States to continue the movement of Mexican aliens out of the country? Los Angeles County serves as an excellent example of a local governmental agency which made persistent efforts to eliminate aliens from its relief rolls through repatriation. In the latter part of the 1930s, however, such repatriation was much more difficult than in the earlier years of the decade. The Los Angeles County Board of Supervisors was on record against coercion of alien indigents, and the sight of trainloads of departing Mexicans was a thing of the past. Apart from occasional families willing to undergo repatriation, by 1937 the Los Angeles Bureau of County Welfare found Mexican aliens most reluctant to leave the United States.

There were ways, however, in which repatriation could be promoted. The bureau added Spanish-speaking employees to the county payroll for the purpose of attempting, "with the assistance of representatives of the Mexican National Government . . . to encourage the acceptance of our offers of repatriation with these indigents, whether the same be employable or non-employable."

Although by 1937, 80 percent of the alien Mexican relief cases in Los Angeles County were being handled by the State Relief Administration and the Works Progress Administration, Superintendent of Charities Rex Thomson noted that the county paid for the cost of medical care and hospitalization for all indigent aliens in the county. While in May 1937 Thomson provided the county board of supervisors with statistics of "Mexican alien cases," "Mexican cases" (defined as Mexican American), and "all alien cases," Los Angeles County made no attempt to break down the statistics for other nationalities than Mexican. "It has not been possible," Thomson noted almost in passing, "to secure data on the various other nationalities represented in the total alien group." His report more than made up for this lack by his detailed analysis of Mexican alien cases in items of clinic visits, average number of patients in sanatoria, and monthly and annual costs.

Thomson's recommendation for another review of the repatriation policy was accepted, and ten Spanish-speaking employees were added to the county payroll. By 1 September 1937, a month after this "special group" (as Thomson called it) went into operation, the following results were reported: seven cases, totaling thirteen people, had been repatriated; another six cases, involving nineteen individuals, were ready to depart; and another thirty-four families were being readied for departure by the end of the year. This accomplishment in repatriation bore little resemblance to the results achieved between 1931 and 1935.

Thomson also reported to the board on whether the State Relief Administration might cooperate with the county agency on the solution of similar problems. The SRA indicated that no one in its case load wished repatriation, however, and declined the county's offer of "every possible repatriation facility."

Undaunted, Thomson's special repatriation unit continued its efforts. By mid-October Thomson could announce to the board of supervisors a monthly saving in relief costs of $2,085, because of the work of the special unit. In the following year, however, repatriation work declined to the point where the repatriates for the most part were unemployables who were blind, tubercular, paralyzed, or were minor children or the aged. This decline in numbers contrasted with the county's interest in continuing repatriation work which was, if anything, intensified in late 1938. Two episodes occurred at that time which involved the county.

L.A. Emissary in Mexico

One of these episodes concerned the board of supervisors, the department of charities, and a private welfare worker named Siegfried Goetze. In early August 1938 Goetze, who was very concerned about the future welfare of Mexicans in the United States, informed the board that he was planning to attend the International Housing and Town Planning Congress in Mexico, D.F., in October. He proposed that while in Mexico he would approach government officials there with the idea of renewing Mexican repatriation from Los Angeles. The board of supervisors authorized the writing of a letter of introduction for him.

Goetze appears to have made the most of his letter of introduction. Presenting himself as "official representative from California" at the congress, Goetze also visited the American Embassy and the Consulate General. He proposed an ambitious scheme called the "Plan of Belvedere," in which substandard housing would be cleared away in the Belvedere area and the inhabitants would be repatriated to Mexico to partake in a program of model rural homestead projects "upon land to be provided by the Mexican government." Goetze's plan provided positive values for everyone: the relief load in Los Angeles County would be lightened, housing projects would be built in Belvedere, the Mexicans would return to their homeland, and new opportunities would be given them by the Mexican government. Goetze spoke to a number of Mexican officials about his plan and even received a promise from one official that the plan would be shown to President Cárdenas. The proposal was unique in that it came from a private citizen with no official sanction for his idea other than a brief letter of introduction. From his letter of 8 October 1938 to H. D. Anderson, director of the California State Relief

Administration, Goetze seems to have believed that if he could convince the Mexican government of the feasibility of his idea, then he could also persuade the officials of Los Angeles County upon his return.

When Goetze returned to Los Angeles he attempted to discuss his proposals with Thomson, but was rebuffed. Thomson, more attuned to the plans of President Cárdenas, knew that Cárdenas was seeking Mexicans with special skills, primarily agricultural, for Mexico's announced repatriation program. Thomson was also put off by Goetze's hope of being subsidized by the county in order to carry out further negotiations. For his efforts, Goetze received a polite letter of appreciation on 9 November 1938 from the board of supervisors, informing him "that this County has on its rolls only non-employable Mexican alien cases, none of whom the Mexican Government would consider as possible candidates for any Mexican Rural Homestead Projects."

At this point an apparent contradiction appeared in Thomson's logic. Over the preceding months he had sponsored the repatriation of indigents in poor health, who were suffering from a variety of illnesses and diseases. Why, then, were "non-employable Mexican alien cases" considered ineligible for organized repatriation programs? The answer must lie in the disparity between what Mexico wanted in the quality of repatriates and what Los Angeles had already been sending south of the border. This distinction becomes clear when the second episode involving Los Angeles County and repatriation in the fall of 1938 is described.

A Second Emissary Departs

At about the same time that Goetze was attending the Town Planning Congress in Mexico, D.F., one of the members of the board of supervisors was planning a trip to the same city. This trip came at the invitation of former Vice Consul Ricardo Hill, now a congressman from the state of Sonora, who wrote to the board of supervisors on 21 September 1938 that he had been informed by the Ministry of the Interior that if a representative from Los Angeles County could visit Mexico, D.F., "with complete data regarding our nationals in your County," plans might be made for an immediate repatriation of those willing to return. This would constitute the vanguard of the new general repatriation program, then still in its theoretical stages, and would redound to the credit of Ignacio García Téllez and his Ministry of the Interior.

Hill's invitation was directed to Rex Thomson, but the superintendent of charities declined to make the trip. Thomson was keenly interested in returning a number of aliens suffering from health problems to Mexico, and he felt that if a supervisor went to Mexico, *both a general repatriation and a repatriation of infirm aliens* could be discussed. Supervisor Gordon L. McDonough accepted the charge and left for Mexico at the same time that Siegfried Goetze was returning from the congress he had attended.

Supervisor McDonough composed a detailed report of his trip to Mexico, which he submitted to the board of supervisors on 21 November 1938. During his stay there he conferred with a number of Mexican government officials, as well as American officials stationed in Mexico. Some of the people with whom he spoke had met with Goetze a month earlier, but McDonough's credentials were far more valid. Working hard to carry out the twofold purpose of his visit, McDonough met Ambassador Josephus Daniels and Consul General James B. Stewart to inform them of the purpose of his visit to Mexico. An interview was arranged with Minister of the Interior García Téllez, with Ricardo Hill present, and with Vice Consul Willard Galbraith acting as interpreter. García Téllez indicated great interest in the possibility of a meaningful program, one in which both the Mexican government and areas such as Los Angeles County could cooperate in making repatriation permanent. Although specific plans for implementing a repatriation program remained as vague as ever, everyone agreed that repatriation would benefit all concerned.

Repatriating the Sick

The trip's second purpose — inducing the Mexican government to accept infirm repatriates — was more complicated. Not wishing to assume the onus of tubercular Mexicans living in the United States, Mexico suggested that the disease (and other ailments as well) had been contracted in the United States, rather than brought over from Mexico. McDonough conferred with Dr. Walter Garnett, the official in the United States Public Health Service who administered medical examinations to Mexican immigrants who sought visas in excess of 180 days. Garnett confessed to the superficiality of the examinations, but blamed insufficient funds allocated for his work. On checking further into the matter, McDonough learned that Mexico's hospital facilities for tubercular patients were quite limited. Left unresolved was the question of who had the legal responsibility of caring for aliens who suffered from contagious diseases. If the patient had originally contracted the disease in Mexico, then the Mexican government was liable, but if the disease had been contracted in the United States, then the United States community, Los Angeles County for example, must bear the expense. But the current practices of the Public Health Service made such liability impossible to determine. McDonough expressed the hope that in the future a more thorough physical examination would be given, but this did little to solve the problem of Mexican aliens cared for in Los Angeles sanatoria. If anything, it only served to alert the Mexican government that Los Angeles had been repatriating infirm Mexicans.

Los Angeles-Mexico Accord

Further conferences were held. In a meeting on 3 November with García Téllez and Landa y Piña, chief of the Mexican Migration Service, McDonough agreed that the Los Angeles County Department of Charities would prepare statistical data on all Mexican aliens on the county's relief rolls as of 1 December 1938. Periodic reports would follow listing all Mexican aliens added to the rolls subsequent to that date. García Téllez agreed that this information would be of great use in providing the Mexican government with valuable information on its nationals. He was interested enough in the possibilities of large-scale repatriation that he agreed to meet with McDonough again, this time in Los Angeles.

On 10 November 1938 McDonough returned to Los Angeles, and on the next day met García Téllez, Landa y Piña, and other high officials of the Mexican government at their consulate. The following agreement was formalized:

1. That the Mexican government will undertake a program of preparing to receive repatriates by organizing the Governors of the various states of Mexico and Labor Unions in the cities of the various states.

2. That Los Angeles County will submit to the Mexican Government through Senior Ignacia [*sic*] García Téllez, Secretary of the Department of Interior, the following statistical data: Names, addresses, number in family, trades,

and city and state of origin in Mexico of all Mexican Nationals on Los Angeles County Relief Rolls as of December 1st, 1938, and after this date the same information of every Mexican National as he becomes eligible for relief in Los Angeles County.

3. That the Mexican government will undertake to make every effort to secure appropriations of large tracts of land on which to rehabilitate their people upon their return to the Republic of Mexico.

4. That the Mexican government through its immigration offices will deny entry to all Mexican citizens both male and female, seeking to enter the United States in the hope of securing employment and who are without means of adequate support.

At a third conference, held on 17 November, all the above points were confirmed and McDonough could state without equivocation, on the assurance of Luis Murillo Coronado of the Mexican Ministry of Labor, "that Mexico would offer every possible cooperation to the County of Los Angeles to repatriate those on the relief rolls as quickly as possible." The matter of infirm aliens was not quite settled; the county counsel was asked to give an opinion as to who was responsible for the administering of medical aid to indigent aliens.

On the basis of McDonough's recommendations, the board of supervisors on 21 November requested the department of charities to submit complete statistical data on all Mexican nationals on relief in the county. From questionnaires completed by relief recipients, the charities department compiled data on 2,161 cases, including name, address, place of origin in Mexico, occupation, length of residence in the United States, length of time on relief, and reason for unemployment. The charities department presented this initial survey to the Mexican Migration Service, with the promise that additional data would be forthcoming when more Mexicans were added to the rolls.

In the months that followed the conducting of the survey, Mexico's repatriation program received much publicity but little response. Ramón Beteta's tour of American cities, calling for his compatriots to return to the homeland, produced negligible results in Los Angeles and elsewhere. Officials in the Mexican Ministry of the Interior grew so pessimistic over this lack of response that they failed to use the data submitted by Los Angeles County.

Since Mexico refused to accept responsibility for the infirm aliens, the charities department continued to care for them. The department also pursued its data gathering, but because the Mexican government had not acted on the first survey, the additional data were not forwarded.

Time passed; the department of charities underwent an organizational change and the county welfare bureau emerged as the bureau of public assistance. Finally, in May 1941 at the request of the new bureau, the board of supervisors rescinded the original survey order. With the abandoning of data gathering, the idea of repatriating significant numbers of Mexican nationals also vanished from the public arena.

APPENDIXES

Appendix A

The Vocabulary of Repatriation

Because classifications are subject to time, circumstance, and law, describing the return of aliens to their homeland can be a complicated undertaking. For example, many more Mexicans were deported in 1932 than in 1922, because in 1929 illegal entry had been made a misdemeanor and the Bureau of Immigration by then had funds more readily available for deporting aliens.[1] A decade earlier, both the law and the funds were lacking. The simplest divisions of alien return are:

I. Deportation (by the federal government)
    A. Formal deportation under warrant proceedings
    B. Voluntary departures without warrant proceedings

II. Repatriation
    A. Voluntary repatriation by the aliens themselves
    B. Repatriation of destitute aliens by the federal government
    C. Organized repatriation by local private and public welfare agencies
    D. Organized repatriation of aliens by the Mexican consul and the Mexican ethnic community
    E. "Coercive," "forced," or "involuntary" repatriation (quotation marks indicate that the repatriation was not actually desired by the alien, but was forced upon him)

Unfortunately, many people involved with the idea of repatriation muddied the definitions, substituting *deportation* for *repatriation,* or elevating motivation (such as homesickness) to the status of a category. Errors in terminology have been perpetuated by the

---

[1] U.S., Department of Labor, Bureau of Immigration, *Annual Report of the Commissioner General of Immigration, 1932,* pp. 28–29.

[166]

few writers who have dealt, however briefly, with Mexican repatriation. To insist that most repatriates were deported or coerced into leaving is to misread the available statistics and to misconstrue the intentions of many of the Mexican repatriates themselves. A brief description of each point under the outline will provide the reader with the way this study uses the vocabulary of repatriation.

Formal deportation was the procedure utilized by the Bureau of Immigration in removing from the country an alien who had violated some law. But deportation was a practice more often proclaimed than performed, as the "Red Scare" following World War I demonstrated. At that time, a much smaller number was actually deported than the numbers of those eligible for deportation as reported by the newspapers. Fearing that with its limited funds and small corps of enforcement officers it would not be able to prevent the return of many deported aliens, the federal government during the 1920s displayed great reluctance to transport Mexican aliens out of the country solely for illegal entry. It therefore deported only those aliens convicted of a crime who were also found to be in the country illegally.[2]

With the onset of the depression, the Bureau of Immigration, reinforced with a border patrol and an increase in funds, intensified its work with deportable aliens — people whose only crime might be illegal entry within the statute period of the law. Because of the expense involved in conducting a hearing and transporting the alien to the border, it became a frequent practice to encourage *voluntary departure*. A deportable alien was allowed to proceed under his own expense to the border, resulting in advantages to both the government and the alien: the government was spared the expense of a hearing and transportation, and the alien could apply to enter the country legally, something he could not do had he been formally deported. Since there was relatively little expense in proceeding to either border, most aliens undergoing voluntary departure were either Mexicans or Canadians, with the former outnumbering the latter about four to one.[3]

---

[2] W. R. Mansfield to Bureau of Immigration, 4 and 5 February 1921 and 8 August 1924, Record Group 85, 55091/6, National Archives. See also other correspondence in this file.

[3] Bureau of Immigration, *Annual Report, 1930,* p. 22; *ibid., 1931,* p. 36; *ibid., 1932,* p. 28.

The practice of repatriation involved far more people than deportation. *Voluntary repatriation* was the return of aliens of their own volition, for whatever reason. Homesickness, the opportunity to participate in a new agrarian reform program, the failure to find employment, the acquisition of wealth, or the inability to obtain it were all factors in the Mexican's decision to return to Mexico. During the 1920s it was possible for Mexicans to make the trip several times, and particularly for those employed in agriculture, there was a degree of validity to the much-touted "cycle of migration" propounded by growers.

The twenties was also a period, however, during which no agreements bound either the United States or Mexico to supervise the contracting of agricultural labor; the *bracero* program lay in the future. Instead, Mexicans in the United States were pretty much on their own. Those who had entered the United States legally but had become destitute found the federal government extremely reluctant to pay their way out of the country, since to do so would have involved appropriating funds for the same purpose for all other immigrant aliens who had failed to gain an economic foothold in their new country. Relatively few aliens, therefore, were ever repatriated by the federal government.[4]

A typical problem concerned the sugar beet companies which brought Mexican aliens into the United States, but then failed to provide for their return. When the Mexican ambassador debated with U.S. officials over who would finance the repatriation, they replied that the federal government would pay to return only those aliens brought in and then cheated by the companies. As a result, when Mexicans who either had deserted or were discharged from their jobs requested repatriation assistance, they were denied it, as were those who had lawfully entered of their own desire, but later became destitute. In defense of the companies, the Michigan Sugar Company maintained that the return fare had been withheld from wages paid, but when the companies met the Mexicans' demands for receipt of their total wages, they would then spend the additional funds on other than return trips to Mexico.[5]

---

[4] Mansfield to Commissioner General of Immigration A. C. Caminetti, 20 January 1922, Record Group 85, 55091/6, National Archives. This file contains numerous letters from cities such as Phoenix, Topeka, Fort Worth, and Houston, requesting assistance for destitute Mexicans who desired repatriation.

[5] See J. W. Fordney to Caminetti, 14 March 1921, *ibid.*

During the 1920s private relief organizations, such as local chapters of the American Red Cross, on occasion appealed to the federal government to return destitute aliens to their countries of origin. Such requests were echoed by public welfare agencies, which complained of intolerable relief burdens.[6] When the depression struck, the need for relief reached a magnitude that dwarfed all previous conceptions of what had been considered "intolerable." *Organized repatriation programs,* of which Los Angeles serves as a model in this study, bore witness to the thousands of destitute Mexicans whose train fares were paid out of relief funds.

Repatriation programs were also carried out by a U.S. locality's Mexican community, supported by donations from Mexican and Mexican-American welfare groups and brotherhoods, and frequently administered by the local Mexican consul. As the Mexican community attempted to care for its own indigents, during the depression years, this form of assistance assumed significant proportions. Money, food, and clothing were raised by sponsoring dances, benefit shows, and solicitations. Repatriation was undertaken by a family when all resources were exhausted.

The final category, that of involuntary repatriation, has possibly been overemphasized. It is more likely that programs were set up primarily to aid possible repatriates, and that efforts to coerce people into leaving were more an abuse of the programs than an original intention. That coercion did occur from time to time can be seen in complaints made against welfare agencies, but it should be noted that such complaints were made during the period following the peak of repatriation rather than before it.[7]

---

[6] *Denver Post,* 19 Jan. 1922; Consul Francisco Pereda to Chicago Mayor W. H. Thompson, 5 April 1921; Fort Worth Chapter, American Red Cross to Bureau of Immigration, 24 May 1921, Record Group 85, 55091/6, National Archives.

[7] Norman D. Humphrey, "Mexican Repatriation from Michigan: Public Assistance in Historical Perspective," *Social Service Review,* 15 September 1941, pp. 512–13.

Visel's Publicity Release

Incident to the present unemployment conditions, official Washington is deeply concerned over the number of aliens now in the United States, illegally, who are holding jobs that rightfully should be available to those having a legal status here; and also over the number of aliens now abroad, who will no doubt seek entry to this country if some additional barriers are not placed in the way of their coming.

Legislation is now before Congress for consideration, looking not only to a complete cessation of immigration for a period of at least two years, but also to the appropriation of sufficient funds to render possible the immediate deportation of aliens who are now here without a legal status.

Los Angeles authorities concerned in Unemployment Relief have wired Secretary Doak, Department of Labor, for help from the surrounding districts. The plan is that trained members of the Immigration Department's Deportation Squad in Nogales, San Francisco, and San Diego be sent to Los Angeles to cooperate with Mr. W. E. Carr, Chief of the Immigration Service here. These men should be here in about ten days.

Chief R. E. Steckel of the Los Angeles Police force and Capt. Hines[1] promise their cooperation in rounding up the deportable aliens as fast as the Immigration Department calls for them.

Charles P. Visel, coordinator of the Los Angeles Citizens Committee on Coordination of Unemployment Relief, to Colonel Arthur Woods, national coordinator of the President's Emergency Committee for Employment, 19 January 1931, with publicity release attached, Record Group 73, entry 3, 040, PECE Papers, National Archives. A copy is also in the George P. Clements Papers, Bundle 15, Box 80, Department of Special Collections, University of California, Los Angeles.

[1]W. J. Hynes, chief of the Los Angeles Police Department's controversial "Red Squad."

Sheriff Wm. Traeger in the County, in conference accompanied with his chief deputies, is very much interested that deportable aliens leave the County, and has promised that his force will be called to constructively help clean up Los Angeles County.

The status of a deportable alien is one who is in this country illegally and subject to deportation by law. These people here are of all races and nationalities. We have some aliens who are not deportable under the law.

The U.S. Immigration law is very definite and inflexible as to the status of a deportable alien and as to the methods of rejecting from the United States.

Deportable aliens include Chinese, Japanese, Europeans, Canadians, Mexicans, and in fact peoples of every nation in the world.

It so happens that many of the deportable aliens in this district are Mexicans; on the other hand, a large majority of Mexicans are not deportable. This article deals only with those who are deportable aliens.

Captain J. F. Lucey, Southwestern Representative of the President's Emergency Committee on Unemployment Relief, is responsible for the following:

> The Mexican Government is helping greatly in the situation. They want their people to come home and stay there. They welcome them and are glad to get them back.
>
> The Mexican Government offers to pay railroad fare from the Mexican border to their homes for any returning Mexicans who apply. They even notified their Consul to look out for unemployed Mexicans in some instances. Particularly from Dallas, Texas, the Mexican Government has paid the fare this side of the border as well as south of the Rio Grande. The action of the Mexican government has helped materially to alleviate this situation.

Los Angeles County Repatriation Shipments and Costs

Date of Departure	Total Ticket Cost	Total Cost	Single Persons	Families	Total Number of Individuals
3–23–31 & 4–24–31	$ 15,262	$ 15,959	29	228	1,350
8–17–31	10,708	11,642	6	149	899
10–29–31	12,885	14,033	13	189	1,059
1–12–32	16,659	18,483	36	227	1,267
3– 8–32	17,415	18,783	62	229	1,295
4–29–32	11,676	12,753	53	155	875
7– 7–32	15,808	16,989	162	217	1,063
8–18–32	12,203	13,125	133	147	845
10– 6–32	10,934	11,879	72	160	758
12– 8–32	13,470	14,380	87	173	932
2– 8–33	7,982	8,687	41	109	546
4–14–33	12,692	13,575	49	177	914
8– 3–33	6,533	7,105	40	82	453
12–12–33	4,340	5,182	49	71	412
4–15–34 [a]	6,804	11,926	47	125	664
Totals	$175,371	$194,501	879	2,438	13,332

Welfare Cases	Aver. No. Persons Per Family[b]	Average Ticket Cost Per Family	Average Total Cost Per Family[c]
257	5.8	$64.58	$67.53
155	6.0	71.10	77.18
202	5.5	66.86	72.81
263	5.4	70.26	78.72
291	5.4	70.71	76.26
208	5.3	68.52	74.85
379	4.2	57.40	61.69
280	4.8	64.97	69.83
232	4.3	58.79	63.88
260	4.9	67.58	72.15
150	4.6	65.57	71.36
226	4.9	66.19	70.80
122	5.0	69.84	75.95
120	5.1	50.79	60.64
172	4.9	49.04	85.94
Totals 3,317	Averages 5.107	$64.94	$72.02

[a] The original analysis incorrectly gives this date as 25 May 1934.

[b] Average does not include single persons.

[c] Items included in the total cost are board and cars, cash, express and cartage, transportation of indigents, and expenses of attendants (exclusive of salaries).

Source: Adapted from "Analysis of Repatriation Trains," 15 June 1934, Division of Accounts and Collections, Statistical Service, Los Angeles County Department of Charities. A carbon copy of this analysis is in Record Group 59, 311.1215/65, National Archives. The original is missing from the files of the board of supervisors.

Total U.S. Repatriation by Months 1929–1937

	1929	1930	1931	1932
JAN	6,868	3,782	6,508	9,115
FEB	4,465	3,472	6,145	6,308
MAR	4,382	3,391	9,400	5,931
APR	4,333	3,830	10,439	5,987
MAY	5,592	3,674	7,201	8,327
JUNE	9,768	5,174	9,639	7,614
JULY	7,101	5,788	8,954	8,018
AUG	6,285	5,775	14,748	6,071
SEPT	6,991	7,134	13,826	3,777
OCT	7,809	8,648	16,448	5,128
NOV	7,850	9,560	20,756	5,460
DEC	7,975	9,899	14,455	5,717
TOTALS	79,419	70,127	138,519	77,453

1933	1934	1935	1936	1937
3,005	1,786	1,339	1,138	467
3,108	1,607	1,014	1,138	515
2,979	1,502	1,241	1,036	558
4,817	2,213	1,275	843	535
2,946	1,489	1,232	981	383
2,741	1,653	1,271	946	552
1,851	1,776	1,266	1,129	714
2,333	1,577	1,369	782	687
1,721	2,320	1,325	926	653
2,283	2,976	1,347	895	788
2,554	2,967	1,413	826	1,026
3,236	2,077	1,276	959	1,159
33,574	23,943	15,368	11,599	8,037

Source: Record Group 59, 811.111 Mexico Reports/59, 80, 99, 122, 141, 142, National Archives, Washington, D.C. These figures were collected by the Mexican Migration Service.

REFERENCES

Source Notes

Complete bibliographic information for the unpublished material in this book is recorded in the author's Ph.D. dissertation, "The Repatriation of Mexican Nationals from the United States During the Great Depression" (University of California, Los Angeles, 1970), which appears in *Dissertation Abstracts* and is on file in University Microfilms, Ann Arbor, Michigan.

CHAPTER 2 — pages 6–10

Unless otherwise documented, quotations, statistics, and other information in this chapter are found in Records of the President's Organization on Unemployment Relief, Record Group 73, National Archives, Washington, D.C., and the George P. Clements Papers, bundles 7, box 62; 8, box 63; and 15, box 80, Department of Special Collections, University of California, Los Angeles.

1. Assumptions about the stereotypes of Mexican Americans are discussed in Edward J. Casavantes, *A New Look at the Attributes of the Mexican American;* and Thomas M. Martinez, "Advertising and Racism" *El Grito* 2 (Summer 1969: 3 –13.
2. Ernesto Galarza, *Merchants of Labor,* pp. 28–29; Roger Dunbier, *The Sonoran Desert,* pp. 340–41.
3. Paul S. Taylor, "Some Aspects of Mexican Immigration," *Journal of Political Economy* 38 (October 1930): 611.
4. Manuel Gamio, "The New Conquest," *Survey,* 1 May 1924, p. 144.
5. Enrique Santibañez, *Ensayo acerca de la inmigración en los Estados Unidos,* pp. 12, 51. The difficulties of modernizing Mexican economic and social life are superbly analyzed in James W. Wilkie, *The Mexican Revolution.*
6. U.S., Department of Labor, Bureau of Labor Statistics, *Monthly Labor Review,* "Wages and Cost of Living of Mexican Agricultural Laborers," November 1926, vol. 23, p. 1056.
7. J. B. Gwin, "Mexican Labor Problems," *Survey,* 20 November 1920, p. 273.
8. Gwin, "Back and Forth to Mexico," *Survey,* 6 October 1917, pp. 9–10.
9. Bureau of Labor Statistics, *Monthly Labor Review,* "Results of Admission of Mexican Laborers, Under Departmental Orders, for Employment in Agricultural Pursuits," November 1920, vol. 11, p. 1097.
10. Charles A. Thomson, "The Man from Next Door," *Century Magazine,* n.s. 89, vol. 111 (January 1926): 279.
11. George P. Clements, "Mexican Immigration and Its Bearing on Calif.'s Agriculture," *California Citrograph* 15 (November 1929): 3. See also Clements, "If Not Mexicans, Who?" *Farm and Garden Magazine of the Sunday Los Angeles Times,* 11 May 1930, p. 3.

12. Taylor, "Mexicans North of the Rio Grande," *Survey,* I May 1931, pp. 135–40; Bureau of Labor Statistics, *Monthly Labor Review,* "Mexican Labor Colony at Bethlehem, Pa.," October 1931, vol. 33, pp. 74–77; Carey McWilliams, *North from Mexico,* p. 184.
13. T. Earl Sullenger, "The Mexican Population of Omaha," *Journal of Applied Sociology* 8 (May-June 1924): 289–90.
14. Norman D. Humphrey, "The Migration and Settlement of Detroit Mexicans," *Economic Geography* 19 (October 1943): 358–61.
15. Emory S. Bogardus, "Second Generation Mexicans," *Sociology and Social Research* 13 (January-February 1929): 282.
16. Max S. Handman, "The Mexican Immigrant in Texas," National Conference of Social Work, *Proceedings* (1926): 333.
17. U.S., Department of Commerce, Bureau of the Census, *Fifteenth Census of the United States, 1930: Population,* vol. 3, pt. 2, p. 941.
18. *Ibid.,* p. 227; Paul Walter, Jr., "The Spanish-Speaking Community in New Mexico," *Sociology and Social Research* 24 (November-December 1930): 150; T. Wilson Longmore and Homer L. Hitt, "A Demographic Analysis of First and Second Generation Mexican Population of the United States: 1930," *Southwestern Social Science Quarterly* 24 (September 1943): 140.
19. Bureau of the Census, *Fifteenth Census, 1930,* vol. 3, pt. 1, pp. 143, 233, and 291. See also the analytical summary by McWilliams, *North from Mexico,* pp. 54–55.
20. U.S., Department of Labor, Bureau of Immigration, *Annual Report of the Commissioner General of Immigration, 1928,* pp. 52–57; *ibid., 1929,* pp. 53–57; *ibid., 1930,* pp. 68–73; and *ibid., 1931,* pp. 89–93.
21. Bureau of Labor Statistics, *Monthly Labor Review,* "Increase of Mexican Population in United States, 1920 to 1930," July 1933, vol. 37, pp. 46–47; McWilliams, *North from Mexico,* pp. 54–55; Bureau of the Census, *Fifteenth Census, 1930,* vol. 2, pp. 27 and 32.
22. Christine Lofstedt, "The Mexican Population of Pasadena, California," *Journal of Applied Sociology* 7 (May–June 1923): 261.
23. McWilliams, *North from Mexico,* pp. 206-207. McWilliams based his charges on the findings reported in the article by Longmore and Hitt, cited in note 18 above.
24. Ernestine M. Alvarado, "Mexican Immigration to the United States," National Conference of Social Work, *Proceedings* (1920), p. 479; Bogardus, "The Mexican Immigrant," *Journal of Applied Sociology* 11 (May-June 1927): 474; Murray, "Mexican Community Service," *Sociology and Social Research* 17 (July-August 1933): 547; Thomson, "Mexicans — An Interpretation," National Conference of Social Work, *Proceedings* (1928), pp. 499–503.
25. *Mexicans in California: Report of C. C. Young's Mexican Fact-Finding Committee,* pp. 105–106, 120; Bureau of Labor Statistics, *Monthly Labor Review,* "Labor and Social Conditions of Mexicans in California," January 1931, vol. 32, pp. 83–89. See also Edwin F. Bamford, "The Mexican Casual Problem in the Southwest," *Journal of Applied Sociology* 8 (July-August 1924): 365–66; Helen W. Walker, "Mexican Immigrants as Laborers," *Sociology and Social Research* 13 (September-October 1928): 55–62; McWilliams, *North from Mexico,* p. 185; and Constantine Panunzio, *How Mexicans Earn and Live,* pp. 10–11.
26. McWilliams, *Factories in the Field;* Taylor, "Mexicans North of the Rio Grande," pp. 135–40; Robert N. McLean, *The Northern Mexican,* p. 15.
27. Gamio, *Mexican Immigration to the U.S.,* pp. 112–22; Francis J. Weber, "Irish-Born Champion of the Mexican-Americans," *California Historical Society Quarterly* 49 (September 1970): 242.
28. Harold Fields, "Where Shall the Alien Work?" *Social Forces* 12 (December 1933): 213–21. This article cites the sources of each law mentioned in the paragraph. The author has focused on states which, with one or two exceptions, had large numbers of Mexicans; the article discusses laws throughout the country.
29. Quoted in McLean, "Rubbing Shoulders on the Border," *Survey,* I May 1924, p. 184. Cf. Clara Smith. "Development of the Mexican People of Watts," p. 59, for an account of a Mexican who became an American citizen despite the fear that his "people" would ostracize him.

30. Cf. Theodore Saloutos, *They Remember America*, and "Exodus U.S.A." in *In the Trek of the Immigrants*, pp. 197–215; and Oscar Handlin, "Immigrants Who Go Back," *Atlantic* 98 (July 1956): 70–74. For a comparison with Japanese immigrants, see Roger Daniels, *The Politics of Prejudice: the Anti-Japanese Movement in California and the Struggle for Japanese Exclusion* (New York, 1968), p. 106.
31. *Mexicans in California*, p. 73.
32. Quoted in "Mexican Invaders Relieving Our Farm-Labor Shortage," *Literary Digest*, 17 July 1920, p. 54.
33. McWilliams, *North from Mexico*, p. 207.
34. Bogardus, "The Mexican Immigrant and Segregation," *American Journal of Sociology* 36 (July 1930): 74. See also Bogardus, "Second Generation Mexicans," p. 277. The distinction between Mexicans and Mexican Americans was further pointed out in O. Douglas Weeks, "The League of United Latin American Citizens: a Texas Mexican Civic Organization," *Southwestern Political and Social Science Quarterly* 10 (December 1929): 270–72. See also Taylor, *Mexican Labor in the United States: Dimmit County, Winter Garden District, South Texas*, p. 411.
35. Taylor, *Mexican Labor in the United States;* there were eleven monographs in all. Taylor also contributed articles to *Survey, Monthly Labor Review, American Journal of Sociology,* and other periodicals. Cf. Santibáñez, *Ensayo,* p. 58, for comments on Taylor's work.
36. Gamio, *Mexican Immigration to the U.S.,* and *The Mexican Immigrant.* For further information on Gamio's research, see Robert Redfield, "The Antecedents of Mexican Immigration to the United States," *American Journal of Sociology* 3 (November 1929): 434.
37. *Mexicans in California*, p. 12.
38. Roy L. Garis, *Immigration Restriction.* Garis took the restrictionist point of view.
39. "Report of the Seventh Annual Conference of the Friends of the Mexicans," Pomona College, 11–12 November 1927; Hazel D. Santiago, "Mexican Influence in Southern California," *Sociology and Social Research* 16 (September-October) 1931: 73; Bogardus, *The Mexican in the United States;* McLean, *That Mexican! As He Really Is;* American Federation of Labor, *Proceedings* (1927), pp. 156, 321–36. The 1 May 1931 issue of *Survey* was devoted to a study of Mexican life in the United States.
40. Galarza, "Life in the United States for Mexican People," National Conference of Social Work, *Proceedings* (1929), pp. 401–404; Santibáñez, *Ensayo,* p. 51.

CHAPTER 3

Unless otherwise noted, material in this chapter is from General Records of the Department of State, Record Group 59, National Archives, Washington, D.C.; and the George P. Clements Papers, bundle 7, box 62, Department of Special Collections, University of California, Los Angeles, California.

1. Norman D. Humphrey, "Mexican Repatriation from Michigan," *Social Service Review* 15 (September 1941): 497; Samuel E. Wood, "California Migrants," *Sociology and Social Research* 24 (January-February 1940): 253; Donald Young, *Research Memorandum on Minority Peoples in the Depression,* pp. 42–43.
2. Saloutos, *They Remember America,* p. vii. U.S., Department of Labor, Bureau of Immigration, *Annual Report of the Commissioner General of Immigration, 1923,* p. 12. A fascinating study of the Back-to-Africa Movement between 1890 and 1910 has been written by Edwin S. Redkey, *Black Exodus: Black Nationalist and Back-to-Africa Movements, 1890–1910* (New Haven, 1969).
3. Maldwyn Allen Jones, *American Immigration,* pp. 290–93; Robert A. Divine, *American Immigration Policy, 1924–1952,* pp. 52–68.
4. U.S., Congress, House, Committee on Immigration and Naturalization, *Hearings on Seasonal Agricultural Laborers from Mexico,* 69th Cong., 1st sess., 1925–1926, pp. 4–27, *passim.*
5. The antirestrictionist article by George Marvin, "Monkey Wrenches in Mexican Machinery," *Independent,* 14 April 1928, pp. 350–52, was rebutted by Richard L. Strout, "A Fence for the Rio Grande," *Indepdt.,* 2 June 1928, pp. 518–20.

The pro-restriction articles by Kenneth L. Roberts in *Saturday Evening Post* were disputed by Charles C. Teague, president of the California Fruit Growers' Exchange, in "A Statement on Mexican Immigration," *Sat. Eve. Post*, 10 March 1928, pp. 169–70. Carleton Beals, "Mexico and the Harris Bill," *Nation*, 9 July 1930, pp. 51–52, also opposed a quota for Mexico.

6. C. M. Goethe, "Other Aspects of the Problem," *Current History* 28 (August 1928): 766–68; idem, "Peons Need Not Apply," *World's Work* 59 (November 1930): 47–48; Remsen Crawford, "The Menace of Mexican Immigration," *Cur. Hist.* 31 (February 1930): 902–907; Chester Rowell, "Why Make Mexico an Exception?" *Survey*, 1 May 1931, p. 180.

7. Roy L. Garis, "The Mexicanization of American Business," *Saturday Evening Post*, 8 February 1930, p. 46; idem, "The Mexican Invasion," *ibid.*, 19 April 1930, pp. 43–44; Garet Garrett, "Government by Tumult," *ibid.*, 16 March 1929, pp. 14–15; Jay S. Stowell, "The Danger of Unrestricted Mexican Immigration," *Current History* 28 (August 1928): 763–66. Some more objectively written articles were McLean, "A Dyke Against Mexicans,"*New Republic*, 14 August 1929, pp. 334–37; Gamio, "Migration and Planning," *Survey*, 1 May 1931, p. 174; Bogardus, "The Mexican Immigrant and the Quota," *Sociology and Social Research* 12 (March-April 1928): 371–78; Thomson, "What of the Bracero?" *Survey*, 1 June 1925, pp. 290–91; Thomson, "Restriction of Mexican Immigration," *Journal of Applied Sociology* 11 (July-August 1927): 574–78; Glenn E. Hoover, "Our Mexican Immigrants," *Foreign Affairs* 8 (October 1929): 99–107; and Louis Bloch, "Facts About Mexican Immigration Before and Since the Quota Restriction Laws," *American Statistical Association Journal* 24 (March 1929): 50–60. See also the brief article by Galarza, "Without Benefit of Lobby," *Survey*, 1 May 1931, p. 181.

8. U.S., Congress, House, *Congressional Record*, 71st Cong., 3d sess., 1931, 74, pt. 7: 6744.

9. Bureau of Immigration, *Annual Report, 1923*, pp. 16–19.

10. *Ibid., 1925*, pp. 14–21; *ibid., 1926*, pp. 16–18; *ibid., 1927*, pp. 16–19; *ibid., 1930*, pp. 34–44.

11. *Ibid., 1930*, p. 41; *ibid., 1931*, p. 60.

12. U.S., *Statutes at Large*, vol. 45, pt. 1, chap. 690, pp. 1551–52; editorial in *Nation*, 24 September 1930, pp. 309–10.

13. Gamio, *Quantitative Estimate*, and *Mexican Immigration to the U.S.*, pp. 30–31.

14. *La Opinión* (Los Angeles), 10 Jan. 1931. See also issues of 11, 12, 13, 15, 19, 20, and 21 Jan. 1931.

CHAPTER 4

Unless otherwise noted, material in this chapter is from the George P. Clements Papers, bundle 15, box 80, Department of Special Collections, University of California, Los Angeles; and General Records of the Department of State, Record Group 59; Records of the President's Organization on Unemployment Relief, RG 73; Records of the Immigration and Naturalization Service, RG 85; General Records of the Department of Labor, RG 174, National Archives, Washington, D.C.

1. Max J. Kohler, "Enforcing Our Deportation Laws," National Conference of Social Work, *Proceedings* (1931), pp. 496–98. See editorials in *Nation*, 22 April 1931, p. 437; 29 April 1931, p. 463; 19 August 1931, p. 170.

2. *New York Times*, 6 Jan. 1931; Gardner Jackson, "Doak the Deportation Chief," *Nation*, 18 March 1931, pp. 295–96.

3. U.S., Department of Labor, Bureau of Immigration, *Annual Report of the Commissioner General of Immigration, 1931*, p. 14.

4. Bureau of Immigration, *Annual Report, 1931*, p. 37; American Civil Liberties Union, *Annual Report, 1930–1931*, p. 22.

5. U.S., *Statutes at Large*, vol. 45, pt. 1, chap. 690, pp. 1551–52.

6. Bureau of Immigration, *Annual Report, 1931*, p. 36.

7. Porter's attitude was satirized in a front-page editorial cartoon in the Los Angeles *Record*, 28 Jan. 1931.

8. For the work of the PECE, see Erving P. Hayes, *Activities of the President's Emergency Committee for Employment, 1930–1931*, especially pp. 103–107.

9. Particular references are to Los Angeles *Record*, 28 Jan., 5 and 6 Feb. 1931; Stanley Rogers, "The Attempted Recall of the Mayor of Los Angeles," *Na-*

tional Municipal Review 21 (July 1932): 416–19; Edmund Wilson, "The City of Our Lady the Queen of the Angels: II," *New Republic,* 9 December 1931, pp. 89–93; Reuben W. Borough, "The Suicide of a Newspaper," *Frontier* 16 (February 1965): 13–14; John Anson Ford, *Thirty Explosive Years in Los Angeles County,* pp. 98–99; and Guy W. Finney, *Angel City in Turmoil.* On the Red marches, see *Record* and *Express,* 20 Jan. 1931, and *Times, Express,* and *Illustrated Daily News,* 21 Jan. 1931, all of Los Angeles; editorial in *Nation,* 6 January 1932, p. 2; also *Record,* 26 Nov. 1931, where the Mexican consul accused Shuler of making "insulting charges against the Mexicans residing here." For charges made against Mayor Frank Shaw, see "Reform Over Los Angeles," *Time,* 5 December 1938, p. 14; and Remi Nadeau, *Los Angeles: From Mission to Modern City,* pp. 259–63.

10. *Ibid.*
11. Los Angeles *Record,* 24 and 25 Nov., 17 Dec 1930, and 17 Apr. 1931; *Express,* 17 Apr. 1931.
12. Quoted in *Los Angeles Times,* 13 Jan. 1931.
13. Editorial in *El Universal* (Mexico, D.F.), 22 Jan. 1931. The movement of repatriates is frequently mentioned in articles in *La Opinión* (Los Angeles).
14. *Evening Express,* 30 Jan. 1931; *Times,* 31 Jan. 1931; *La Opinión,* 30 Jan. 1931, all of Los Angeles.
15. Los Angeles *Illustrated Daily News,* 31 Jan. 1931.
16. *Los Angeles Times,* 31 Jan. 1931.
17. *Los Angeles Evening Herald,* 30 Jan. 1931.
18. *Los Angeles Examiner,* 3 Feb. 1931.
19. Cf. *La Opinión* (Los Angeles), 6, 7, and 10 Feb. 1931.
20. *Examiner* and *Times,* 15 Feb. 1931. See also *La Opinión,* 15 Feb. 1931, and *Evening Express,* 16 Feb. 1931, all of Los Angeles.
21. *La Opinión,* 16 Feb. 1931; *Evening Express,* 17 Feb. 1931; *Record,* 24 Feb. 1931, all of Los Angeles.
22. *La Opinión* (Los Angeles), 17, 19, and 28 Feb. 1931.
23. *Los Angeles Evening Express,* 19 Feb. 1931.
24. *La Opinión,* 28 Feb. 1931; *Heraldo de Mexico,* 28 Feb. 1931; *Japanese-American News,* 24 Feb. 1931, all of Los Angeles.
25. The substance of this description is taken from the National Commission on Law Observance and Enforcement, Report No. 5, "Report on the Enforcement of the Deportation Laws of the United States," 27 May 1931, pp. 59–60, *passim.* The fact that aliens did not share the same civil liberties as American citizens has been studied in depth by Milton R. Konvitz, *Civil Rights in Immigration,* pp. 99, 106–109.
26. *La Opinión* (Los Angeles), 28 Feb. 1931.

CHAPTER 5

Unless otherwise documented, material in this chapter is from the George P. Clements Papers, bundle 15, box 80, Department of Special Collections, University of California, Los Angeles; and General Records of the Department of State, Record Group 59; Records of the President's Organization on Unemployment Relief, RG 73; and Records of the Immigration and Naturalization Service, RG 85, National Archives, Washington, D.C.

1. *El Informador* (Guadalajara), 20 Feb. 1931, and *El Universal* (Mexico, D.F.), 24 Feb. 1931, are earlier examples. See also *Excelsior* (Mexico, D.F.), 1 and 31 May and 10 June 1931.
2. *Los Angeles Times,* 29 May and 7 June 1931; *La Opinión* (Los Angeles), 13 May 1931. See also *Los Angeles Evening Express,* 19 May 1931; Santiago, "Mexican Influence in Southern California," 71 n. News of Kerr's statement also reached Mexico, D.F., where *Excelsior* covered it in its 2 June 1931 edition.
3. *Los Angeles Evening Herald,* 25 Mar. 1931.
4. Secretaría de Relaciones Exteriores, *Apéndice a la Memoria de la Secretaría de Relaciones Exteriores de Agosto de 1931 a Julio de 1932* (Mexico, 1932), table facing p. 984.
5. *Los Angeles Times,* 7 June 1931; *El Universal* (Mexico, D.F.), 15 and 20 June 1931.
6. *Los Angeles Times,* 8 June 1931; *Excelsior* (Mexico, D.F.), 10 June 1931.

7. *La Opinión* (Los Angeles), 7 and 8 Jan. 1931.
8. Los Angeles *Record,* 20 and 21 Mar. 1931.
9. *Ibid.,* 19 June 1931.
10. *Ibid.,* 20 June 1931.
11. *Ibid.,* 22 June 1931.
12. *Ibid.,* 23 June 1931.
13. Reuben Oppenheimer, "The Deportation Terror," *New Republic,* 13 January 1932, p. 232.
14. *Los Angeles Evening Express,* 21 June 1931.
15. *New York Times,* 17 July 1931.
16. Bureau of Immigration, *Annual Report, 1931,* pp. 12, 35–36.

CHAPTER 6

Unless otherwise documented, material in this chapter is drawn from the George P. Clements Papers, bundle 7, box 62, and bundle 15, box 80, Department of Special Collections, University of California, Los Angeles; General Records of the Department of State, Record Group 59; Records of the President's Organization on Unemployment Relief, RG 73; Records of the Immigration and Naturalization Service, RG 85; and General Records of the Department of Labor, RG 174, National Archives, Washington, D.C.; Los Angeles County Board of Supervisors, file #40.31/340 and minute books, beginning with vol. 167 in 1931 and concluding with vol. 208 in 1935, Los Angeles County Hall of Administration.

1. An example of the then-current view of unassimibility of Mexican aliens is found in Murray, "Mexican Community Service," p. 547.
2. *Christian Science Monitor,* 17 Jan. 1931, quoting W. H. Holland, superintendent of the Los Angeles County Department of Charities.
3. Bogardus, "Mexican Repatriates," *Sociology and Social Research* 17 (November-December 1933): 174.
4. *La Opinión* (Los Angeles), 27 and 29 Jan., 8 Feb. 1931; *Los Angeles Evening Express,* 16 and 19 Feb. 1931. On the work of the Los Angeles Diocese in the depression, see Weber, "Irish-Born Champion of the Mexican-Americans," pp. 238–39. McLean, "Goodbye, Vicente," pp. 183 and 195, credits the Mexican consul with obtaining low charity fares for Mexicans wishing to repatriate themselves by train to the border.
5. *Los Angeles Evening Herald,* 30 Jan. 1931; McLean, "Goodbye, Vicente," p. 183. See also Louis B. Perry and Richard S. Perry, *A History of the Los Angeles Labor Movement, 1911–1941,* p. 227.
6. Los Angeles *Record,* 28 Jan. and 6 Feb. 1931.
7. Harvey C. Fremming, "Los Angeles Meets Unemployment," *American Federationist* 38 (July 1931): 855–57. For a report of the friction between Fremming and Shaw, see Finney, *Angel City in Turmoil,* p. 110.
8. *California Political Code,* sec. 4041.16 (4); *Statutes of California,* chap. 239, sec. 2. McWilliams, "Getting Rid of the Mexican," *American Mercury* 28 (March 1933): 322–24, oversimplifies the origins of the repatriation program.
9. McWilliams, *Southern California Country,* pp. 315–17, is highly generalized and the figures he gives are questionable. The train departure he described as occurring in February 1931 either was not a county-sponsored departure, or else he was confused as to the date. He repeated the same account in *North from Mexico,* p. 193. See also *Los Angeles Evening Express,* 24 April, and *Record,* 16 June 1931.
10. *Los Angeles Evening Express,* 24 April, and *New York Times,* 25 April 1931.
11. *New York Times,* 12 April, *La Opinión* (Los Angeles), 12 Jan. 1931, and McLean, "Goodbye, Vicente," pp. 183 and 195.
12. *Los Angeles Times,* 8 June, and *Evening Express,* 10 Aug. 1931.
13. *Los Angeles Times,* 8 June 1931.
14. McWilliams, *Southern California Country,* p. 317, and *Factories in the Field,* p. 129. Cf. *North from Mexico,* p. 193, where the same anecdote is repeated, followed by McWilliams discussing repatriations as being instigated by agricultural interests in an effort to stop unionization. It seems that here he attempted to link together too many disparate factors.
15. The investigation can be followed in *Los Angeles Evening Express,* 4 July, 16, 18, 20, and 28 Aug., and *Record,* 25 Aug. 1931.
16. Historical Society of Southern California, *Annual Publications* 15 (1931), a special issue commemorating "the One Hundred Fiftieth Anniversary of the

Founding of Los Angeles, September 4, 1781." See the Los Angeles newspapers, 1 to 10 Sept. 1931, for many more examples of how a city diverts itself from thoughts of economic depression. See also Leonard Pitt, *Decline of the Californios,* chap. XVI, "Schizoid Heritage," especially pp. 290–93; Marion Parks, "La Fiesta de Los Angeles — Retrospect," *Overland and Out West Magazine,* 89 (October 1931): 11, 32.

17. Los Angeles *Record* and *Times,* 29 Oct., and *New York Times,* 30 Oct. 1931.
18. McWilliams, *North from Mexico,* p. 193; *Southern California Country,* pp. 315–17; "Getting Rid of the Mexican," pp. 322–24.
19. Cf. Jack Starr-Hunt, "The Mexicans Who Went Home," *Los Angeles Times Sunday Magazine,* 26 March 1933, p. 20.
20. The departure date of 25 May 1934, as given in the "Analysis of Mexican Repatriation Trains," copy in Record Group 59, 311.1215/65, National Archives, is incorrect.
21. *El Universal,* 5 and 9 May; *Excelsior,* 5 and 6 May; and *El Nacional,* 8 May 1934, all of Mexico, D.F.

CHAPTER 7

Unless otherwise cited, material in this chapter is drawn from General Records of the Department of State, Record Group 59, and Records of the Immigration and Naturalization Service, RG 85, National Archives, Washington, D.C.

1. Harry Schwartz, *Seasonal Farm Labor in the United States,* p. 61; Adena Miller Rich, "Case Work in the Repatriation of Immigrants," *Social Service Review* 10 (December 1936): 602; *La Opinión* (Los Angeles), 14 Jan., 7, 20, and 25 Feb., 12 March, and 9 May 1931.
2. Taylor, *Mexican Labor in the United States: Migration Statistics,* p. 48.
3. Schwartz, *Seasonal Farm Labor in the United States,* pp. 102–39.
4. Herschel T. Manuel, "The Mexican Child in Texas," *Southwest Review* 17 (April 1932): 291–92; H. T. Manuel, "The Mexican Population of Texas," *Southwestern Social Science Quarterly* 15 (June 1934): 36–38.
5. Governor's Interracial Commission, "Mexicans in Minnesota," in *Race Relations in Minnesota,* p. 41; "Back to the Homeland," *Survey* 69 (January 1933): 39.
6. *New York Times,* 20 March 1934.
7. "Back to the Homeland," p. 39. See also Lawrence L. Waters, "Transient Mexican Agricultural Labor," *Southwestern Social Science Quarterly* 22 (June 1941): 61; and Powell A. Moore, *Calumet Region: Indiana's Last Frontier,* Indiana Historical Bureau, 1959, pp. 568–569.
8. *Detroit News,* 10 Oct. 1931.
9. Michigan State Welfare Department, *Repatriation* (Lansing, n.d.), quoted in Norman D. Humphrey, "Mexican Repatriation from Michigan: Public Assistance in Historical Perspective," *Social Service Review* 15 (September 1941): 498.
10. Humphrey, "The Migration and Settlement of Detroit Mexicans," *Economic Geography* 19 (October 1943): 360.
11. Humphrey, "Mexican Repatriation from Michigan," pp. 512–13.
12. *Ibid.,* pp. 505–11.
13. U.S., Department of Commerce, Bureau of the Census, *Fifteenth Census of the U.S., 1930: Population,* vol. 3, sect. 1, p. 143.
14. Taylor, *Mexican Labor in the United States: Migration Statistics,* p. 47.
15. U.S., Department of Labor, *Annual Report of the Secretary of Labor, 1933,* p. 54.
16. *Annual Report of the Secretary of Labor, 1934,* p. 51. See also *Annual Report, 1935,* p. 90, and National Commission on Law Observance and Enforcement, "Report on the Enforcement of the Deportation Laws of the United States," Report No. 5, 1931, p. 154.
17. *Annual Report of the Secretary of Labor, 1934,* p. 52.
18. *Ibid.,* p. 47.
19. *Ibid.,* p. 48; G. C. Wilmoth, "Mexican Border Procedure," U.S., Department of Labor, Immigration and Naturalization Service, Lecture No. 23, Second Series, dealt with procedures involving all categories of people crossing the border.
20. Joan W. Moore and Ralph Guzman, "The Mexican-Americans: New Wind from the Southwest," *Nation,* 30 May 1965, pp. 645–48, cite a figure of "at least

100,000" while Louisa R. Shotwell, *The Harvesters: The Story of the Migrant People,* p. 74, gives (without documentation) a figure of half a million. Leo Grebler, "Mexican Immigration to the United States: The Record and Its Implications," Advance Report 2 of the Mexican-American Study Project (UCLA, 1966), pp. 25–29, grossly underestimates the total number of Mexicans leaving the United States. John H. Burma estimates between 300,000 and 400,000 repatriates, but does not give his source, in *Spanish-Speaking Groups in the United States,* pp. 43–44.

21. McWilliams, *North from Mexico,* p. 185, and *Factories in the Field,* p. 285. Examples are Ruth Landes, *Latin Americans of the Southwest,* pp. 56–57, and Earl Pomeroy, *The Pacific Slope,* p. 283. Beatrice Griffith, *American Me,* p. 115, follows McWilliams, *Southern California Country,* p. 317, in describing the departure of Mexicans from the United States, but she confuses the terms repatriation and deportation. Cf. Abraham Hoffman, "Mexican Repatriation Statistics: Some Suggested Alternatives to Carey McWilliams," *Western Historical Quarterly* 3 (October 1972), pp. 391–404.

22. *Annual Report of the Secretary of Labor, 1932,* p. 72.

23. The Mexican Migration Service figures given herein and in the following paragraphs are from Record Group 59, 811.111, Mexico Reports/59, 80, 99, 122, 141, 142, National Archives, Washington, D.C. See appendix D.

24. *Annual Report of the Secretary of Labor, 1933,* p. 53.

25. *Ibid., 1934,* p. 65.

26. This figure is obtained by adding the figures for deportation and voluntary departures to Mexico found in the Department of Labor's nineteenth through twenty-third *Annual Reports, 1931–1935.*

27. Dean L. Williams, "Some Political and Economic Aspects of Mexican Immigration into the United States" (Master's thesis, University of California, Los Angeles, 1950), p. 15, n. 15.

28. *La Opinión* (Los Angeles) provides many such descriptions. Good examples can be found in the 10 and 21 Jan., 8 Feb. and 9 May 1931 editions. Marta Roberts' novel *Tumbleweeds* (New York: G. P. Putnam's Sons, 1940) depicts the struggles of a Mexican family in the United States during the depression.

29. Taylor, *Mexican Labor in the United States: Migration Statistics,* p. 24.

CHAPTER 8

Material in this chapter, unless otherwise documented, is from General Records of the Department of State, Record Group 59, and Records of the Immigration and Naturalization Service, RG 85, National Archives, Washington, D.C.; Los Angeles County Board of Supervisors, file #40.31/340, and minute books, vol. 208, 1935, Los Angeles County Hall of Administration.

1. *El Universal,* 27 Dec. 1930, 10 Jan. 1931; *Excelsior,* 10 Jan. 1931; *El Nacional,* 8 May 1934, all of Mexico, D.F.

2. *Excelsior,* 10 Feb. 1931, 26 April 1932; *El Universal,* 12 Feb. 1931, 26 July 1934; *El Nacional,* 21 Aug. 1934, all of Mexico, D.F.

3. *New York Times,* 13 Nov. 1931; Edna E. Kelley, "The Mexicans Go Home," *Southwest Review* 17 (April 1932): 303–304; *Excelsior* (Mexico, D.F.), 26 April 1932.

4. Kelley, *Southwest Review* 17 (April 1932): 304–307.

5. James C. Gilbert, "A Field Study in Mexico of the Mexican Repatriation Movement" (Master's thesis, University of Southern California, 1934), p. 104. Gilbert had interviewed Gamio personally. Gamio had no connection with the National Repatriation Committee. President Rodríguez is quoted as professing an opposite view in Jack Starr-Hunt, "The Mexicans Who Went Home," *Los Angeles Times Sunday Magazine,* March 26, 1933, p. 10. Starr-Hunt was the English language section editor of *Excelsior* (Mexico, D.F.).

6. Gilbert, "Field Study," pp. 108–10.

7. *El Universal* (Mexico, D.F.), 9 March 1934. The figures were as of December 31, 1933.

8. See also *Excelsior,* 5 May 1934, and *El Nacional,* 8 May and 21 Aug. 1934, (Mexico, D.F.); and Secretariá de Relaciones Exteriores, *Informe de la Secretariá de Relaciones Exteriores, 1933–34,* (Mexico, 1934), pp. 415–21.

9. *Diario Oficial* (Mexico, D.F.), 12 March 1935.

10. Bogardus, *Mexican in the U.S.,* p. 91.
11. Enrique Mexia, "Irrigation Works in Mexico; Capacity of the 'Don Martin' Dam," *Pan Pacific Progress* 14 (February 1931): 85; Gilbert, "Field Study," pp. 113–14.
12. Gilbert, "Field Study," pp. 114–19.
13. Frank Tannenbaum, *Mexico,* pp. 190–92, reviews the development of the irrigation projects. By 1950 there were 28 irrigation districts covering almost a million hectares of land.
14. *El Porvenir* (Monterrey), 12 and 15 Nov. 1931.
15. Paul S. Taylor, *A Spanish-Mexican Peasant Community,* especially pp. 55–58. This monograph is No. 4 in the Ibero-Americana series.
16. Osgood Hardy, "Los Repatriados," *Pomona College Magazine* 21 (January 1933): 71–73; Emma R. Stevenson, "The Emigrant Comes Home," *Survey,* 1 May 1931, pp. 175–77; Bogardus, "Mexican Repatriates," *Sociology and Social Research* 18 (November-December 1933): 169–76. Bogardus' article, slightly revised, appears as a chapter in his *Mexican in the U.S.* See also Starr-Hunt, *Los Angeles Times Sunday Magazine,* 26 March 1933, pp. 10, 20.
17. Gilbert, "Field Study," pp. 6–17.
18. *Ibid.,* p. 164.
19. *Ibid.,* pp. 47, 60–61.
20. *Ibid.,* p. 71. Cf. the experiences of returned European immigrants in Oscar Handlin, "Immigrants Who Go Back," *Atlantic* 198 (July 1956): 70–74.
21. Stevenson, *Survey,* 1 May 1931, p. 177. Cf. Taylor, *Spanish-Mexican Peasant Community,* p. 56.
22. Gilbert, "Field Study," p. 126.
23. *Ibid.,* p. 158.
24. Agnes K. Hanna, "Social Services on the Mexican Border," National Conference of Social Work, *Proceedings* (1935), pp. 698–99; Taylor, *Spanish-Mexican Peasant Community,* p. 53.
25. Paul S. Taylor, *An American-Mexican Frontier,* p. 349, n. 10.
26. The story is told in a biographical note on the author, Julian Nava, *Mexican-Americans: Past, Present, and Future* (Los Angeles, 1969), p. iv.
27. Hanna, National Conference of Social Work, *Proceedings* (1935), p. 699.
28. Carrie Belle H. MacCarthy, "A Survey of the Mexican Hardship Cases Active in the Los Angeles County Department of Charities, Los Angeles, California" (Master's thesis, University of Southern California, 1939), pp. 93–94. Cf. Marie Pope Wallis, "A Study of Dependency in One Hundred Cases Taken from Files of Bureau of County Welfare, Catholic Welfare Bureau, Los Angeles County Relief Administration (Torrance and Watts Districts)" (Master's thesis, University of Southern California, 1935). The Wallis study suffers from subjective generalizations and stereotypes about Mexicans.

CHAPTER 9

Unless otherwise documented, material in this chapter is from General Records of the Department of State, Record Group 59, National Archives, Washington, D.C.; Los Angeles County Board of Supervisors, File #40.31/340 and minute books, beginning with volume 234 in 1937 and concluding with volume 268 in 1941, Los Angeles County Hall of Administration.

1. Howard F. Cline, *The United States and Mexico,* does not mention Mexican repatriation in the 1930s; neither does Lesley Byrd Simpson, *Many Mexicos,* nor Joe C. Ashby, *Organized Labor and the Mexican Revolution Under Lázaro Cárdenas.*
2. Ernesto Hidalgo, *La Protección de mexicanos en los Estados Unidos: Defensorías de oficio anexas a los consulados — un proyecto,* pp. 5–6.
3. *Excelsior* and *El Universal,* 22 Oct. 1937, both of Mexico, D.F.
4. *El Continental* (El Paso), 13 April 1939.
5. *La Prensa* (San Antonio), 11 April 1939.
6. *El Universal* (Mexico, D.F.), 15 April 1939.
7. See *Times* and *Herald-Express,* 20 July 1939, both of Los Angeles.
8. "Mexican Exodus," *Newsweek,* 31 July 1939, p. 11.

Bibliography

Archival Sources

Los Angeles. Department of Special Collections, University of California, Los Angeles. George P. Clements Papers.
Los Angeles. Hall of Administration. County Board of Supervisors. Minute Books, 1930–1941.
————. Supervisors' Decimal File 40.31/340.
Washington, D.C. National Archives. Record Group 59. General Records of the Department of State.
————. Record Group 73. Records of the President's Emergency Committee on Employment (PECE).
————. Record Group 85. Records of the Immigration and Naturalization Service.
————. Record Group 174. General Records of the Department of Labor.

Published Works, Theses, and Dissertations

Adamic, Louis. "Aliens and Alien-Baiters." *Harper's* 173 (November 1936): 561–74.
Ahl, Frances N. "Los Angeles Mayor Survives Recall." *National Municipal Review* 31 (June 1932): 400.
Albig, William. "Opinions Concerning Unskilled Mexican Immigrants." *Sociology and Social Research* 15 (September-October 1930): 62–72.
Allen, Robert S. "One of Mr. Hoover's Friends." *American Mercury* 35 (January 1932): 53–62.
Almada, Baldomero A. "Agriculture in Mexico, Present and Future." *Pan Pacific Progress* 8 (January 1928): 11.
Alvarado, Ernestine M. "Mexican Immigration to the U.S." National Conference of Social Work, *Proceedings* (1920): 479–80.
American Federation of Labor. *Proceedings,* 1925–1932.
Ashby, Joe C. *Organized Labor and the Mexican Revolution Under Lázaro Cárdenas.* Chapel Hill: University of North Carolina Press, 1967.

Babson, Roger W. *Washington and the Depression: Including the Career of W. N. Doak.* New York: Harper and Brothers, 1932.

"Back to the Homeland." *Survey* 69 (January 1933): 39.

Bamford, Edwin F. "The Mexican Casual Problem in the Southwest." *Journal of Applied Sociology* 8 (July–August 1924): 363–71.

Barker, Frederick F. "Colonization of Mexico by Americanized Mexicans." *Pan Pacific Progress* 10 (January 1929): 6.

"Barring Aliens to Aid Our Jobless." *Literary Digest,* 25 April 1931, p. 10.

Batten, James H. "The Mexican Immigration Problem." *Pan Pacific Progress* 8 (February 1928): 39, 52.

Beals, Carleton. "Mexico and the Harris Bill." *Nation,* 9 July 1930, pp. 51–52.

Bennett, Marion T. *American Immigration Policies: A History.* Washington: Public Affairs Press, 1963.

Bernstein, Irving. *The Lean Years: A History of the American Worker, 1920–1933.* Boston: Houghton Mifflin Company, 1960.

Bloch, Louis. "Facts About Mexican Immigration Before and Since the Quota Restriction Law." *American Statistical Association Journal* 24 (March 1929): 50–60.

Bogardus, Emory S. "Current Problems of Mexican Immigrants." *Sociology and Social Research* 25 (November–December 1940): 166–74.

———. "From Immigration to Exclusion." *Sociology and Social Research* 24 (January–February 1940): 272–78.

———. "The Mexican Immigrant." *Journal of Applied Sociology* 11 (May–June 1927): 470–88.

———. "The Mexican Immigrant and Segregation." *American Journal of Sociology* 36 (July 1930): 74–80.

———. "The Mexican Immigrant and the Quota." *Sociology and Social Research* 12 (March–April 1928): 371–78.

———. *The Mexican in the United States.* Los Angeles: University of Southern California Press, 1934.

———. "Mexican Repatriates." *Sociology and Social Research* 18 (November–December 1933): 169–76.

———. "Second Generation Mexicans." *Sociology and Social Research* 13 (January–February 1929): 276–83.

Borough, Reuben W. "The Suicide of a Newspaper." *Frontier* 16 (February 1965): 13–14.

Brown, Lawrence G. *Immigration, Cultural Conflicts and Social Adjustments.* New York: Longmans, Green and Company, 1933.

Bryan, Samuel. "Mexican Immigrants in the United States." *Survey,* 7 September 1912, pp. 726–30.

Burma, John H. *Spanish-Speaking Groups in the United States.* Durham: Duke University Press, 1954.

California. Commission of Immigration and Housing. *Annual Report of the Commission of Immigration and Housing of California.* Sacramento, 1927.

———. *Mexicans in California: Report of C. C. Young's Mexican Fact-Finding Committee.* San Francisco, October 1930.

———. State Relief Administration of California. *Review of Activities of the State Relief Administration of California, 1933–1935.* Sacramento, 1936.

California State Federation of Labor. *Proceedings, 1925–1932.*

Carillo, Alfonso R. "Mexico Looks at the United States." *Sociology and Social Research* 15 (July–August 1931): 558–61.

Carroll, Raymond G. "The Alien on Relief." *Saturday Evening Post,* 11 January 1936, pp. 16–17.

Casavantes, Edward J. *A New Look at the Attributes of the Mexican American.* Albuquerque: Southwestern Cooperative Research Laboratory, Inc., 1969.

"Changes Among Mexican Officials." *Pan Pacific Progress* 13 (September 1930): 92.

Clark, Victor. "Mexican Labor in the United States." U.S. Bureau of Labor Statistics, *Bulletin* 78 (September 1908): 464–522.

Clements, George P. "If Not Mexicans, Who?" *Farm and Garden Magazine of the Sunday Los Angeles Times,* 11 May 1930, p. 3.

————. "Mexican Immigration and Its Bearing on Calif.'s Agriculture." *California Citrograph* 15 (November 1929): 3, 28–31.

Cline, Howard F. *The United States and Mexico.* New York: Atheneum, 1963.

Collins, Henry H., Jr. *America's Own Refugees: Our 4,000,000 Homeless Migrants.* Princeton: Princeton University Press, 1941.

"Commissioner Hull, Exporter." *Saturday Evening Post,* 18 January 1930. p. 24.

Crawford, Remsen. "The Menace of Mexican Immigration." *Current History* 31 (February 1930): 902–907.

Daniels, Roger. *The Politics of Prejudice: The Anti-Japanese Movement in California and the Struggle for Japanese Exclusion.* New York: Atheneum, 1968.

Davila, José M. "The Mexican Migration Problem." *Pan Pacific Progress* 10 (January 1929): 7, 25.

Day, George M. "Races and Cultural Oases." *Sociology and Social Research* 18 (March–April 1934): 326–39.

Diario Oficial (Mexico, D.F.).

Dimock, Marshall E. "Recall Movement Against Mayor Porter of Los Angeles." *National Municipal Review* 20 (December 1931): 742–43.

Divine, Robert A. *American Immigration Policy, 1924–1952.* New Haven: Yale University Press, 1957.

" 'Doakery' and Deportations." *Literary Digest,* 22 August 1931, p. 6.

Dulles, John W. F. *Yesterday in Mexico: A Chronicle of the Revolution, 1919–1936.* Austin: University of Texas Press, 1961.

Dunbier, Roger. *The Sonoran Desert: Its Geography, Economy, and People.* Tucson: University of Arizona Press, 1968.

El Nacional (Mexico, D.F.).

El Universal (Mexico, D.F.).

Elac, John C. "The Employment of Mexican Workers in U.S. Agriculture, 1900–1960: A Binational Economic Analysis." Ph.D. dissertation, University of California, Los Angeles, 1961.

Erdman, H. C. "The Development and Significance of California Cooperatives." *Agricultural History* 32 (July 1958): 179–84.

Excelsior (Mexico, D.F.).

Fields, Harold. "Where Shall the Alien Work?" *Social Forces* 12 (December 1933): 213–21.

Finney, Guy. *Angel City in Turmoil.* Los Angeles: American Press, 1945.

Ford, John Anson. *Thirty Explosive Years in Los Angeles County.* San Marino: Huntington Library, 1961.

Fremming, Harvey C. "Los Angeles Meets Unemployment." *American Federationist* 38 (July 1931): 855–57.

"Friends of Mexico Meet at Claremont." *Pan Pacific Progress* 8 (January 1928): 14–15.

"Friends of the Mexicans Conference." *Pan Pacific Progress* 9 (December 1928): 205.

Fuller, Levi V. "The Supply of Agricultural Labor as a Factor in the Evolution of Farm Organizations in Cailifornia." Ph.D. dissertation, University of California, 1939.

Galarza, Ernesto. "Life in the United States for Mexican People: Out of the Experiences of a Mexican." National Conference of Social Work, *Proceedings* (1929): 399–404.

———. *Merchants of Labor: The Mexican Bracero Story.* Santa Barbara: McNally and Loftin, 1964.

———. "Without Benefit of Lobby." *Survey,* 1 May 1931, p. 181.

Gamio, Manuel. *The Mexican Immigrant: His Life Story.* Chicago: University of Chicago Press, 1931.

———. *Mexican Immigration to the United States: A Study of Human Migration and Adjustment.* Chicago: University of Chicago Press, 1930.

———. "Migration and Planning." *Survey,* 1 May 1931, pp. 174–75.

———. "The New Conquest." *Survey,* 1 May 1924, p. 144.

———. *Quantitative Estimate: Sources and Distribution of Mexican Immigration into the United States.* Mexico, D.F., 1930.

Garis, Roy L. *Immigration Restriction: A Study of the Opposition to and Regulation of Immigration into the United States.* New York: Macmillan, 1927.

———. "The Mexican Invasion." *Saturday Evening Post,* 19 April 1930, pp. 43–44.

———. "The Mexicanization of American Business." *Saturday Evening Post,* 8 February 1930, p. 46.

Garrett, Garet. "Government by Tumult." *Saturday Evening Post,* 16 March 1929, pp. 14–15.

Gilbert, James C. "A Field Study in Mexico of the Mexican Repatriation Movement." Master's thesis, University of Southern California, 1934.

Goethe, C. M. "Peons Need Not Apply." *World's Work* 59 (November 1930): 47–48.

———. "Other Aspects of the Problem." *Current History* 28 (August 1928): 766–68.

González Navarro, Moisés. "Efectos sociales de la crisis de 1929." *Historia Mexicana* 19 (April–June 1970): 536–558.

Grebler, Leo. "Mexican Immigration to the United States: The Record and Its Implications." Advance Report 2 of the Mexican-American Study Project. University of California, Los Angeles, 1966.

Grebler, Leo; Moore, Joan; and Guzman, Ralph. *The Mexican-American People: The Nation's Second-Largest Minority.* New York: Macmillan, 1970.

Griffith, Beatrice. *American Me.* Boston: Houghton Mifflin Co., 1948.

Gwin, J. B. "Back and Forth to Mexico." *Survey,* 6 October 1917, pp. 9–10.

———. "Immigration Along Our Southwest Border." American Academy of Political and Social Science, *Annals* 93 (January 1921): 126–30.

———. "Mexican Labor Problems." *Survey,* 20 November 1920, pp. 272–73.

———. "Social Problems of Our Mexican Population." National Conference of Social Work, *Proceedings* (1926): 328–32.

Handlin, Oscar. "Immigrants Who Go Back." *Atlantic* 198 (July 1956): 70–74.

Handman, Max S. "Economic Reasons for the Coming of the Mexican Immigrant." *American Journal of Sociology* 35 (January 1930): 601–11.

———. "The Mexican Immigrant in Texas." National Conference of Social Work, *Proceedings* (1926): 332–38.

Hanna, Agnes K. "Social Services on the Mexican Border." National Conference of Social Work, *Proceedings* (1935): 692–702.

Hardy, Osgood. "Los Repatriados." *Pomona College Magazine* 21 (January 1933): 71–73.

Hayes, Erving P. *Activities of the President's Emergency Committee for Employment, 1930–1931.* Concord: Rumford Press, 1936.

Hernández Alvarez, José. "A Demographic Profile of the Mexican Immigration to the United States, 1910–1950." *Journal of Inter-American Studies* 8 (July 1966): 471–96.

Hidalgo, Ernesto. *La protección de mexicanos en los Estados Unidos: Defensorías de oficio, anexas a los consulados — un proyecto.* Mexico, D.F., 1940.

Higham, John. *Strangers in the Land: Patterns of American Nativism, 1860–1925.* New York: Atheneum, 1965.

Hill, Laurance L. "A Great City Celebrates Its 150th Anniversary." Historical Society of Southern California, *Annual Publications* 15 (1931): 7–55.

Hoffman, Abraham. "The El Monte Berry Strike: International Involvement in a Local Labor Dispute." *Journal of the West* 12 (January 1973): 71–84.

———. "Mexican Repatriation Statistics: Some Suggested Alternatives to Carey McWilliams." *Western Historical Quarterly* 3 (October 1972): 391–404.

———. "Stimulus to Repatriation: The 1931 Federal Deportation Drive and the Los Angeles Mexican Community." *Pacific Historical Review* 42 (May 1973): 205–19.

———. "The Trinidad Incident." *Journal of Mexican American History* 2 (Spring 1972): 143–51.

Holmes, Samuel J. "An Argument Against Mexican Immigration." Commonwealth Club of California, *Transactions,* 23 March 1926, pp. 21–27.

———. "Perils of the Mexican Invasion." *North American Review* 227 (May 1929): 615–23.

Hoover, Glenn E. "Our Mexican Immigrants." *Foreign Affairs* 8 (October 1929): 99–107.

Hoover, Herbert C. *The Memoirs of Herbert Hoover: The Great Depression, 1929–1941.* Vol. 3. New York: Macmillan, 1952.

Humphrey, Norman D. "Mexican Repatriation from Michigan: Public Assistance in Historical Perspective." *Social Service Review* 15 (September 1941): 497–513.

———. "The Migration and Settlement of Detroit Mexicans." *Economic Geography* 19 (October 1943): 358–61.

"The Immigrant from Mexico." *Outlook,* 19 May 1920, p. 131.

Indiana. Lake County Relief Committee. *The Story of Unemployment Relief Work in Lake County, Indiana.* East Chicago: Lake County Relief Committee, 1932.

"Is Mexican Labor Cheap?" *Saturday Evening Post,* 21 July 1934, p. 22.

Jackson, Gardner. "Doak the Deportation Chief." *Nation,* 18 March 1931, pp. 295–96.

Jones, Anita E. "Mexican Colonies in Chicago." *Social Service Review* 2 (1928): 579–97.

Jones, Maldwyn A. *American Immigration.* Chicago: University of Chicago Press, 1960.

Jones, Robert C., and Wilson, Louis R. *The Mexican in Chicago.* Chicago: Comity Commission of the Chicago Church Federation, 1931.

Kane, Francis F. "The Challenge of the Wickersham Deportations Report." *Journal of Criminal Law and Criminology* 23 (November–December 1932): 575–613.

Kelley, Edna E. "The Mexicans Go Home." *Southwest Review* 17 (April 1932): 303–11.

Kirkbride, William H. "An Argument for Mexican Immigration." Commonwealth Club of California, *Transactions,* 23 March 1926, pp. 11–20.

Kohler, Max J. "Enforcing Our Deportation Laws." National Conference of Social Work, *Proceedings* (1931): 495–505.

Konvitz, Milton R. *Civil Rights in Immigration.* Ithaca: Cornell University Press, 1953.

Landes, Ruth. *Latin Americans of the Southwest.* St. Louis: Webster Division, McGraw-Hill, Inc., 1965.

La Opinión (Los Angeles).

"The League's Investigations and Arizona's Demands Concerning Mexican Immigration." *Municipal League of Los Angeles Bulletin,* 1 April 1928, pp. 1–3.

Levenstein, Harvey A. "The AFL and Mexican Immigration in the 1920s: An Experiment in Labor Diplomacy." *Hispanic American Historical Review* 48 (May 1968): 206–20.

————. *Labor Organizations in the United States and Mexico: A History of Their Relations.* Westport, Conn.: Greenwood Press, Inc., 1971.

Lofstedt, Christine. "The Mexican Population of Pasadena, California." *Journal of Applied Sociology* 7 (May–June 1923): 260–68.

Longmore, T. Wilson, and Hitt, Homer L. "A Demographic Analysis of First and Second Generation Mexican Population of the United States: 1930." *Southwestern Social Science Quarterly* 24 (September 1943): 138–49.

Lopez, Ron W. "The El Monte Berry Strike of 1933." *Aztlán: Chicano Journal of the Social Sciences and the Arts* 1 (Spring 1970): 101–14.

Los Angeles Evening Express.

Los Angeles Evening Herald.

Los Angeles Examiner.

Los Angeles *Illustrated Daily News.*

Los Angeles *Record.*

Los Angeles Times.

MacCarthy, Carrie Belle H. "A Survey of the Mexican Hardship Cases Active in the Los Angeles County Department of Charities, Los Angeles, California." Master's thesis, University of Southern California, 1939.

McLean, Robert N. "A Dyke Against Mexicans." *New Republic,* 14 August 1929, pp. 334–37.
————. "Goodbye, Vicente!" *Survey,* 1 May 1931, pp. 182–83.
————. "Hard Times Oust the Mexican." *Mexican Life* 7 (September 1931): 19–21.
————. "The Mexican Return." *Nation,* 24 August 1932, pp. 165–66.
————. "Mexican Workers in the United States." National Conference of Social Work, *Proceedings* (1929): 531–38.
————. *The Northern Mexican.* New York: Home Missions Council, n.d.
————. "Rubbing Shoulders on the Border." *Survey,* 1 May 1924, pp. 184–85.
————. *That Mexican! As He Really Is, North and South of the Rio Grande.* New York: Fleming H. Revell Company, 1928.
————. "Tightening the Mexican Border." *Survey,* 1 April 1930, pp. 28–29.
McWilliams, Carey. *Factories in the Field: The Story of Migratory Labor in California.* Boston: Little, Brown and Company, 1939.
————. "The Forgotten Mexican." *Common Ground* 3 (Spring 1943): 65–78.
————. "Getting Rid of the Mexican." *American Mercury* 28 (March 1933): 322–24.
————. *Ill Fares the Land: Migrants and Migratory Labor in the United States.* Boston: Little, Brown and Company, 1942.
————. *North from Mexico: The Spanish-Speaking People of the United States.* Philadelphia: J. B. Lippincott Company, 1949.
————. *Southern California Country: An Island on the Land.* New York: Duell, Sloan and Pearce, 1946.
Manuel, Herschel T. "The Mexican Child in Texas." *Southwest Review* 17 (April 1932): 290–302.
————. "The Mexican Population of Texas." *Southwestern Political and Social Science Quarterly* 15 (June 1934): 29–51.
Martinez, John R. "Mexican Emigration to the United States, 1910–1930." Ph.D. dissertation, University of California, Berkeley, 1957.
Martinez, Thomas M. "Advertising and Racism: The Case of the Mexican American." *El Grito* 2 (Summer 1969): 3–13.
Marvin, George. "Monkey Wrenches in Mexican Machinery." *Independent,* 14 April 1928, pp. 350–52.
Meier, Matt S., and Rivera, Feliciano. *The Chicanos: A History of Mexican Americans.* New York: Hill and Wang, 1972.
Mexia, Enrique. "Irrigation Works in Mexico; Capacity of the 'Don Martin' Dam." *Pan Pacific Progress* 14 (February 1931): 113–14.
"The Mexican Conquest." *Saturday Evening Post,* 22 June 1929, p. 26.
"Mexican Exodus." *Newsweek,* 31 July 1939, p. 11.
"Mexican Immigration and the Farm." *Outlook,* 7 December 1927, p. 423.
"Mexican Invaders Relieving Our Farm-Labor Shortage." *Literary Digest,* 17 July 1920, pp. 53–54.
"Mexican Rights in the United States." *Nation,* 12 July 1922, pp. 51–53.
Mexico. Secretaría de Relaciones Exteriores. *Informe de la Secretaría de Relaciones Exteriores, 1933–34.* Mexico, D.F., 1934.
————. *Memoria de la Secretaría de Relaciones Exteriores.* Mexico, D.F., 1929–1937.
"Migration to and from Mexico in 1930." *International Labour Review* 24 (November 1931): 612–13.
Minnesota. Governor's Interracial Commission. "The Mexican in Minnesota." *Race Relations in Minnesota: Reports of the Governor's Interracial Commission.* St. Paul, 1948.

Moore, Joan W., and Guzman, Ralph. "The Mexican-Americans: New Wind from the Southwest." *Nation,* 30 May 1966, pp. 645–48.

Moore, Powell A. *The Calumet Region: Indiana's Last Frontier.* Indianapolis: Indiana Historical Bureau, 1959.

"Move to Restrict Mexican Immigration." *Pan Pacific Progress* 7 (July 1927): 51.

Murray, Katherine K. "Mexican Community Service." *Sociology and Social Research* 17 (July–August 1933): 545–60.

Nadeau, Remi. *Los Angeles: From Mission to Modern City.* New York: Longmans, Green and Company, 1960.

Nation, 24 September 1930, pp. 309–10; 10 December 1930, p. 636; 22 April 1931, p. 437; 29 April 1931, p. 463; 19 August 1931, p. 170; 9 December 1931, p. 627; 30 December 1931, p. 712; 6 January 1932, p. 2; 10 February 1932, pp. 169–70; 7 December 1932, p. 544.

Neal, Joe W. "The Policy of the United States Toward Immigration from Mexico." Master's thesis, University of Texas, 1941.

New Republic, 13 May 1931, pp. 338–39; 29 July 1931, p. 271; 19 August 1931, p. 2.

New York Times.

"The Old Mistake." *Saturday Evening Post,* 20 June 1931, p. 24.

Oppenheimer, Reuben. "The Deportation Terror." *New Republic,* 13 January 1932, pp. 231–34.

"Our New Mexican Consul." *Pan Pacific Progress* 13 (December 1930): 154.

Panunzio, Constantine. *How Mexicans Earn and Live: A Study of the Incomes and Expenditures of One Hundred Mexican Families in San Diego, California.* University of California Publications in Economics, vol. 13, no. 1. Berkeley: University of California Press, 1933.

Park, Joseph F. *Mexican Labor in Arizona During the Territorial Period.* Tucson: University of Arizona Press, forthcoming.

Parks, Marion. "La Fiesta de Los Angeles — Retrospect." *Overland and Out West Magazine* 89 (October 1931): 11, 32.

Perry, Louis B., and Perry, Richard S. *A History of the Los Angeles Labor Movement, 1911–1941.* Berkeley: University of California Press, 1963.

Pitt, Leonard. *The Decline of the Californios: A Social History of the Spanish-Speaking Californians, 1846–1890.* Berkeley: University of California Press, 1966.

Pomeroy, Earl. *The Pacific Slope: A History of California, Oregon, Washington, Idaho, Utah, and Nevada.* New York: Alfred A. Knopf, Inc., 1965.

"The President Violates the Law." *Nation,* 30 December 1931, p. 712.

"Protection for Skilled Labor." *Saturday Evening Post,* 7 January 1928, p. 32.

Rak, Mary K. *Border Patrol.* Boston: Houghton Mifflin Company, 1938.

Raley, Helen. "Guardians of Our Border." *Sunset* 57 (November 1926): 30–31.

Redfield, Robert. "The Antecedents of Mexican Immigration to the United States." *American Journal of Sociology* 35 (November 1929): 433–38.

Redkey, Edwin S. *Black Exodus: Black Nationalist and Back-to-Africa Movements, 1890–1910.* New Haven: Yale University Press, 1969.

"Reform Over Los Angeles." *Time,* 5 December 1938, p. 14.

Rich, Adena M. "Case Work in the Repatriation of Immigrants." *Social Service Review* 10 (December 1936): 569–605.

Roberts, Kenneth L. "The Docile Mexican." *Saturday Evening Post,* 19 March 1928, pp. 39–41.
———. "Mexicans or Ruin." *Saturday Evening Post,* 18 February 1928, pp. 14–15.
———. "Wet and Other Mexicans." *Saturday Evening Post,* 4 February 1928, pp. 10–11.
Rogers, Stanley. "The Attempted Recall of the Mayor of Los Angeles." *National Municipal Review* 21 (July 1932): 416–19.
Rowell, Chester H. "Why Make Mexico an Exception?" *Survey,* 1 May 1931, p. 180.
Saloutos, Theodore. "Exodus U.S.A." *In the Trek of the Immigrants: Essays Presented to Carl Wittke.* Edited by O. F. Ander. Rock Island: Augustana College Library, 1964.
———. *They Remember America: The Story of the Repatriated Greek-Americans.* Berkeley: University of California Press, 1956.
Samora, Julian. *Los Mojados: The Wetback Story.* South Bend: University of Notre Dame Press, 1971.
Santiago, Hazel D. "Mexican Influence in Southern California." *Sociology and Social Research* 16 (September–October 1931): 68–74.
Santibañez, Enrique. *Ensayo acerca de la inmigración mexicana en los Estados Unidos.* San Antonio: Clegg Company, 1930.
Schwartz, Harry. *Seasonal Farm Labor in the United States, with Special Reference to Hired Workers in Fruit and Vegetable and Sugar-Beet Production.* New York: Columbia University Press, 1945.
Scruggs, Otey M. "Evolution of the Mexican Farm Labor Agreement of 1942." *Agricultural History* 34 (July 1960): 140–50.
———. "The First Mexican Farm Labor Program." *Arizona and the West* 2 (Winter 1960): 319–26.
Servín, Manuel P. "The Pre-World War II Mexican-American." *California Historical Society Quarterly* 45 (December 1966): 325–38.
"Shall We Apply the Quota to Our Nearest Neighbors." *Literary Digest,* 27 August 1927, p. 12.
Shotwell, Louisa R. *The Harvesters: The Story of the Migrant People.* Garden City: Doubleday & Co., Inc. 1961.
Simpich, Frederick. "The Little Brown Brother Treks North." *Independent,* 27 February 1926, pp. 237–39.
Simpson, Eyler N. *The Ejido: Mexico's Way Out.* Chapel Hill: University of North Carolina Press, 1937.
Simpson, Lesley Byrd. *Many Mexicos.* Berkeley: University of California Press, 1964.
Slayden, James L. "Some Observations on Mexican Immigration." American Academy of Political and Social Science, *Annals* 93 (January 1921): 121–26.
Smith, Clara. "Development of the Mexican People in Watts, California." Master's thesis, University of Southern California, 1933.
Spaulding, Charles B. "The Mexican Strike at El Monte, California." *Sociology and Social Research* 18 (July–August 1934): 571–80.
Starr-Hunt, Jack. "The Mexicans Who Went Home." *Los Angeles Times Sunday Magazine,* 26 March 1933, pp. 10, 20.
Stevenson, Emma R. "The Emigrant Comes Home." *Survey,* 1 May 1931, pp. 175–77.

Stevenson, Philip. "Deporting Jesús." *Nation,* 18 July 1936, pp. 67–69.

Stowell, Jay S. "The Danger of Unrestricted Mexican Immigration." *Current History* 28 (August 1928): 763–66.

———. *The Near Side of the Mexican Question.* New York: George H. Doran Company, 1921.

Strout, Richard L. "A Fence for the Rio Grande." *Independent,* 2 June 1928, pp. 518–20.

Stump, Frank V. "Fighting Battles for the Farmer." *Southern California Business* 4 (March 1925): 17.

Sturges, Vera L. "Mexican Immigrants." *Survey,* 2 July 1921, pp. 470–71.

Suastegui, F. "Irrigation Projects in Mexico." *Pan Pacific Progress* 9 (July 1928): 14.

Sullenger, T. Earl. "Mexican Population of Omaha." *Sociology and Social Research* 8 (May–June 1924): 289–93.

Tannenbaum, Frank. *Mexico: The Struggle for Peace and Bread.* New York: Alfred A. Knopf, 1950.

Taylor, Paul S. *An American-Mexican Frontier: Nueces County, Texas.* Chapel Hill: University of North Carolina Press, 1934.

———. *Mexican Labor in the United States: Dimmit County, Winter Garden District, South Texas.* University of California Publications in Economics, vol. 6, no. 5. Berkeley: University of California Press, 1930.

———. *Mexican Labor in the United States: Imperial Valley.* University of California Publications in Economics, vol. 6, no. 1. Berkeley: University of California Press, 1928.

———. *Mexican Labor in the United States: Migration Statistics.* University of California Publications in Economics, vol. 6, no. 3. Berkeley: University of California Press, 1929.

———. *Mexican Labor in the United States: Migration Statistics, IV.* University of California Publications in Economics, vol. 12, no. 3. Berkeley: University of California Press, 1934.

———. "Mexicans North of the Rio Grande." *Survey,* 1 May 1931, pp. 135–40.

———. "More Bars Against Mexicans?" *Survey,* 1 April 1930, pp. 26–27.

———. "Note on Streams of Mexican Migration." *American Journal of Sociology* 36 (September 1930): 287–88.

———. "Some Aspects of Mexican Immigration." *Journal of Political Economy* 38 (October 1930): 609–15.

———. *A Spanish-Mexican Peasant Community: Arandas in Jalisco, Mexico.* Berkeley: University of California Press, 1933. Ibero-Americana series, no. 4.

Teague, Charles C. "A Statement on Mexican Immigration." *Saturday Evening Post,* 10 March 1928, pp. 169–70.

Thomson, Charles A. "The Man from Next Door: The Mexican Who is Filling the Cheap Labor Vacuum." *Century Magazine* 111 (n.s. 89, January 1926): 275–82.

———. "Mexicans — An Interpretation." National Conference of Social Work, *Proceedings* (1928): 499–503.

———. "The Restriction of Mexican Immigration." *Sociology and Social Research* 11 (July–August 1927): 574–78.

———. "What of the Bracero? The Forgotten Alternative in Our Immigration Policy." *Survey,* 1 June 1925, pp. 290–93.

"To End the Deportation Terror." *New Republic,* 13 January 1932, pp. 229–30.

"To Put Mexico on a Quota Basis." *Literary Digest,* 7 April 1928, p. 14.

U.S. Congress. House. Committee on Immigration and Naturalization. *Hearings on Immigration from Countries of the Western Hemisphere.* 70th Cong., 1st sess., 1928.

———. *Hearings on Seasonal Agricultural Laborers from Mexico.* 69th Cong., 1st sess., 1925–26.

U.S. Congress. Senate. Committee on Immigration. *Hearings on Restriction of Western Hemisphere Immigration.* 70th Cong., 1st sess., 1928.

U.S. Congress. Senate. Subcommittee of the Committee on Education and Labor. *Hearings on Violations of Free Speech and Rights of Labor.* 74th Cong., 2d sess., 1940, part 53.

U.S. *Congressional Record.* 69th Cong., 1st sess., 1926; 71st Cong., 2d and 3d sess., 1930.

U.S. Department of Commerce. Bureau of the Census. *Fifteenth Census of the United States: 1930, Population.*

U.S. Department of Justice. *Report of the Commissioner of Immigration and Naturalization, 1970.*

U.S. Department of Labor. *Annual Report of the Secretary of Labor, 1931–1935.*

———. Bureau of Immigration. *Annual Report of the Commissioner General of Immigration, 1908–1932.*

———. Bureau of Labor Statistics. *Monthly Labor Review:* "Increase of Mexican Population in United States, 1920 to 1930," 37 (July 1933): 46–47; "Labor and Social Conditions of Mexicans in California," 32 (January 1931): 83–89; "Mexican Labor Colony at Bethlehem, Pa.," 33 (October 1931); 74–78; "Results of Admission of Mexican Laborers, Under Departmental Orders, for Employment in Agricultural Pursuits," 11 (November 1920): 1095–97; "Wages and Cost of Living of Mexican Agricultural Laborers," 23 (November 1926): 1055–56.

U.S. National Commission on Law Observance and Enforcement. *Report on the Enforcement of the Deportation Laws of the United States.* Report No. 5, 1931.

U.S. *Statutes at Large,* vol. 45.

Walker, Helen W. "Mexican Immigrants and American Citizenship." *Sociology and Social Research,* 13 (May–June 1929): 465–71.

———. "Mexican Immigrants as Laborers." *Sociology and Social Research* 13 (September–October 1928): 55–62.

Wallis, Marie P. "A Study of Dependency in One Hundred Cases Taken from Files of Bureau of County Welfare, Catholic Welfare Bureau, Los Angeles County Relief Administration (Torrance and Watts Districts)." Master's thesis, University of Southern California, 1935.

Walter, Paul, Jr. "The Spanish-Speaking Community in New Mexico." *Sociology and Social Research* 24 (November–December 1939): 150–57.

Ward, Stuart R. "The Mexican in California." Commonwealth Club of California, *Transactions,* 23 March 1926, pp. 4–10.

Waters, Leslie L. "Transient Mexican Agricultural Labor." *Southwestern Social Science Quarterly* 22 (June 1941): 49–66.

Weber, Francis J. "Irish-Born Champion of the Mexican-Americans." *California Historical Quarterly* 49 (September 1970): 233–49.

Weeks, O. Douglas. "The League of United Latin-American Citizens: A Texas Mexican Civic Organization." *Southwestern Political and Social Science Quarterly* 10 (December 1929): 258–78.

"What of the Mexican Immigrant?" *Literary Digest,* 24 August 1929, p. 11.

Wilkie, James W. *The Mexican Revolution: Federal Expenditure and Social Change Since 1910.* 2nd ed. Berkeley: University of California Press, 1970.

Williams, Dean L. "Some Political and Economic Aspects of Mexican Immigration into the United States Since 1941, with Particular Reference to this Immigration into the State of California." Master's thesis, University of California, Los Angeles, 1950.

Wilson, Edmund. "The City of Our Lady the Queen of the Angels: II." *New Republic,* 9 December 1931, pp. 89–93.

Woehlke, Walter V. "Don't Drive Out the Mexicans." *American Review of Reviews* 81 (May 1930): 66–68.

Wollenberg, Charles. *"Huelga,* 1928 Style: The Imperial Valley Cantaloupe Workers' Strike." *Pacific Historical Review* 38 (February 1969): 45–58.

———. "Race and Class in Rural California: The El Monte Berry Strike of 1933." *California Historical Quarterly* 51 (Summer 1972): 155–64.

Wood, Samuel E. "California Migrants." *Sociology and Social Research* 24 (January–February 1940): 248–61.

———. "The California State Commission of Immigration and Housing: A Study of Administrative Organization and the Growth of Function." Ph.D. dissertation, University of California, 1942.

Young, Donald R. *Research Memorandum on Minority Peoples in the Depression.* New York: Social Science Research Council, 1937.

Index